# Street by Street

CW00327685

# DERBY

## BELPER, CASTLE DONINGTON, DUFFIELD, MICKLEOVER

Aston-on-Trent, Borrowash, Breaston, Draycott, Findern, Kilburn, Kirk Langley, Melbourne, Ockbrook, Spondon

1st edition May 2001

© Automobile Association Developments Limited 2001

This product includes map data licensed from Ordnance Survey® with the permission of the Controller of Her Majesty's Stationery Office. © Crown copyright 2000. All rights reserved. Licence No: 399221.

Published by AA Publishing (a trading name of Automobile Association Developments Limited, whose registered office is Norfolk House, Priestley Road, Basingstoke, Hampshire, RG24 9NY. Registered number 1878835).

Mapping produced by the Cartographic Department of The Automobile Association.

ISBN 0 7495 2617 3

A CIP Catalogue record for this book is available from the British Library.

Printed by GRAFIASA S.A., Porto, Portugal

The contents of this atlas are believed to be correct at the time of the latest revision. However, the publishers cannot be held responsible for loss occasioned to any person acting or refraining from action as a result of any material in this atlas, nor for any errors, omissions or changes in such material. The publishers would welcome information to correct any errors or omissions and to keep this atlas up to date. Please write to Publishing, The Automobile Association, Fanum House, Basing View, Basingstoke, Hampshire, RG21 4EA.

Ref: ML084

| | |
| --- | --- |
| Key to map pages | ii-iii |
| Key to map symbols | iv-1 |
| Enlarged scale pages | 2-3 |
| Street by Street | 4-77 |
| Index – towns & villages | 78 |
| Index – streets | 79-90 |
| Index – featured places | 90-92 |

ii

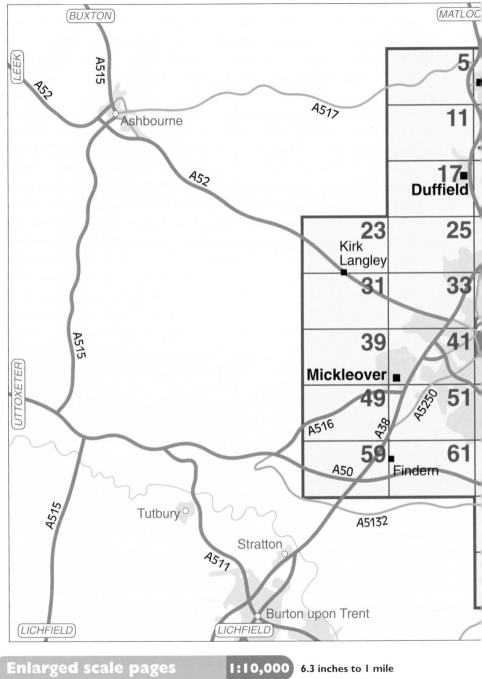

**Enlarged scale pages**  1:10,000  6.3 inches to 1 mile

0    1/4    miles    1/2    3/4
0    1/4    1/2    kilometres    3/4    1    1 1/4

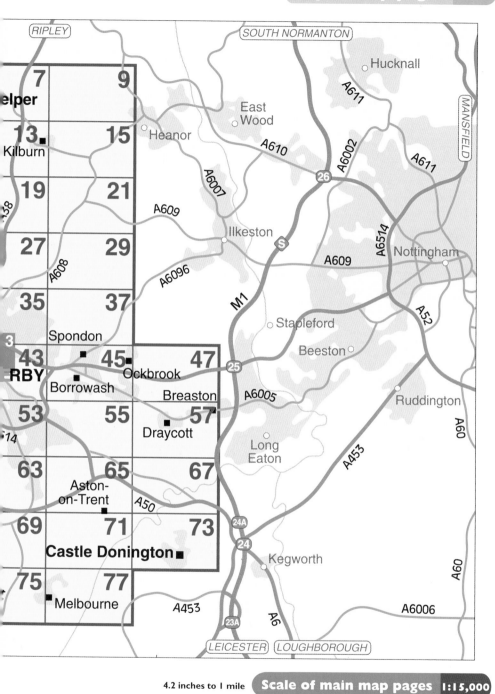

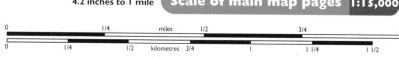

4.2 inches to 1 mile **Scale of main map pages** **1:15,000**

| 0 | | 1/4 | | miles | 1/2 | | 3/4 | | 1 |

| 0 | | 1/4 | | 1/2 | kilometres | 3/4 | | 1 | | 1 1/4 | | 1 1/2 |

| | |
|---|---|
| **Junction 9** | Motorway & junction |
| **Services** | Motorway service area |
| | Primary road single/dual carriageway |
| **Services** | Primary road service area |
| | A road single/dual carriageway |
| | B road single/dual carriageway |
| | Other road single/dual carriageway |
| | Restricted road |
| | Private road |
| ← ← | One way street |
| | Pedestrian street |
| - - - - - | Track/ footpath |
| | Road under construction |
| [ - - = = ] | Road tunnel |
| **P** | Parking |

| | |
|---|---|
| **P+** | Park & Ride |
| | Bus/Coach station |
| | Railway & main railway station |
| | Railway & minor railway station |
| ⊖ | Underground station |
| ⊖ | Light Railway & station |
| +++++++++ | Preserved private railway |
| *LC* | Level crossing |
| •—•—•—•—• | Tramway |
| - - - - - - | Ferry route |
| ................ | Airport runway |
| — · — · — · — | Boundaries- borough/ district |
| ▾▾▾▾▾▾▾▾▾ | Mounds |
| **93** | Page continuation 1:15,000 |
| **7** | Page continuation to enlarged scale 1:10,000 |

River/canal, lake, pier

Aqueduct, lock, weir

465
▲
Winter Hill
Peak (with height in metres)

Beach

Coniferous woodland

Broadleaved woodland

Mixed woodland

Park

Cemetery

Built-up area

Featured building

City wall

A&E Accident & Emergency hospital

Toilet

Toilet with disabled facilities

Petrol station

PH Public house

PO Post Office

Public library

Tourist Information Centre

Castle

Historic house/ building

Wakehurst Place NT National Trust property

Museum/ art gallery

† Church/chapel

Country park

Theatre/ performing arts

Cinema

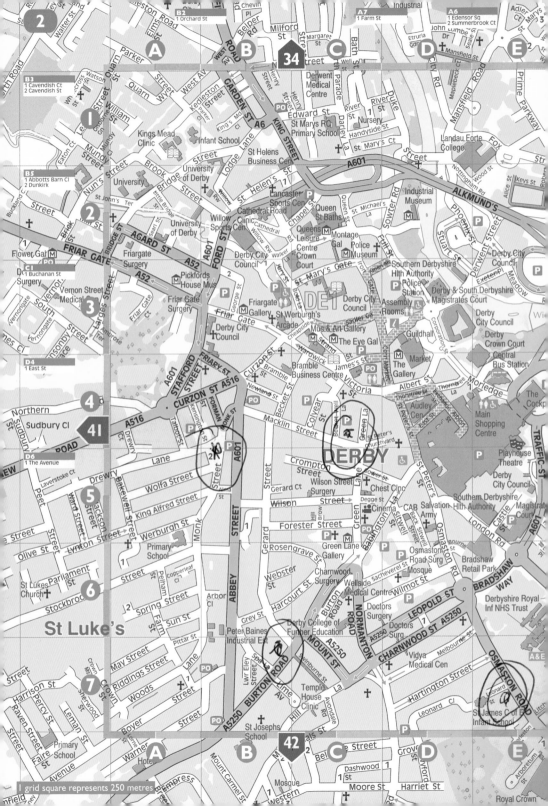

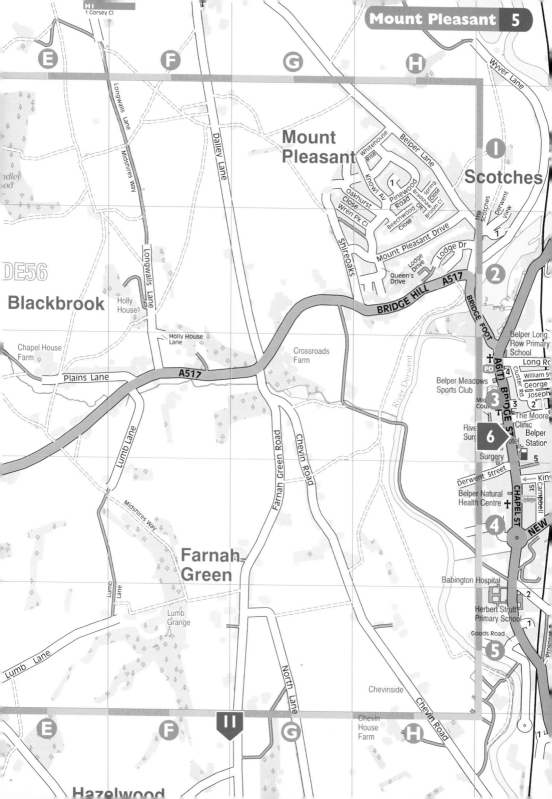

H1
1 Corsey Cl

E    F    G    H

**I**

**Mount Pleasant**

**Scotches**

Wyver Lane

Longwalls Lane

Dalley Lane

Midshires Way

Whitehouse Rise
Belper Lane
Knowl Av
Pinewood Road
Spring Close
Bradshaw Cft
Broom Cl
Oakhurst Close
Beechwood Close
Wren Pk Cl

The Scotches

Derwent View

1

Shireoaks

Mount Pleasant Drive

Lodge Drive
Lodge Dr

**2**

Queen's Drive

BRIDGE HILL
A517

BRIDGE FOOT

A6(T)

**DE56**

**Blackbrook**

Holly House

Longwalls Lane

Holly House Lane

Chapel House Farm

Plains Lane    A517

Crossroads Farm

River Derwent

Belper Long Row Primary School

Long Ro

✝
PO

Cluster Rd

William St

Belper Meadows Sports Club

George
Joseph

**3**

BRIDGE ST

The Moore
Clinic

Belper Station

Rive
Surg

**6**

otel

5

Surgery

Derwent Street

Kin
Campbell

Belper Natural Health Centre ✝

St

Lumb Lane

Midshires Way

Farnah Green Road

Chevin Road

**4**

CHAPEL ST

NEW

**Farnah Green**

Lumb Grange

Babington Hospital

2

Herbert Strutt Primary School

1

Lumb Lane

Goods Road

**5**

Lumb Lane

North Lane

Chevinside

Chevin Road

E    F    **II**    G    H

Chevin House Farm

**Hazelwood**

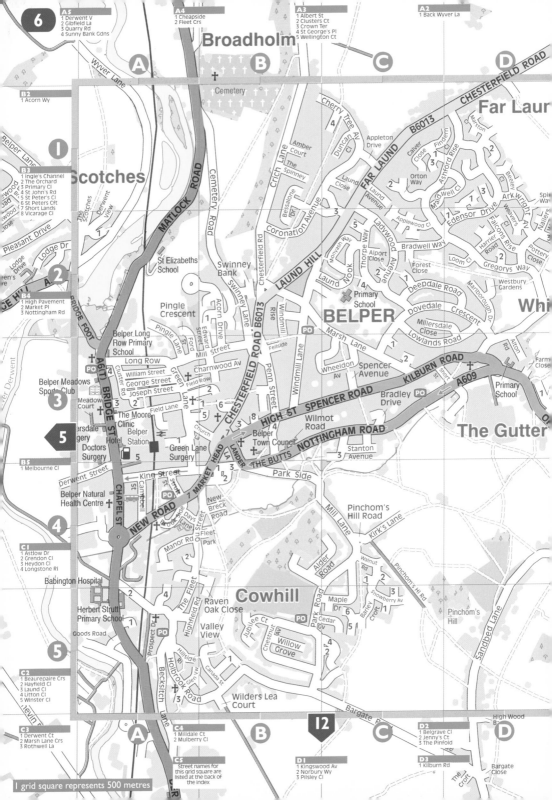

## Boothgate

E2
1 Blenheim Ct
2 Courtney Wy
3 Harewood Cl
4 Kendray Cl
5 Martindale Ct
6 Moulton Cl
7 Salisbury Dr
8 Sherbourne Dr
9 Whitemoor Hall

E3
1 Barton Knowle
2 Brampton Ct
3 Chatham Ct
4 Culworth Cl
5 Leys Ct
6 Overstone Cl
7 Pytchley Cl
8 Ryegrass Cl
9 St James Cl
10 Whilton Ct

E   F   G   H

## Morley Park

Iron Works Farm

I   Marehay Hall

F2
1 Bretton Rd
2 Hoyland Ct
3 Morrell Wood Dr

Whitemoor Hall

Boothgate

Knob Farm

Street Lane

Morley Close

Morrell Wood Farm

✝ Street Lane Primary School

2treet

G5
1 Blackthorne Cl
2 Hawthorne Cl

Whitemoor Lane

Hunter Road

Moor

Wicksteed Close

Scott Drive
Hilary Cl
Cook Close
Morrell Wd Dr

Warwick Gdns
John O'Gaunts Way
Royston Drive
Ashop Road
Over Lane

Belper Sports Centre

Burbage Close
Stoke Close
Beackden Cl

LeChe Cft
Ash Acre
Yardley Way
Byfield Close

Ashton Wy
Naseby Road
High Gv
Royal Gate

Jodrell Avenue

## Openwoodgate

✝ Openwood Rd

A38(T)

Street Lane

3

8

Station Road

4

PO   S

PO

KILBURN LANE

Ireton Houses

Park Hall Road

Derby Road

Rykneild Hill

## Rawson Green

John Flam Community chool

5

A609 BELPER ROAD

## Cinderhill

Hilltop Lane

Belper Rd

Blackberry Way

Bramble Way

Brickyard Lane
Belper Rise

Brookvale Rd
Brookvale Avenue
Brookvale Rise

Northfield

Danesby Rise

Danesby Crescent

## Denby Bottles

E   F   13   G   H

WSON GREEN

Ticknall Lane

Prospect Road

Bottlebrook Houses

PO

Queen

Church Street

Pit Lane

**H3**
1 Draycott Cl
2 Groome Av
3 The Nook

**H4**
1 Clarke Av

West Hill

Hollywell Avenue

Pinewood

Cross Lane

MARKET PL HEANOR RO

NOTTINGHAM

**E** **F** **G** **Waingroves** **H**

Waingroves Road

Station Lane

Waingroves Hall

Codnor-Denby Lane

Cemetery

Middleton Avenue

**Cross Hill**

CROSSHILL

**I** **Woodl**

Highfield Close

Springfield Avenue

Brook Street

A6007

Sheldon Road

Kirkman Road

Lake Av

Clayton

Tristam

**2**

Primrose Hill Farm

**Codnor Breach**

Grammer Street

Weldon Street

Loscoe-Denby

Loscoe C of E Primary School

Lane

Wilson Av

Flamstead Avenue

Church View

Egreaves Avenue

Leniscar Av

1

2

Ford Av

HIGH

Furnace

Grandfield Street

Birchwood

**Loscoe** **3**

Flamstead Avenue

STREET

Taylor

Breach Road

Heanor Road

Common

Denby

Dumbles

Lane

**Denby Common**

HEANOR ROAD

Loscoe Cr

**4**

Clarke Av

Purchase Avenue

Milward Road

Wellington Rd

Watki

Cottage G

Communi School

Douglas Av

eens Av

Northern Rd

Holmes St

Park

**5**

Kingsway

Balmoral Close

Monarch Way

4

Sovereign Way

Indust Estate

per rd

High Bank

**E** **F** **15** **G** **H**

Robey Fields Farm

Pinburn

Kensin Av

Hallington Drive

Hazel Cl

Peatburn Av

1

2

3
4

Heanor Gate School

A60

GS
1 Richmond Dr

HS
1 Ash Tree Cl

Goods Road

E  F  **5**  G  Chevinside  H

Chevin
House
Farm

Hazelwood

Goodwin's Lane

Hob Hill

Hazelwood Hill

Firestone

Spring Hollow

Hazelwood Hall
Farm

Midshires Way

Chevin Road

Derwe
Indust
Estate

1

2

Found
Lane

Hazelwood Road

North Lane

Courthouse
Farm

Jacksons Lane

Chevin Road

3

**12**  Sunny
Wood La

Hazelbrow

Midshires Way

4

Chevin Bank

The
Oaks

Chevin
Vale

Chevin
Road

Chevin Golf
Club

Golf Lane

Mosco
Farm

DERBY ROAD

5

Spring
Hill

Centenary Way

1

Nether
Close

Hazeldene C

Chadfield Rd

Avenue Road

River

Cemetery

Lime Avenue

Castle Hill

ORD ROAD A6(T)

River

E  WIRKSWORTH ROAD  F  **17**  G  H  Primary
School

Phillips Cror

The
Pastures

Holloway

King Street

Vicarage La

2

1

Duffield

12

A B 6 C D

Goods Road
PO
B4
1 Holly Bush La
A1
1 Goods Yd
Prospect
Willow
Grove
Chestnut
2 4

Sandbed

Beckitch Lane

Holbrook Road
Illside
Glen Vw
Canada St
3
Wilde Lea
Court

Bargate Road
High Wood
Bank
Highwood
Avenue

DERBY ROAD A6(T)

1

D2
1 East Crs

Derwentside
Industrial
Estate

Derwent
Avenue

Bargate
Close

The Croft

Bargat

2

D3
1 Horsley Crs
2 Moorpool Crs
3 The Nook
4 Vicarwood Av

Vicarage Road

Hopping Hill

Orchard
Close

Shaw Lane

Holbrook
Moor

Belper Road
Blackbird Row
Moor
Rise
Moorside
Chapel Street
3 PO
1
Chestnut
Avenue
Glen
Avenue
Ruffstone
close
4

Jacksons Lane

Chevin Road

Foundry
Lane

Bridge View

Orangewood Dr

North Lane

3

II

Milford
County
School

Well

Sunny Hill

Wood La

River
View

PO

Milford

Makeney Road

Pond
Road
Bradshaw Dr
The
Paddock
2
1

D4
1 Lower Hall Cl
2 St Michael's Cl

Dark Lane

Mellor's Lane
Upper Hall
Close
Church St
1 2
Town St

4

DERBY ROAD A6(T)

Makeney Road
1

Makeney

Hotel

Red Lane

hevin
ale

Moscow
Farm

Chevin
Golf
Club

Golf Lane

River Derwent

Save Penny Lane

Duffield Bank

Road
1 7
adfield Rd
enue Road
Avenue

5

Castle Hill
Castle Orch
2
Vicarage La
Primary

Duffield

A B 18 C D

1 grid square represents 500 metres

Daypark

**Cinderhill**

F3
1 Brookfields
2 Derby Rd

A609 BELPER ROAD

Hilltop Lane

Northfield

G2
Black1 1 Dale Ct
Way      2 Kerry's Yd
         3 Shaw's Yd
         4 Top Farm Ct

Brick Lane

Bramble W.

E          F

7

RAWSON   GREEN

BYWELL LANE

H

Brookvale Rd

Brookvale Rise

Danesby Rise

**Denby Bottles**

Danesby Crescent

Prospect    Road

Bottlebrook Hous

I

Ticknall Lane

H2
1 Coppice Cl
2 Dove Cl
3 Farm Cl
4 Holbrook Vw
5 Kingsway Crs
6 Mill Cl
7 St John's Dr
8 Vincent Cl

Junior & Infant School

The Flat

**KILBURN**

Edwards Crescent

Chapel  Street

Highfield Road

2

PO

Hunter Drive

Dale Vw

Park Gdns

3

Dale Vw

7

4

2

Alfred Road

Bown Ct

High  Street

Windmill Av

5

Mayfield Av

Hillcrest Drive

8

6

Dale Park Avenue

3

4

1

1

Rowan Dr

2

1

H3
1 Bowler Dr
2 Meadow Ct
3 Sitwell Dr

The Walk

Elm Tree  Av

Fairview

2

1

Cl

Larch Road

Field Ct

Rykneld Road

2

3

**Lower Kilburn**

A609 WOODHOUSE ROAD

14

Ladylea Industrial Estate

The Ce

**Holbrook**

Watering   Lane

Nether Lane

Killis Lane

Brown's Lane

Infant

2

1

Tants Meadow

Horsley Road

Horsley C of E Primary Sch

The Dovecote

Lady  Lea  Hill

Lady Lea Road

Golden Valley

4

Church  Street

French Lane

French Lane

**Horsley**

5

DERBY ROAD B6179

A38(T)

Coxbench Road

Parkgate Farm

E          F

19

G

H

**Coxbench**

The Rockety

Horsley Lane

Old

Smalley Mill

B6179

E4
1 Richardson Dr

H1
1 Banksburn Cl
2 Kings Cl
3 Platts Av
4 Poynter Cl

E F 9 G H

Robey Fields
Farm

Peatburn
Avenue

Heanor Gate
School

Industr
Estate

A608

Heanor Gate
Industrial Estate

I

Heanor
Ga

Adale Rd

The Beeches

Twyford
Close

The Grange

Marina
Road

2

**Heanor Gate**

Sinclair
Close

Adams

3

HEANOR ROAD

Holly Mount
Farm

moor
m

A608

4

Flatm
Farm

Old Pit Lane

1

Dix Av

Bradford Road

Kerry

PO

Stafford
Cl

OBHOLES
LANE

MAIN ROAD

Richardson Endowed
Primary School

icarage
Cl

e Av

Laurel
Crs

**Smalley**

St Johns
Road

Prospect
Farm

ine
Close

Bell Lane

5

Bell Lane

21

Whitehouse
Fa

E F G H

Smalley
Hall

**16**

The Clouds

d Green Lane
Moseyley

**A** Gun Hills **B** **10** **C** **D**

Windley Meadows

Windleyhill Farm

**1**

**2**

Newlands

Centenary Way

Cocks-hut-hill

Woodfall Lane

Centenary Way

**3**

Cu
Co

**4**

Hall Close

**5**

Ireton Farm

Hall Close

**A** Kedleston Road **B** **24** **C** **D**

edleston

Hay Wood

Kedleston Road

1 grid square represents 500 metres

Coxbench

Drum Hill

Breadsall
Moor

Golf
Club

Parkgate
Farm

Brackley Gat
Farm

Morley
Almshouses
Lane

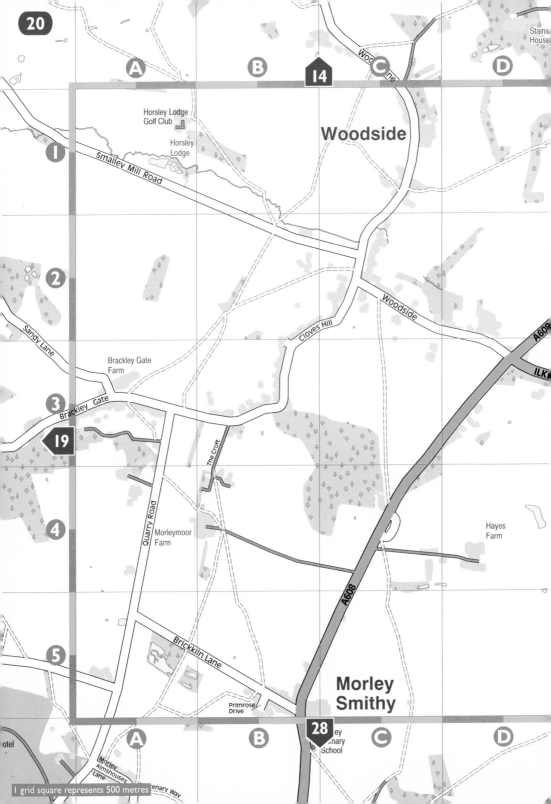

20

A    B    14    C    D

Stains
House

Horsley Lodge
Golf Club

Horsley
Lodge

Woodside

1    Smalley Mill Road

Woodside

2    Cloves Hill    Woodside

Sandy Lane

Brackley Gate
Farm

A608

ILK

3    Brackley Gate

19    The Croft

Quarry Road

Hayes
Farm

4    Morleymoor
Farm

A608

Bricklin Lane

5    Primrose
Drive

Morley
Smithy

A    B    28    C    D

otel

Morley
Almshouses
Lane    enary Way

ey
inary
School

A  B  C  D

Slade Lane

Centenary Way

Wildpark

Wood

1

2

3

4  **Over Burrows**

5

**Nether Burrows**

Wildpark Lane

Windy Arbour

ASHBOURNE ROAD A52(T)

A52(T)

Hilltop Farm

Snapes Farm

The Burma Rd

The Burma Road

Flagsh

A  B  C  D

30

Kirk La

Petty

Clos

Ch

E F G H

**Kedleston**

Moodersley

Mercaston Lane

I

Buckhazels Lane

Lodge Lane

Wildpark Lane

Buck
Hazels

2

Meynell Langley

Priestwood
Farm

3

24

Meynell
Langley

4

Lodge Lane

Lodge Farm

5

Flagshaw Lane

E F G H

31

The Cunnery

Kirk Langley
C of E
Primary School

ASHBOURNE

ley

1

**24**

**A**   **B**   **16**   **C**   **D**

Ireton
Farm

Kedleston Road

dleston

Lane

**1**

*Hay
Wood*

Kedleston Road

Kedleston Park
Golf Club

**2**

*Golf Course*

*Kedleston
Park*

**3**

Kedleston
Hall (NT)

**23**

nell
gley

**4**

Upper
Vicarwood

**5**

Lower
Vicarwood

**A**   **B**   **32**   **C**   **D**

P
M

I grid square represents 500 metres

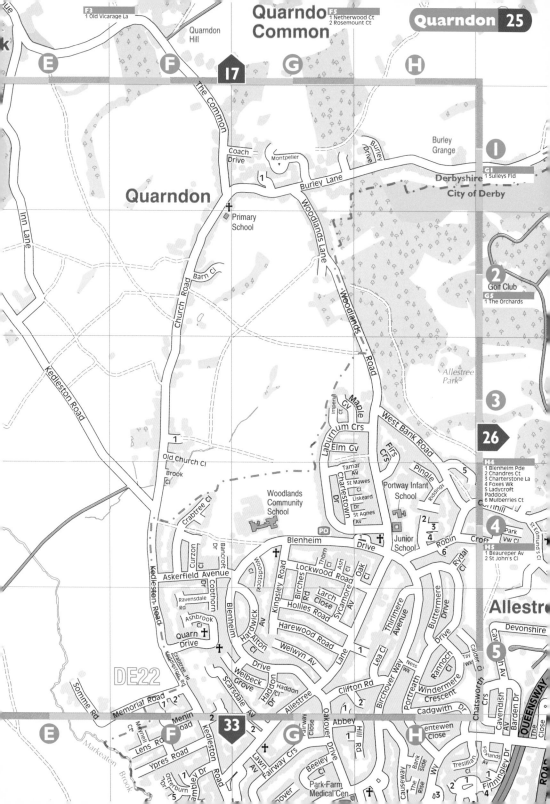

Quarndo
Common

**F5**
1 Netherwood Ct
2 Rosemount Ct

**F3**
1 Old Vicarage La

Quarndon
Hill

E  F  **17**  G  H

The Common

Coach
Drive

Montpelier

Burley
Drive

Burley
Grange

**I**

**Quarndon**

Burley Lane

Derbyshire
City of Derby

**G1**
1 Sulleys Fld

Inn Lane

Primary
School

Woodlands Lane

**2**
Golf Club

**G5**
1 The Orchards

Kedleston Road

Barn Cl

Church Road

Woodlands Road

Allestree
Park

**3**

Maple
Gv

Imperial
Ct

**26**

West Bank Road

Old Church Cl

Laburnum Crs

Elm Gv

Firs
Crs

**H4**
1 Blenheim Pde
2 Chandres Ct
3 Charterstone La
4 Foxes Wk
5 Ladycroft
Paddock
6 Mulberries Ct

Brook
Cl

Tamar
Av

Pingle

5

Charlestown Dr

St Mawes
Cl

Liskeard
Dr

St Agnes
Av

Riddings

Portway Infant
School

Crabtree Cl

Woodlands
Community
School

Cornhill

**4**  Park
Vw Cl

**H5**
1 Beaureper Av
2 St John's Cl

Curzon
Dr

Bancroft
Dr

**PO**

Blenheim

Drive

3
4

Robin

Croft

Junior
School

2

6

**Allestre**

Askerfield Avenue

Cobthorn

Blenheim

Woodstock
Av

Thorn

Kingsley Road

Lockwood
Road

Ash
Cl

Oak

Rydal

Ravensdale
Rd

Hardwick
Av

Birches
Rd

Larch
Close

Sycamore
Av

Thirlmere
Avenue

Buttermere
Drive

Devonshire

Ashbrook
Cl

Alton
Cl

Hollies Road

Cavn Av

**5**

Quarn
Drive

Harewood Road

Lane

Lea Cl

Rannoch
Cl

Windermere

Tay Wk

Calder Cl

Welwyn Av

Ness
Wk

Cavendish
Av

**DE22**

Drive

Birchover Way

Portreath

Chatsworth
Crs

Barden Cl

Welbeck
Grove

Clifton Rd

Windermere
Crescent

Cadgwith Dr

**QUEENSWAY**

The
Close

Somme Rd

Scarsdale Av

Haddon
Dr

Haddon
Cl

Allestree

Memorial Road

7

Menin
Road

Kedleston Road

Crabtree Hi

Maplebrook

**33**

Lawn
Av

Fairway Crs

Oakover
Drive

Abbey

Fairway
Close

Hill
Rd

**H**  Hentewen
Close

Finningley Dr

Markeaton Brook

Lens
Rd

Ypres Road

Otterburn
Tce

Beeley
Cl

Park-Farm
Medical Cen.

Causeway

The
Bank
Side

Rise

Wy

Tresillian
Av

Hands
Rd

Little Eaton

A    B    18    C    D

A5
1 Church La North

A4
1 Siddals La

Woodla
Close

Park
Close

Vicarage Lane

Church
Lane

Little Eaton
Primary
School - 1

Doc
Surg

Station Rd

PO

Burley
Hill

Burley
Gran

1

B3
1 Padley Cl
2 Rushup Cl

hire County

City of Derby

Old Hall Mill
Business Park

New Inn
La

Bern
Aven

ALFRETON ROAD

B6

Duffield Road
Industrial Est

2

B4
1 Derwent Cl
2 Fountains Cl
3 Poplar Nook
4 Portway Cl

Golf Club

BURLEY HILL

Eaton
Avenue

Eaton
Close

Chester
Av

Ford  Lane

3

Allestree
Park

25

B5
1 Lambourn Cl
2 Nutwood Cl

Main  Av

Short  Av

Evans  Avenue

DUFFIELD ROAD

Froggatt
Cl

Spenbeck Dr

Medway

Waverley
Cl

Severndale

Cuckmere
Close

Windrush
Close

Lambourn  Drive

Ford  Lane

y Infant
hool

Roddings

Cornhill

Park Lane
Surg

Park Lane

Rockingham  Cl

Farnborough

Wharfedale Cl

ABBEY    HILL

A61

k Road

Derwent Avenue

Gisborne

Doctors
Surgery

Home  Farm
Dr

Woodside

Derwent
Av

Gdns

4

D1
1 Hollow Brooks
2 The Town
3 Wood Cl Camp

obin

Croft

Park
Vw Cl

Road

St Edmund's Cl

Crs

Doctors
Surgery

Lambourn
Cl

Cama
Cl

Derwent
Dr  Drive

A38(T)

A6(T)

Holme
Nook

Kings Croft

Buttermere  Drive

Ness

Pannock  Cl

Calder Cl

Allestree

Devonshire Av

Cavendish Av

Chatsworth
Crs

Cavendish
Dr

Barden Dr

Baslow Dr

QUEENSWAY

River  Derwent

A61

5

Portreath

Windermere  Crescent

Cadgwith  Dr

Pentewen
Close

Cadgwith
Close

North Av

South
Av

Old Vicarage
School

2

Alfreton  Road

Wheatcroft
Wy

SIR FRANK WHITTLE RD

Bank
Side
Wy

Tresillian

nior
hool

Langley Dr

Portlands
Av

Walter Evans
C of E School

D2
1 Bermuda Av

A    B    34    C    D

Darley
Abbey

1 grid square represents 500 metres

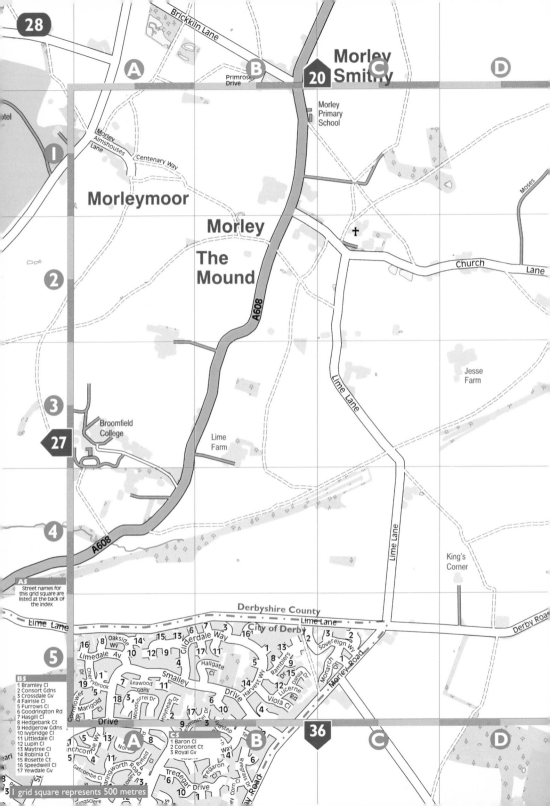

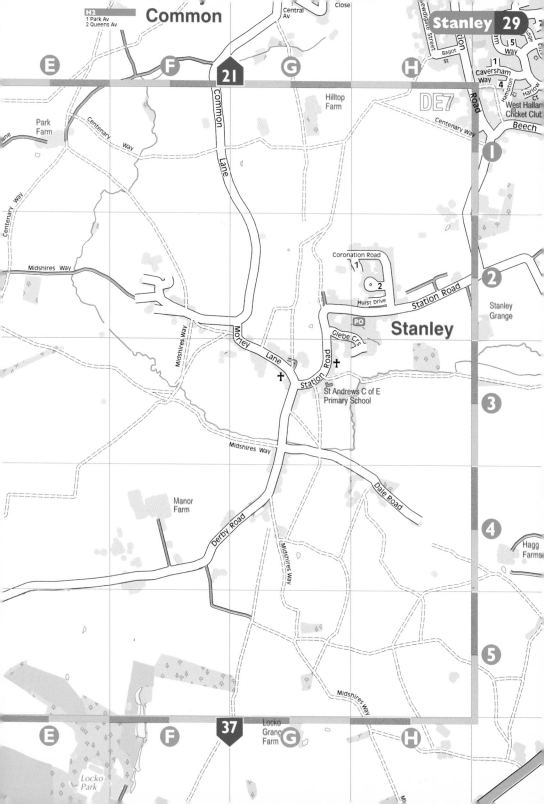

**30**

Nether Burrows

A  B  **22**  C  D

Petty

Riddings Lane

Close

Lane

church

Kirk La

**1**

Langley Green

The Green

**2**

Petty  Close  Lane

The Pastures

Long Lane

Long Lane

**3**

Lees

**4**

Foxfields Farm

**5**

Woodhouse Lane

Bonnie Prince Charlie Walk

A  B  **38**  C  D

Woodhouse Farm

Radbourne

E1
1 Fieldon Cl

E   F   23   G   H

Flagshaw Lane

✝
PO
The Cunnery
ley
Kirk Langley
C of E
Primary School
1
ASHBOURNE   ROAD   A52(T)

I

MOOR LANE

B5020

Poyser Lane

Adam's Road
Pimm's
Road

Pole's Road

Brun   Lane

Bowbridge
Fields Farm

Bowbridge
House Farm

ASHBOURNE

2

Wheathill
Farm

**Langley
Common**

3

32

B5020

4

*Radbourne
Common*

5

E   F   39   G   H

RADB

Silverhill
Farm

Bonnie Prnce Charlie Walk

Radbourne   Lane

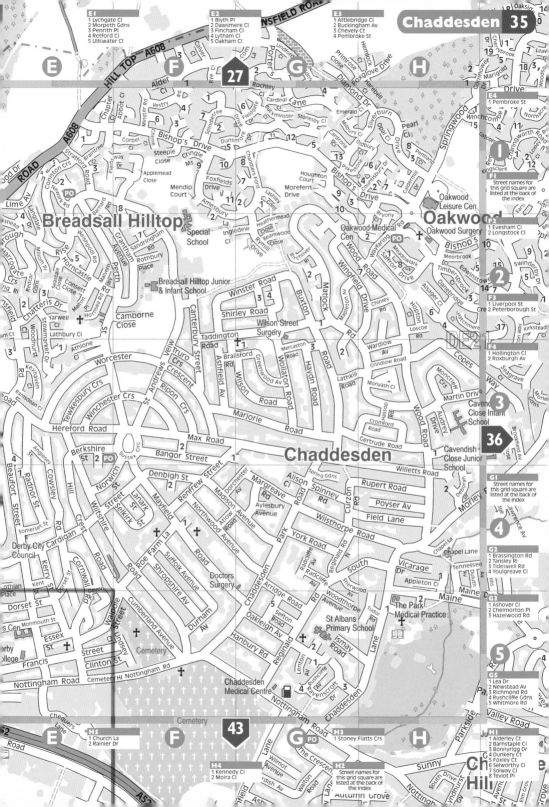

**36**

A1, A2
Street names for
these grid squares
are listed at the
back of the index

**28**

C

D

I

A3
1 Kibworth Cl
2 Sandfield Cl

Oakwood
Leisure Cen

# Oakwood

Oakwood Surgery

Moor Farm

Bishop's

2

A4
1 Atchison Gdns

DE21

Copes

3 Cavendish
Close Infant
School

35

Lees Brook
Community
School

Ca
Close Junior

A5
1 Carson Rd
2 Lansing Gdns
3 Sanderson Rd
4 Trenton Green Dr
5 Washington Av

4

B1
1 Aberdare Cl
2 Biscay Ct
3 Leominster Dr
4 Porthcawl Pl
5 Shrewsbury Cl
6 Wheatsheaf Cl

Maine

cal Practice

5

Derbyshire County
City of Derby

Oregon

Derbyshire County
Council

PO

Longley
Lane

Longley La

Lousie Greaves
La

Sancroft Avenue

1

Junior School

A

44

C

1 Heronswood Dr

D

B5
1 J F Kennedy Gdns
2 Vermont Dr

Springfield
Primary School

# Cherrytree

West Road

West Park

St Werburghs

1 grid square represents 500 metres

E5
1 Badger Cl
2 Gerard Cl
3 Greenfinch Cl
4 Linnet Cl

F5
1 Lancaster Wk
2 Pheasant Field Dr

E F 29 G H

Locko
Grange
Farm

Midshires Way

Locko
Park

Midshires Way

Midshires Way

Dunnshill

Midshires Way

I

Deer Park

2

The
Lake

Bartlewood
Farm

3

A6096

Brunswood
Farm

Spondon
Wood Farm

4

Spondon
Wood

Moor

5

Chaffinch
Close

Deer Pk Vw

Fallow Rd

Goldcrest

Redstart

4

Huntley

Upholl

Eland Cl

Deincourt

Avenue

3 1

Cl

Cl

2

Lane

Sancroft

Hamilton
Road

Hazel Drive

Birch

1

ROAD

Green Lane

End

Fellside

Windsor Dr

Wd Rd

Dale Road

Dale Road

The

2

Dale Rd

DALE

Ridings

E 45 F G H

Holyrood
Close

**Spondon**

Oak Cl

5 7

Way

Beaumaris

1

Ryal

Columbel

Av

Farningham
Cl

Caernarvon
Cl

2

Hampton

Homefarm

2

4

Pares

Top

Yew

Lawnside

Ockbrook
School

3

**H2**
1 Saxondale Av

**H3**
1 Ashton Cl
2 Chelmsford Cl
3 Lingfield Ri
4 Seaton Cl
5 Southgate Cl
6 Wigmore Cl

**H4**
1 Barnwood Cl
2 Staines Cl
3 Taplow Cl
4 Whenby Cl

**H5**
1 Alverton Cl
2 Chantry Cl
3 Uffa Magna

E    F    **31**    G    H

I

**B5020**

RAT

Silverhill Farm

Bonnie Prnce Charlie Walk

Radbourne Lane

Hackwood Farm

City of Derby
Derbyshire County

Potlocks Farm

**2**

Fairbourne Dr

Camellia Cl

Wellan

Belvedere

Langford Rd

Westhall Rd

**3**

Olton Rd
Roydon Cl
Milton Cl
Stanstead Rd
Barnwell
Ladybank Road
Chilson
Rigsby Ct
Sandown Av
Shelford
Branston
Kingsmuir Rd
Daventry
Starcross Ctr
Doctors Surgery
Naseby Close
Draycott Dr
Primary School
Hoylake Dr
Hoylake Ct

Rothwell Rd

**40**

West    Drive

Station

Swayfield Cl
Adwick Cl

Farnworth

Hope Av

Fenton Rd
Vicarage Rd

**4** ckleover Primary School

Chertsey Rd
Dresden
Lambrook Close
Cookham Close
Greenside Cl
Glenfield
Burnham Drive
DE3
Parkstone Ct
Farnham Close
Wendover Cl
Brunton

Park Rd
Medical Centre

Vicarage Rd

Ladybank Road
Lidgate
Prescot Close
Catterick Drive
Cromer Close

Hilton Rd

**5**

Uttoxe

P
m

Howden Cl
Cumbria Wk
Etwall Road
The Square
The Green
The Orchard St

Ardleigh Cl
Ingham Way

el

Hedingham

**49**
E    F    G    H

Bannell's Lane

nerrills rm

Bonehill Farm

**A516(T)**

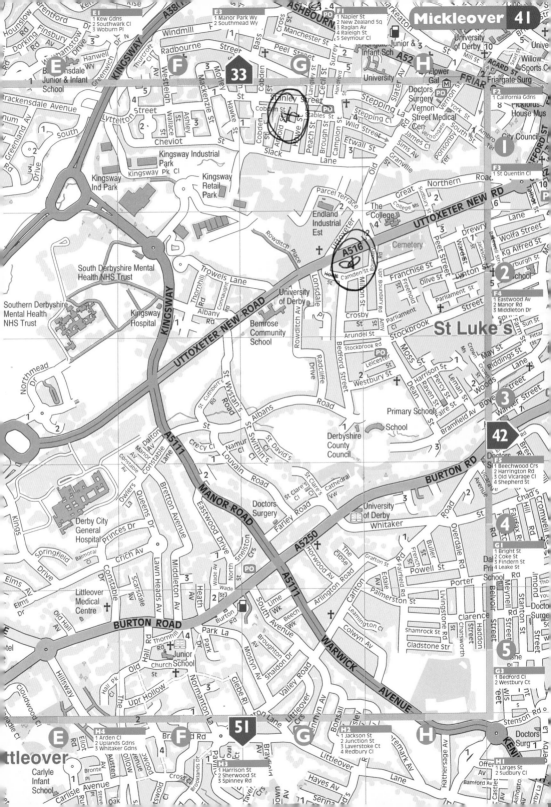

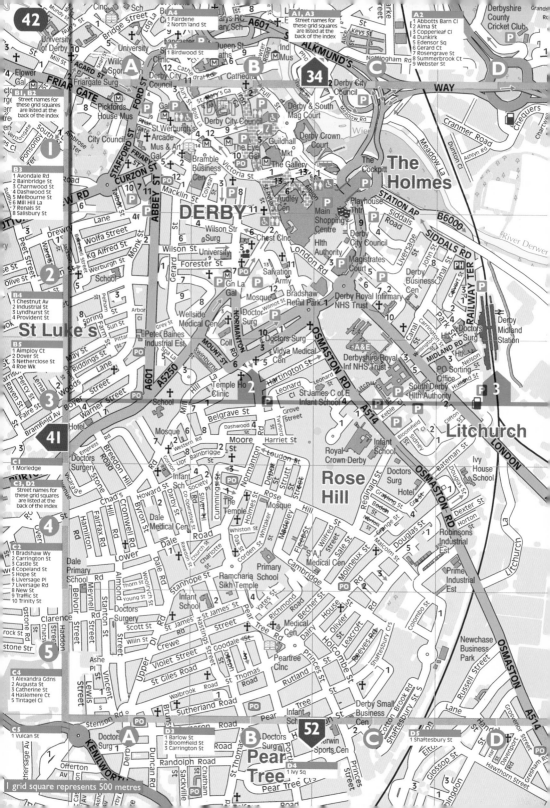

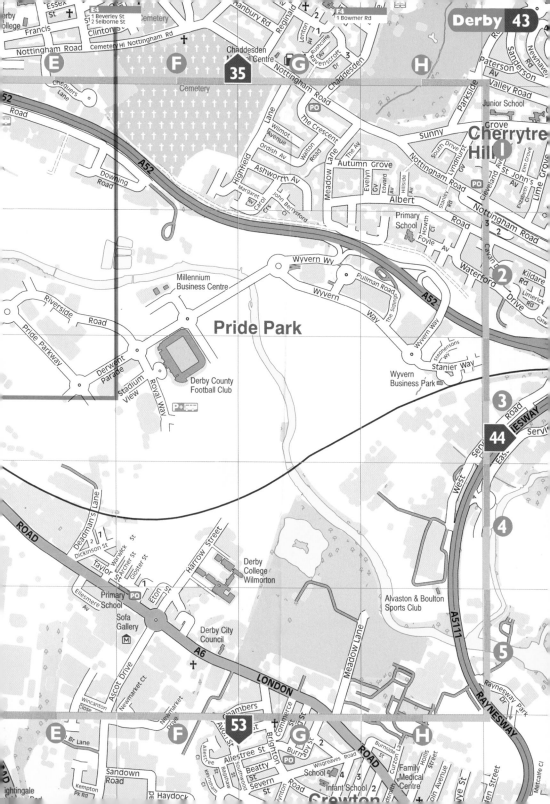

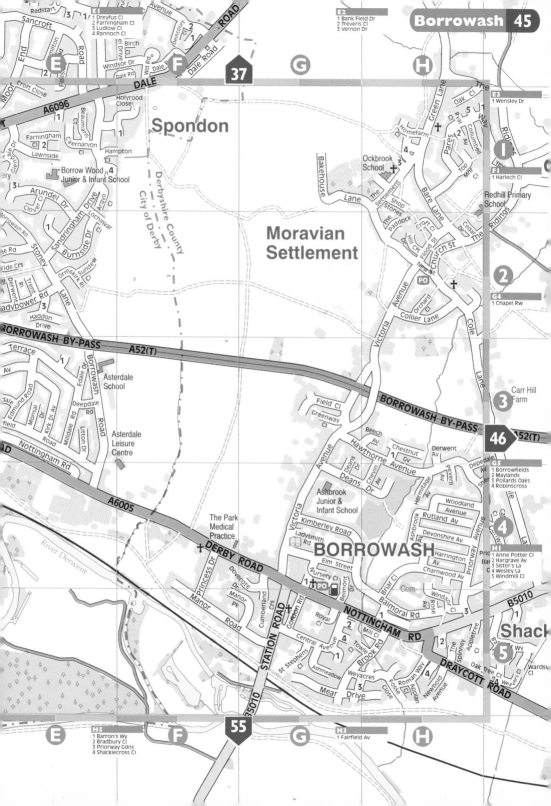

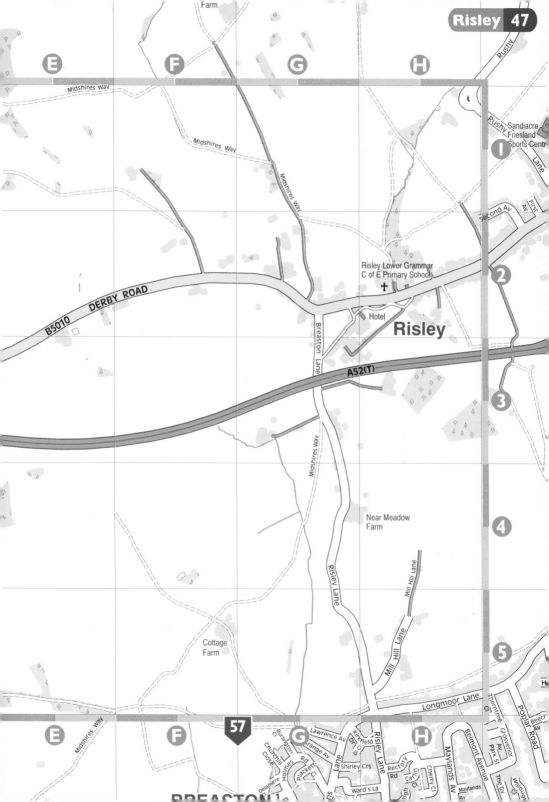

E F G H

Midshires Way

Midshires Way

Midshires Way

Rushy

Rushy

Sandiacre
Friesland
Sports Centr

**I**

Second Av

First Av

Lane

Risley Lower Grammar
C of E Primary School

**2**

DERBY ROAD

B5010

Hotel

**Risley**

Breaston Lane

A52(T)

**3**

Midshires Way

Near Meadow
Farm

**4**

Risley Lane

Mill Hill Lane

Cottage
Farm

**5**

Longmoor Lane

Thorntree Ct

Grosvenor

Poplar Road

Beech

E F **57** G H

Midshires Way

Lawrence Av

Burlington Rd

Churchill Close

Holmes

Plackett

Delamere Rd

Grange Av

Shirley Crs

Ward's La

Kirkfield
Cl

Risley Lane

Rectory
Rd

Cherry Cl

Calvin

Belmont Avenue

Maylands Av

Maylands
Av

Park St

The Gv

Willow

Av

BREASTON

E4
1 Walnut Cl

G2
1 Kingfisher Cl

Bonehill Farm

E   F   39   G   H

I

Hotel

A516(T)

ETWALL ROAD

A516(T)

Prest
Park Cl

Uttoxe

Howard
Cl

Gon Close

Road

Cumbria Wk

Etwall Road

The

The
Square

The
Green

Hedingham

Ardleigh
Cl

Ingham

Way

Orchard
St

The Grange

Wilson
Close

Finch Crs

Mallard Walk

Hospital Lane

Linnet Hill

Merlin Way

Watergo

2

3

50

Grassy Lane

Dee Lane

**Burnaston**

Main Street

New Buildings
Farm

Findern Lane

Green Lane

Bannell's Lane

4

Staker Lane

Burton Road

ROAD

5

E   F   59   G   Park
House   H

BURTON

Doles Lane

Burns Cl
1 Greenacres

E1
1 Burns Cl
2 Greenacres

E2
1 Greenfields Av
2 Lothlorien Cl
3 Moorway Cft

Ploughfield Cl
1 Ploughfield Cl
2 Tiller Cl

WARWICK AVENUE

E

F

41

G

H

ttleover

Carlyle
Infant
School

Hillcross

Derby Moor
Community
School

DE23

St Georges
RC School

NORMANTON

Cemetery

Doctors
Surgery

Junior
School

F1
1 Edgbaston Ct
2 Fernwood Cl
3 Headingley Ct
4 Lawnswood Cl
5 Richmond Av
6 Trent Bridge Ct

I

F2
1 Highfield Rd
2 Rowley Gdns
3 Shireoaks Cl

F3
1 Carisbrooke Gdns
2 Garfield Cl
3 Kegworth Av

2

F4
1 Norbury Crs
2 Plantain Gdns

F5
1 Serina Av
2 Wood Cft

3

52

Sunnyhill
Infant
School

Sunny
Hill

G2
1 Leander Cl
2 Redwing Cft
3 Whitstable Cl

4

G3
1 Alexandre Cl
2 Corfe Cl
3 Lulworth Cl
4 St Stephen's Cl
5 Witham Dr

G4
1 New Mount Cl
2 Rodsley Crs
3 Sapperton Cl

5

G5
1 Avocet Cl
2 Bluebird Ct
3 Coriander Gdns
4 Curlew Cl
5 Glenmore Gn
6 Merlin Gn
7 Peregrine Cl

E

H5
1 Aviemore Wy

F

61

G

H3
1 Bosworth Av
2 Bradgate Ct
3 Cuttlebrook Cl
4 Oadby Ri

H

H1
1 Stenson Rd

H4
Street names for
this grid square are
listed at the back of
the index

Sinfin

H2
1 Caxton Ct

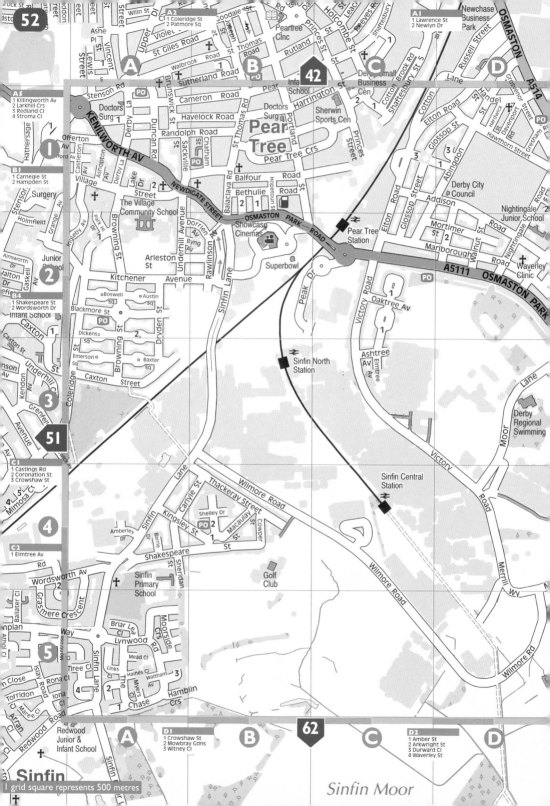

E5
1 Hanslynn
2 Yew Tree La

E

F

45

STATION

St Stephens
Cl

Central Ave
Ashmeadow

F4
1 Barrons Ct

G

Brook

Weyacres
Fosse Close
Mear
Drive
3

Roman Way
Wear Cl

Oak Tree Ct
Wers Cl

H

Arboid Avenue
4

DRAYCOTT ROAD

Wardsw
Cl

I

2

The Park

M

Home
Farm

Elvaston Castle

Elvaston Cricket
Club

Elvaston Castle
Country Park

Elvaston Castle
Working Estate
Museum

M

B5010

MAIN ROAD

3

56
Ambasto

Mere Be

1

Elvaston

Silver La

BALL LANE

Ambaston Lane

4

Brook Road

OAK ROAD

1

Thulston

2

Grove Cl
The Pinfold
Sturges La

BROAD LA

A6

Thurlestone
Grange

Bellington
Hill

5

E

F

65

G

H

Bellington
Farm

56

4

Spinney Cl

Appletree Cl

Ballards WN

2 3

Oak Tree Ct

Weavers CI

West's Cl

DRAYCOTT ROAD

Newbold Avenue

Shacklecross

Wardswood Cl

Grange Farm

**D2**
1 Mcneil Gv
2 St Mary's Av
3 Victoria Av

Draycott Fields Farm

**A**

Gypsy Lane

**B**

46

**C**

Hopwell Road

**D**

I

A6005

DERBY

Nooning Lane

ROAD

WEST WAY

Arthur St

Mapleton Rd

Walter St

Gertrude Rd

Clay St

Cem

Primary School

Meadow Gv

Wallis Cl

2

Lime Grove

Doctors Surg

Thoresby Crs

Cleveland Av

Garfield Av

Mons St

A6005

Market St

Walk Cl

Mills Cl

Sy

VICTORIA RD

PO

3

**Draycott**

Milner Av

1

Holly Cl

South Street

Derwent St

The

3

Meadow Ct

Derwent Crt

Mere Beck

Main

Wilne Road

55

**Ambaston**

Street

River Derwent

4

DE72

5

ington Hill

Ambaston

Ambaston Grange

**A**

**B**

66

**C**

**D**

Bellington Farm

Cottage
Farm

HC

E   F   **47**   G   H

Mill Hill Lane
Longmoor Lane
Thorntree
Grosvenor
Beech
Park St

Midshires Way

Lawrence Av
Burlington
Grange Av
Kirkfield Dr
Risley Lane
Belmont Avenue
Maylands Av
Poplar Road

Churchill
Close
Holmes
Packhert
Shirley Crs
Rectory
Rd
Cherry Cl
Maylands
Av

**BREASTON**

Delamere
Cl
Ward's La
Manoreigh

1

Stevens
Lane
Manor
Ct
Cave

**I**
**H1**
Willow

1 Bourne Sq

Far Cft
Holmes Rd
Blind La
**PO**
**WILSTHORPE ROAD**
Orchard Cl
Maxwell St

Gregory Av
Hind Av
Spring
Festival
Av
**MAIN
ST**
1
Mount St

Stevenson
Av
Hills
Road
Albert
Hayes
Av
**A6005**
**DRAYCOTT ROAD**
Marlborough Rd
Firfield Av
**2**

Villa St
1
**Draycott Parish
Council**
Doctors
Surgery
The Crs
Meadow Cl
Firfield Primary
School

Town End Rd
Elvaston St
2
**STATION ROAD**
Bridge
Field
Belvoir Cl

Fowler
St
3
Attewell Cl
The
Elms
LC
Breaston
Farm

The
Pines
Sawley
Road
LC
Sawley Road
**3**

**M1**

Midshires Way
Wilne Road
Church
Wilne Water
Sports Club
**4**

Midshires Way
Ingle
Hilton Close

**Church
Wilne**

Haddon
Wy
e Lane
**5**

E   **F**   **67**   G   H   S

Midshires Way
Wilne Lane

River Derw

**58**

Derby Road

Leisure Centre

Hilton Road

**Etwall**

Etwall Primary School

B1
1 Courtland Rd

Lodge Close

A1
1 Blakelow Dr
2 Melville Ct

**A**    **B**    **48**    **C**    **D**

New Close Farm

Mill Meadow Way

The Bancroft

Chestnut Grove

Windmill Road

Pine Ct

Road

Belfield Grove

Elms Grove

Springfield Road

Willington Road

**I**

Eggington Road

Grove Park

**A50(T)**

Jacksons Lane

Etwall Common

**2**

Blakeley Lane

Eggington Road

**A50(T)**

Blakeley Lodge

**A50(T)**

**3**

Eggington Road

Boundary Road

**4**

LC

**HILTON ROAD**

**Egginton Common**

**5**

Etwall Road

**A5132**   **CARRIERS**

Grove Lane

**A**    **B**    **ROAD**    **C**    **D**

**A38(T)**

1 grid square represents 500 metres

H2
1 Thrushton Cl

H3
1 Cloverslade

E    F    49    G    H

Park
House

BURTON

Doles Lane

I

BURTON ROAD

A38(T)

Burton Road

Barn Cl

2

W
Lawn   Hillside

Cromwell
Av

Mill
Cl   3

2

The
Hayes

Butts
Close

Porter's Lane

Castle Hill

1

Wren
Pk Cl

2

Aldersley

1

Main   Street

Heath Lane

3

Longlands Lane

60

A38(T)

A50(T)

4

Willington Road

B5008

Road

ETWALL   ROAD

Hill
Farm

Findern Lane

5

BURTON

LC

LC

E    F    G    H

**Willington**

Cemetery

BRIDGE

Derwent
Cl

**60**

**A3**
1 Gorsty Leys
2 Willowsend Cl

**A2**
1 Cardales Cl
2 Green Wy
3 Hawthorn Crs
4 Meadow Cl

A    B    **50**    C    D

BURTON ROAD

Burton

Doles Lane

**I**

**B2**
1 Hazel Cl

BURTON

Bakeacre Lane

Hell Brook

Wallfields Cl

Barn Cl    1   4

**2**

East Lawn

**Findern**

W Lawn    Hillside    Cromwell Av

Mill Cl    3

Porter's Lane    2

Aults Close    1

**The Hayes**    Wren    Pk Cl

Aldersley Cl    7   2

Castle Hill    The Green

Main Street

Heath Lane

Sycamore Av    1    Beech Dr

Lower Green    Common Piece Lane

PO

Brook Close

A50

**3**

Longlands L

**59**

Cemetery

**4**

Willington Road

Heath Lane

**Stensor**

**5**

Buckford    Lane

Findern CP School

Frizams Lane

A    B    C    D

Power Station

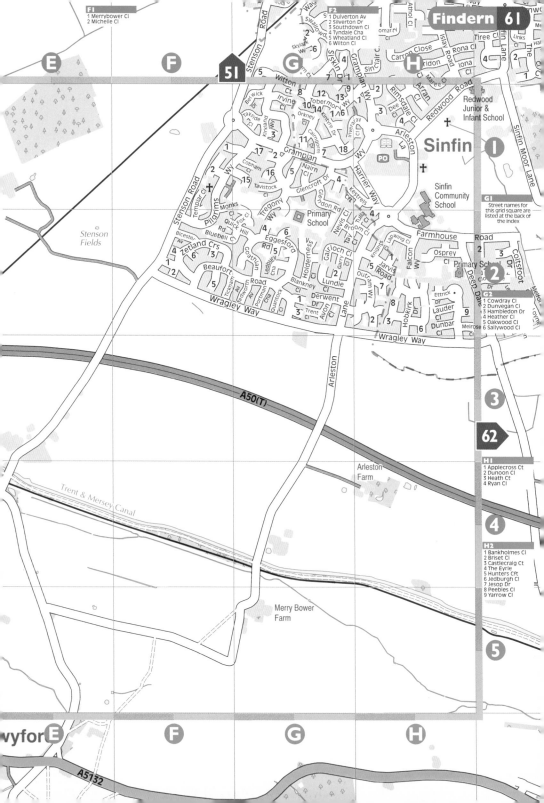

Sinfin

**F1**
1 Merrybower Cl
2 Michelle Cl

**F2**
1 Dulverton Av
2 Silverton Dr
3 Southdown Cl
4 Tyndale Cha
5 Wheatland Cl
6 Wilton Cl

**G1**
Street names for
this grid square are
listed at the back of
the index

**G2**
1 Cowdray Cl
2 Dunvegan Cl
3 Hambledon Dr
4 Heather Cl
5 Oakwood Cl
6 Sallywood Cl

**H1**
1 Applecross Ct
2 Dunoon Cl
3 Heath Ct
4 Ryan Cl

**H2**
1 Bankholmes Cl
2 Briset Cl
3 Castlecraig Ct
4 The Eyrie
5 Hunters Cft
6 Jedburgh Cl
7 Jesop Dr
8 Peebles Cl
9 Yarrow Cl

Redwood
Junior &
Infant School

Sinfin
Community
School

Primary School

Primary
School

Stenson
Fields

Arleston
Farm

Trent & Mersey Canal

Merry Bower
Farm

A50(T)

Wragley Way

A5132

62

52

A2
1 Ashwater Cl
2 Vetchfield Cl
3 Willowherb Cl

Wilmore Rd

Lynwood Rd

Montrose

Mead Cl

Tiree Cl

Links

Haines

Waltham

Islay Road

Athol Cl

Rona Road

Iona

Thirlmere

Myers

Chase

Marie Cl

Torridon

Redwood Road

Hamblin Crs

A

B

C

D

Redwood Junior & Infant School

Sinfin Moor Lane

Sinfin Moor

Sinfin

Sinfin Community School

Sinfin Moor Lane

Farmhouse Road

Coltsfoot Cl

Osprey Cl

Primary School

Lea Farm

Falcon W

Cloverdale Dr

2

3

Melfort

Ettrick Dr

Lauder Cl

Dunbar Cl

Leven Cl

Sunart

Lorne

Watten Av

Lomond

Av

Deep Dale La

9

Melrose

6

Moy

City of Derby
Derbyshire County

Way

3

61

Ashlea Farm

4

A50(T)

The Lowes Farm

5

Barrow-hill

Moor Lane

Moor Lane

Trent & Mersey Canal

A

B

68

C

D

Sinfin Lar

SWARKE

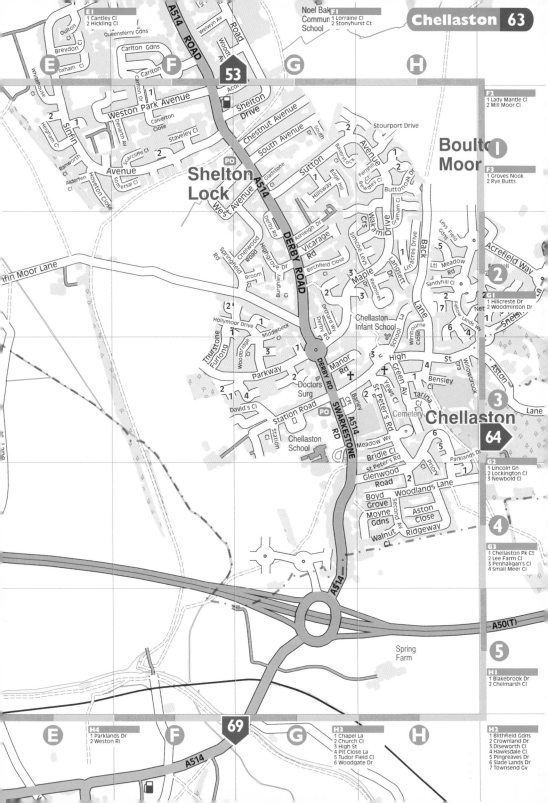

E1
1 Cantley Cl
2 Hickling Cl

F1
Noel Bak
Commun
School
1 Lorraine Cl
2 Stonyhurst Ct

**53**

Quilton Cl
Breydon
Foxham Cl

Queensferry Gdns
Welwyn Av
Carlton Gdns
Carlton
Carlton Dr

Woodi
ACO
Shelton
Drive

Whitehouse
Cl
Simfin
Helpham Cl
Ranworth
Alderfen
Hoveton Close
Avenue
Somersal Cl

Weston Park Avenue
Denarth Av
Calverton
Close
Staveley Cl

S Carcliffe Dr

Chestnut Avenue
South Avenue
Gladstone

Sutton
South
Avenue

Baverstock
Fernhill
Ct
Bardey Cl
Oak Dr
Button

Stourport Drive

**Boulto
Moor**

F2
1 Lady Mantle Cl
2 Mill Moor Cl

F3
1 Groves Nook
2 Rye Butts

**I**

**Shelton
Lock**

PO

West Avenue

Derby Rd

Highgrove Dr

Chelwood Road

Ashleigh Dr

Springfield Rd

Vicarage
Rd

Hillsway
Edge Hill

Wakam
Crs
Simcoe Leys
Drive

Graham Cl
Langsett Cl
Reedmere
Unacres Drive
Back
Ltl Meadow
Rd
Sandyhill Cl
Leys Field Gdns

Acrefield Way

Fairfell

Hill Meadow
Fellow Lands Wy

**2**

G1
1 Hillcreste Dr
2 Woodminton Dr

Ifin Moor Lane

Hollymoor Drive

Thurstone
Furlong

Broom
Burghley
Cl

Orchard Dr
Birchfield Close
Cl

Maple
Dr

Chellaston
Infant School

School

High
Green Av

St
Bensley

Willowbrook
St Gra

Aston
Lane

**3**

Woodbridge
Middlebeck
Cl
Parkway
David's Cl
Station Road
Station
Cl

Derby RD

Manor
Rd

Doctors
Surg

Bailey

PO

A514

Yews Cl
St Peter's Rd

Wimbourne
Close

Tarina

**Chellaston**

**64**

G2
1 Lincoln Gn
2 Lockington Cl
3 Newbold Cl

Chellaston
School

St Peter's Rd
Glenwood
Road

Boyd
Grove
Moyne
Gdns
Walnut
Cl

Meadow Wy
Bridle Cl

Aston
Close
Ridgeway

Second Av

Priory

Parklands Dr

**4**

G3
1 Chellaston Pk Ct
2 Lee Farm Cl
3 Penhaligan's Cl
4 Small Meer Cl

A514

A50(T)

Spring
Farm

**5**

H1
1 Blakebrook Dr
2 Chelmarsh Cl

**E**
**F**
**69**
**G**
**H**

H4
1 Parklands Dr
2 Weston Ri

H3
1 Chapel La
2 Church Cl
3 High St
4 Pit Close La
5 Tudor Field Cl
6 Woodgate Dr

H2
1 Blithfield Gdns
2 Crownland Dr
3 Diseworth Cl
4 Hawksdale Cl
5 Pingreaves Dr
6 Slade Lands Cl
7 Townsend Gv

A514

**64**

**54**

**A2**
1 Bradmoor Gv
2 Leveret Cl
3 Newgate Cl

Mill Hill
Sevenlands Drive
Cl

A6(T)

Derbyshire County
City of Derby

Stubble
Close

Thulston Fields
Farm

Snelsmoor Lane

**B**lton
Moor

**1**

Leys Field Gdns
Laurels Drive
Back
Ltl Meadow
5
Foxdell
Way
**2**
Sandyhill Cl
Acrefield Way
Netherside Dr
2
3
Snelsmoor La
1
7
Fenrow Lands Wy
Lane
6
4

Marsh
Flatts

A50

St
Gra
Willowbrook
**3**
Bensley
Cl
Tarina Cl
ery
**Chellaston**
**63**
Aston
Lane
Chellaston        Lane

Chellaston

6
5
Priory
Parklands
Cl
1
dlands Lane

Aston
Close
dgeway
**4**

Knob
Farm

Weston Fields Farm

**5**

A50(T)

Glebe Farm
**70**

1 grid square represents 500 metres

Thulston

Thurlestone
Grange

E F **55** G H

**I**

A6

B4

STURNTON LA

Derby Road

Bellington
Farm

**2**

Glebe
Farm

A50(T)

Fox Covert
Farm

Manor
Farm

Shardlow
Business
Park

Bird's Nest
Farm

A50(T)

**3**

Aston Hill

Alderslade
Cl

**66**

Aston Hill
Farm

Hanger
Bank
Cem
1

Derby

**Aston-
on-Trent**

Moor Lane

Aston Lane

**4**

Lane

Aston-on-Trent
Primary School

Long Croft

Leas

Compton Avenue

Road

Walnut Cl

Clarkes
Lane

Manor
Farm

Ash Cl

Willow
Close

Acre

Holden
Avenue

**2**

PO

1

Ellison
Avenue

Bell
Avenue

Posy
Lane

Rectory Gdns

Park View

**2**

**5**

Valerie Road

Willow Park
Way

Aston Hall Drive

Shardlow Road

E F **71** G H

Breaston Road

Aston Hall
Hospital

Trent & Mersey Canal

**66**
Bellington Hill

**A**   **B**   **56**   **C**   **D**

D3
1 Cavendish Ct
2 The Maltings

Ambaston Grange

Bellington Farm

**I**

Glebe Farm

**2**

Manor Farm

PO   **LONDON ROAD**   **Shardlow**

Clover Ct

Shardlow Business Park

Glenn Wy

Alts Nook Wy

The Grove Hospital

Shardlow County Primary School

W End Drive

Wakelyn Cl

The Wharf

The Whf

**LONDON ROAD**

**A50(T)**

**3**

Aston Lane

Cowlishaw Cl

Canal Bank

**65**

Trent & Mersey Canal

Aston Lane

Roydon Hall Farm

**4**

**A50(T)**

Aston Lane

Acre Lane

**5**

River Trent

**A**   Derbyshire County   **B**   **72**   **C**   **D**

Leicestershire County

Back Lane

1 grid square represents 500 metres

Church
Wilne

E    F    57    G    H

I

Great
Wilne

Midshires Way

River Derwent

Long Row Lane

Millfield

Midshires Way

2 M1

3

Marina

River Trent

B6540

Hemington
Fields House

Cavendish
Bridge

LONDON    ROAD

PH

Donington Lane

TAMWORTH ROAD

Netherfield

4

A50(T)

Rycroft    Road

5

Donington Lane

Station Road

A50(T)

E    F    73    G    H

A    B    62    C    D

B2
1 Beaumont Cl

Barrow-hill

Moor

B1
1 Walnut Cl

Trent & Mersey Canal

Sinfin Lane

**1**

SWARKESTONE ROAD

A5132    A5132    BARROW    LANE

Twyford Road

Cemetery

Brookfield

The Nook

Chapel Lane

Doctors
Surgery

Church La

Sale & Davys
C of E
School

Hall

Park

Church    Lane

**2**

Barrow upon
Trent

Green Lane

**3**

River Trent

**4**

Ingleby

**5**

Ingleby Toft

A    B    74    C    D

E    F    **63**    G    H

**I**

A514

Woodshop Lane

e Water Mdw

✝ **Swarkestone**

The Hall

**2**

SWARKESTONE BRIDGE

**3**

Swarkestone
Boat Club

**70**

Stanton
y Bridge

A514

River Trent

**4**

✝

The Hills

Ward's Lane

**5**

B587

E    F    **75**    G    H

Breach
Lane

**DE73**

D3
1 Park La

D2
1 Old Gate Av

A   B   64   C   D

Glebe Farm

1

2

Trent & Mersey Canal

Hill
Farm

3

69

Weston-on-Tre
Parochial
Primary School

Wilmot Av

Main

Park Lane

Rectory
Farm

Trent & Mersey Ca

4

5

Trent Lane

Sleepy Lane

A   B   76   C   D

King's
Newton

Hall Leys Lane

Main Str

1 grid square represents 500 metres

E2
1 Forrester Av

Rectory

Shardlow Road
2

Willow Park Way

Aston Hall Drive

**65**

E

F

G

H

Weston Road

Aston Hall
Hospital

Trent & Mersey Canal

I

Weston
Grange

**Weston-on-Trent**

2

River Trent

Lane

King's

Mill

Lane

3

**King's Mills**

Hotel

**72**

Home
Farm

4

River Trent

Donington
Hall

5

E

F

**77**

G

H

Newton's
Corner

...shire County
...ire County

D4
1 Carrs Cl
2 Delven La
3 Lothian Pl
4 Peartree Cl

D3
1 Loudoun Pl
2 Rawdon Cl
3 Selina Cl
4 The Spinney

A
B
66
C
D

1

D5
1 Cavendish Cl

River Trent

Derbyshire County
Leicestershire County

River Trent

LC

2

Trent

Short Lane

3

71

Bentley Road
Hazelrigg Cl
Walton Hl
Spittal
Campion Hill
Shirley Cl
Darsway
Fox Road
Salter Cl
Fosbrook Dr
Staunton Cl
School Lane
Huntingdon Dr
Haul
Roby Lea
Queensway
Orchard CP School
Drive
Minton Rd
Studbrook Close
The Green
Cordwell Cl
Kirkland Close
Ferrers Close
Grange
Drive
Tipnal Road
4

Park Lane

Paddock Cl
Bosworth Road
Starkie Avenue
Park Av
Shields Cresent
Orchard Avenue
Park Lane
Towles Pastures
Cheribough Road
Cooks Av
High Street
Crabtree Close

5

A
B
C
Hill Top Farm
Hill Top
PH
D
Disel Road

1 grid square represents 500 metres

E3
1 The Moat
2 Monteith Pl
3 Montford Ms

E4
1 The Biggin
2 Mount Pleasant
3 St Anne's La

Rycroft

Road

**E** **F** **67** **G** **H**

A50(T)

**I**

E5
1 Routh Av
2 Windmill Cl

**2**

Trent Lane
Industrial Estate

Station Road

New Delight

**Hemington**

Main

Hemington Lane

Station Road

Gasny
Av

Newbold
Drive

Sycamore Road

Willow Road

Hawthorn Road

Station Road

Victoria
Street

Grange Farm Cl

Lockington Road

Hemington
Primary School

PO

Main Street

1

1

PO

Chur

**3** **Loc**

Tanyard
Close

The Horse
Shoes

Church Lane

Harcourt
Place

Bondgate

The Hollow

Castle
Hill

1 3

The Barroon

Hemington Hill

Cem

**4**

PO

St

Borough

3

Apiary
Gate

Clapgun Street

Garden Crs

1

Charnwood
Avenue

Moira Dale

Eastway

ctors
rg

Hotel

Raven Lane

St Edwards
Junior School

2

Castle Donington
Community
College

Eaton
Road

Hastings St

1

Harvey
Rg

2

ward's

Meadow
Crs

Stonehill

Cedar Road

**CASTLE
DONINGTON**

**DE74**

**5**

**E** **F** **G** **H**

A  B  C  D

Ingleby Toft  68

1

2

Warsick Lane

Seven
Spouts
Farm

Robin
Wood

3

Knowle Hill
Farm

4

Woodside

5

STANTON HILL

Dame Catherine
Harpurs School

Chapel Street

Melbourne Lane

MAIN  STREET

A  B  C  D

BURTON ROAD

A514

PO

Grange Cl

Church La

Rose La

Ingleby La

Banton's Lane

Harpur
Avenue

Narrow Lane

Ticknall

1 grid square represents 500 metres

H2
1 Benbow Av
2 Blackthorn Cl
3 The Croft
4 Hardacre Cl
5 Lampad Cl
6 Redway Cft

H3
1 Hatton Ct
2 Moira St
3 Orchard Cl
4 Quick Cl
5 Thomas Cook Cl

E  F  69  B587  G  H

I

PH

Netfield Cft
Smith Av
Pack
The Woodlands
Woodlands Ct
Horse
Oakland
Cem
Me
Ju
Sc

Breach Lane
DE73
DERBY ROAD

Melton Av
Windsor Av
Doctors Surg
Woodlands
Coronation Close
Grange Close
Queensway
2
Beech Av
Grange
Road

Acacia Drive
7
4
6
5
Spinney Hill
3
8
Derby
Victoria Street
North St
Alma
South Street
Dunnicliffe La
Chapel Street
Jubilee Cl
Road
3
Potter Stre
3

Cockshut Lane Business Centre
2
Cockshut Lane

Highfield House

Hope St
Union St
Commerce Street
George Street
South Street
MELBOURNE
4
5
Selina St
High Str
Penn
Church str
4
1
Lane
76

St Brides

Riding Bank

Washington Close
Peniston Rise
Ashby Road

Shaw House

ROBINSON'S HILL  B587

4

Bleak House

Shepherd's Lane

Bog Lane

B587

5

Derby Hills House Farm

**Woodhouses**

E  F  G  H

Staunton Harold Reservoir

**A3**
1 Bishops Ct
2 Market Pl
3 Palmerston Ct
4 Salisbury La

**A2**
1 Blakemore Av

A    B    C    D

# King's Newton

Sleepy

**A4**
1 Church Sq

I

PH

Trent Lane

Hall Leys Lane

Main Street

Woodlands Cl

Netfield Cl

PACK

Smith Av

Cem

The Woodlands

Horse Road

Jawbone La

Station Road

Melton Av

Windsor Av

Doctors

Woodlands Way

Grange Cl

Oaklands Wy

Huntingdon Ct

2

**D4**
1 Wilson Ri

1

Queensway

Coronation

Derby

Beech Av

Melbourne Junior & Infant School

1

3

Pimney Hill

Victoria Street

North St

South Street

George Street

Alma Street

Huntcliffe La

Blanch Cft

Chapel Street

Jubilee Cl

Castle Street

Castle Lane

3

PO

3

2

Potter Street

Castle Mews

Bianca Cft

Selina St

Street

2

4

5

ington

Penistone Rise

Church Street

Blackwell La

4

1

1

Melbourne Hall

Derby Road

Lane

Pool Road

Fort Street

4

Main Street

Green Lane

Breedon Priory Golf Club

B58

5

Pool Road

A    B    C    D

*Melbourne Parks*

Derbyshire County

Leicestershire County

1 grid square represents 500 metres

E    F    **71**    G    H

I

Newton's
Corner

Derbyshire County
Leicestershire County

Donington Park
Motor Racing Circuit

The Donington
Racing Car Mu

2    M

Donington Park
Farm

Foot Lane

Forty

Slade Lane

3    WALTON HILL

Isley

Wilson Hall
Farm

Slade Lane

✝

4

Slade Lane

Wilson

A453

5

E    F    G    H

MOOR LANE

| | | | |
|---|---|---|---|
| Allenton | 52 D5 | Denby Bottles | 13 H1 |
| Allestree | 26 A5 | Denby Common | 9 F4 |
| Alvaston | 54 A2 | Derby | 2 C5 |
| Ambaston | 55 H3 | Draycott | 56 C2 |
| Aston-on-Trent | 65 G4 | Drum Hill | 19 G4 |
| Bargate | 12 D1 | Duffield | 17 H2 |
| Barrow upon Trent | 68 B2 | Duffieldbank | 18 B1 |
| Belper | 6 C2 | Eaton Hill | 18 D4 |
| Blackbrook | 5 E2 | Egginton Common | 58 B5 |
| Borrowash | 45 G4 | Elvaston | 55 H4 |
| Boulton | 53 H3 | Etwall | 48 A5 |
| Boulton Moor | 63 H1 | Far Laund | 6 D1 |
| Breadsall | 27 F4 | Farnah Green | 5 F4 |
| Breadsall Hilltop | 35 E2 | Findern | 60 A2 |
| Breaston | 57 F1 | Flaxholme | 18 A4 |
| Burnaston | 49 E4 | Great Wilne | 67 E2 |
| Castle Donington | 73 F5 | Gun Hills | 10 A5 |
| Cavendish Bridge | 67 F4 | The Gutter | 6 D3 |
| Chaddesden | 35 G3 | Hazelwood | 11 E1 |
| Chellaston | 63 H3 | Heanor Gate | 15 H2 |
| Cherrytree Hill | 43 H1 | Hemington | 73 G2 |
| Church Wilne | 57 E5 | Hillcross | 51 E2 |
| Cinderhill | 7 E5 | Holbrook | 13 E4 |
| Codnor Breach | 9 F3 | Holbrook Moor | 12 C3 |
| Cowers Lane | 4 A4 | The Holmes | 3 F4 |
| Cowhill | 6 B5 | Horsley Woodhouse | 14 B4 |
| Crewton | 53 C1 | Ingleby | 68 B4 |
| Cross Hill | 9 H1 | Kedleston | 23 H1 |
| Cumberhills Cottages | 16 D4 | Kilburn | 13 H2 |
| Dalbury | 38 A5 | King's Mills | 71 G3 |
| Darley Abbey | 34 B1 | King's Newton | 76 B1 |
| Denby | 14 B1 | Kirk Langley | 30 D1 |

| | | | |
|---|---|---|---|
| Langley Common | 31 G3 | Quarndon Common | 17 G |
| Langley Green | 30 C2 | Radbourne | 38 |
| Lees | 30 A4 | Rawson Green | 7 G |
| Litchurch | 42 D3 | Risley | 47 H |
| Little Chester | 34 B4 | Rose Hill | 42 G |
| Little Eaton | 18 D5 | St Luke's | 41 H |
| Littleover | 50 D1 | Scotches | 5 |
| Lower Kilburn | 13 G3 | Shacklecross | 46 A |
| Mackworth | 32 B4 | Shardlow | 66 B |
| Makeney | 12 B4 | Shelton Lock | 63 F |
| Marehay | 8 C1 | Shottlegate | 4 |
| Markeaton | 33 E3 | Sinfin | 61 H |
| Melbourne | 75 G3 | Smalley | 15 |
| Mickleover | 40 A4 | Smalley Common | 21 H |
| Milford | 12 B3 | Smalley Green | 21 |
| Moravian Settlement | 45 G2 | Smithy Houses | 8 A |
| Morley | 28 B2 | Spondon | 45 H |
| Morleymoor | 28 A1 | Spring Hill | 11 G |
| Morley Park | 7 H1 | Stanley | 29 H |
| Morley Smithy | 20 C5 | Stanley Common | 21 H |
| Mount Pleasant | 5 G1 | Stanton by Bridge | 69 E |
| Nether Burrows | 22 A5 | Stenson | 60 D |
| Normanton | 51 G2 | Street Lane | 8 A |
| The Oaks | 11 G4 | Sunny Hill | 51 G |
| Oakwood | 35 H2 | Swarkestone | 69 H |
| Ockbrook | 46 A1 | Thulston | 55 |
| Openwoodgate | 7 E4 | Weston-on-Trent | 71 E |
| Osmaston | 53 E2 | White Moor | 6 D |
| Park Nook | 16 D5 | Wilson | 77 E |
| Pear Tree | 52 B1 | Windley | 10 A |
| Pride Park | 43 F2 | Woodhouses | 75 G |
| Quarndon | 25 F1 | Woodside | 20 C |

## USING THE STREET INDEX

Street names are listed alphabetically. Each street name is followed by its postal town or area locality, the Postcode District, the page number, and the reference to the square in which the name is found.

Example: **Abbeyfields CI** *DERBYW* DE22 ........**34** B1 **1**

Some entries are followed by a number in a blue box. This number indicates the location of the street within the referenced grid square. The full street name is listed at the side of the map page.

## GENERAL ABBREVIATIONS

| | | | | | | | |
|---|---|---|---|---|---|---|---|
| ACC | ACCESS | CUTT | CUTTINGS | HOL | HOLLOW | NW | NORTH WEST |
| ALY | ALLEY | CV | COVE | HOSP | HOSPITAL | O/P | OVERPASS |
| AP | APPROACH | CYN | CANYON | HRB | HARBOUR | OFF | OFFICE |
| AR | ARCADE | DEPT | DEPARTMENT | HTH | HEATH | ORCH | ORCHARD |
| ASS | ASSOCIATION | DL | DALE | HTS | HEIGHTS | OV | OVAL |
| AV | AVENUE | DM | DAM | HVN | HAVEN | PAL | PALACE |
| BCH | BEACH | DR | DRIVE | HWY | HIGHWAY | PAS | PASSAGE |
| BLDS | BUILDINGS | DRO | DROVE | IMP | IMPERIAL | PAV | PAVILION |
| BND | BEND | DRY | DRIVEWAY | IN | INLET | PDE | PARADE |
| BNK | BANK | DWGS | DWELLINGS | IND EST | INDUSTRIAL ESTATE | PH | PUBLIC HOUSE |
| BR | BRIDGE | E | EAST | INF | INFIRMARY | PK | PARK |
| BRK | BROOK | EMB | EMBANKMENT | INFO | INFORMATION | PKWY | PARKWAY |
| BTM | BOTTOM | EMBY | EMBASSY | INT | INTERCHANGE | PL | PLACE |
| BUS | BUSINESS | ESP | ESPLANADE | IS | ISLAND | PLN | PLAIN |
| BVD | BOULEVARD | EST | ESTATE | JCT | JUNCTION | PLNS | PLAINS |
| BY | BYPASS | EX | EXCHANGE | JTY | JETTY | PLZ | PLAZA |
| CATH | CATHEDRAL | EXPY | EXPRESSWAY | KG | KING | POL | POLICE STATION |
| CEM | CEMETERY | EXT | EXTENSION | KNL | KNOLL | PR | PRINCE |
| CEN | CENTRE | F/O | FLYOVER | L | LAKE | PREC | PRECINCT |
| CFT | CROFT | FC | FOOTBALL CLUB | LA | LANE | PREP | PREPARATORY |
| CH | CHURCH | FK | FORK | LDG | LODGE | PRIM | PRIMARY |
| CHA | CHASE | FLD | FIELD | LGT | LIGHT | PROM | PROMENADE |
| CHYD | CHURCHYARD | FLDS | FIELDS | LK | LOCK | PRS | PRINCESS |
| CIR | CIRCLE | FLS | FALLS | LKS | LAKES | PRT | PORT |
| CIRC | CIRCUS | FLS | FLATS | LNDG | LANDING | PT | POINT |
| CL | CLOSE | FM | FARM | LTL | LITTLE | PTH | PATH |
| CLFS | CLIFFS | FT | FORT | LWR | LOWER | PZ | PIAZZA |
| CMP | CAMP | FWY | FREEWAY | MAG | MAGISTRATE | QD | QUADRANT |
| CNR | CORNER | FY | FERRY | MAN | MANSIONS | QU | QUEEN |
| CO | COUNTY | GA | GATE | MD | MEAD | QY | QUAY |
| COLL | COLLEGE | GAL | GALLERY | MDW | MEADOWS | R | RIVER |
| COM | COMMON | GDN | GARDEN | MEM | MEMORIAL | RBT | ROUNDABOUT |
| COMM | COMMISSION | GDNS | GARDENS | MKT | MARKET | RD | ROAD |
| CON | CONVENT | GLD | GLADE | MKTS | MARKETS | RDG | RIDGE |
| COT | COTTAGE | GLN | GLEN | ML | MALL | REP | REPUBLIC |
| COTS | COTTAGES | GN | GREEN | ML | MILL | RES | RESERVOIR |
| CP | CAPE | GND | GROUND | MNR | MANOR | RFC | RUGBY FOOTBALL CLUB |
| CPS | COPSE | GRA | GRANGE | MS | MEWS | RI | RISE |
| CR | CREEK | GRG | GARAGE | MSN | MISSION | RP | RAMP |
| CREM | CREMATORIUM | GT | GREAT | MT | MOUNT | RW | ROW |
| CRS | CRESCENT | GTWY | GATEWAY | MTN | MOUNTAIN | S | SOUTH |
| CSWY | CAUSEWAY | GV | GROVE | MTS | MOUNTAINS | SCH | SCHOOL |
| CT | COURT | HGR | HIGHER | MUS | MUSEUM | SE | SOUTH EAST |
| CTRL | CENTRAL | HL | HILL | MWY | MOTORWAY | SER | SERVICE AREA |
| CTS | COURTS | HLS | HILLS | N | NORTH | SH | SHORE |
| CTYD | COURTYARD | HO | HOUSE | NE | NORTH EAST | SHOP | SHOPPING |

(WY ........ SKYWAY
MT ........ SUMMIT
OC ........ SOCIETY
P ........ SPUR
PR ........ SPRING
Q ........ SQUARE
T ........ STREET
TN ........ STATION
TR ........ STREAM
TRD ........ STRAND
SW ........ SOUTH WEST
TDG ........ TRADING
TER ........ TERRACE
THWY ........ THROUGHWAY
TNL ........ TUNNEL
TOLL ........ TOLLWAY
TPK ........ TURNPIKE
TR ........ TRACK
TRL ........ TRAIL
TWR ........ TOWER
U/P ........ UNDERPASS
UNI ........ UNIVERSITY
UPR ........ UPPER
V ........ VALE
VA ........ VALLEY
VIAD ........ VIADUCT
VIL ........ VILLA
VIS ........ VISTA
VLG ........ VILLAGE
VLS ........ VILLAS
VW ........ VIEW
W ........ WEST
WD ........ WOOD
WHF ........ WHARF
WK ........ WALK
WKS ........ WALKS
WLS ........ WELLS
WY ........ WAY
YD ........ YARD
YHA ........ YOUTH HOSTEL

## POSTCODE TOWNS AND AREA ABBREVIATIONS

SHB ........ Ashbourne
PR/DUF ........ Belper/Duffield
WSH/BRSTN ........ Borrowash/Breaston
DON/KEG ........ Castle Donington/Kegworth
ERBY ........ Derby
DERBYE ........ Derby east
DERBYSE ........ Derby southeast
DERBYW ........ Derby west
HEANOR ........ Heanor
ILK ........ Ilkeston
LGEAT ........ Long Eaton
MCKLVR ........ Mickleover
MELB/CHEL ........ Melbourne/Chellaston
NORM/LIT ........ Normanton/Littleover
RDERBYSW ........ Rural Derby southwest
RIPLEY ........ Ripley

## Index - streets

## Abb - Bar

## A


bbeyfields Cl *DERBYW* DE22 .... 34 B1
bbey Hl *DERBYW* DE22 .... 26 C4
bbey Hill Rd *DERBYW* DE22 .... 33 G1
bbey La *DERBYW* DE22 .... 34 B2
bbey St *DERBYW* DE22 .... 2 B6
bbey Yd *DERBYW* DE22 .... 34 B2
bbot Cl *DERBYE* DE21 .... 35 F1
bbotts Barn Cl *DERBYW* DE22 .. 2 B5
bells *RIPLEY* DE5 .... 14 B1
berdare Cl *DERBYE* DE21 .... 36 B1
bingdon St *DERBYSE* DE24 .... 52 D1
bney Cl *MCKLVR* DE3 .... 40 C4
cacia Av *MCKLVR* DE3 .... 40 B5
cacia Dr *MELB/CHEL* DE73 .... 75 H2
cer Cft *DERBYE* DE21 .... 27 F5
corn Cl *DERBYSE* DE24 .... 63 F1
corn Dr *BPR/DUF* DE56 .... 6 B2
corn Wy *BPR/DUF* DE56 .... 6 B2
*DERBYE* DE21 .... 36 B2
*DERBYE* DE21 .... 44 B1
crefield Wy *MELB/CHEL* DE73 .... 64 A2
cre La *BWSH/BRSTN* DE72 .... 66 A5
cton Rd *DERBYW* DE22 .... 32 C5
dale Rd *HEANOR* DE75 .... 15 G2
dam's Rd *ASHB* DE6 .... 31 F3
ddison Rd *DERBYSE* DE24 .... 52 C1
delaide Cl *MCKLVR* DE3 .... 40 B2
delphi Cl *NORM/LIT* DE23 .... 50 D3
dler Ct *DERBY* DE1 .... 34 C4
drian St *DERBYSE* DE24 .... 53 E3
dwick Cl *MCKLVR* DE3 .... 39 H4
gard St *DERBY* DE1 .... 2 A2
mploy Ct *NORM/LIT* DE23 .... 42 B5
inley Cl *DERBYSE* DE24 .... 53 G2
insworth Dr *NORM/LIT* DE23 .... 51 H2
lbany Rd *DERBYW* DE22 .... 41 F2
lbemarle Rd *DERBYE* DE21 .... 36 A5
lbert Crs *DERBYE* DE21 .... 44 A2
lbert Rd *BWSH/BRSTN* DE72 .... 57 E2
*DERBYE* DE21 .... 43 H1
lbert St *BPR/DUF* DE56 .... 6 A3
*DERBY* DE1 .... 2 D4
lbion St *DERBY* DE1 .... 2 D4
lder Cl *DERBYE* DE21 .... 35 F1
lderfen Cl *DERBYSE* DE24 .... 63 E1
lderley Ct *DERBYE* DE21 .... 35 H1
lder Rd *BPR/DUF* DE56 .... 6 B4
ldersgate *DERBYW* DE22 .... 32 C4
lderslade Cl *BWSH/BRSTN* DE72 .. 65 G3
ldersley Cl *RDERBYSW* DE65 .... 59 H3
ldwych *DERBYW* DE22 .... 32 D5
lexandra Gdns
*NORM/LIT* DE23 .... 42 C4
lexandre Cl *NORM/LIT* DE23 .... 51 G3
lfred Rd *BPR/DUF* DE56 .... 13 H2
lfreton Rd *DERBYE* DE21 .... 19 E3
*DERBYE* DE21 .... 26 D2
*DERBYE* DE21 .... 34 C3
lice St *DERBY* DE1 .... 2 E2
lison Cl *DERBYE* DE21 .... 35 G4
llan Av *NORM/LIT* DE23 .... 50 B1
llen St *DERBYSE* DE24 .... 53 F4
llestree Cl *DERBYSE* DE24 .... 53 F1
llestree La *DERBYW* DE22 .... 33 G1
llestree St *DERBYSE* DE24 .... 53 F1
ll Saints Ct *MCKLVR* DE3 .... 40 A5
Alma Hts *MCKLVR* DE3 .... 40 B5
Alma St *DERBYW* DE22 .... 2 B5
*MELB/CHEL* DE73 .... 75 H3
Almond St *NORM/LIT* DE23 .... 42 A4
Alport Cl *BPR/DUF* DE56 .... 6 C2
Alsager Cl *DERBYE* DE21 .... 35 H2
Alstonfield Dr *DERBYW* DE22 .... 33 H2
Alton Cl *DERBYW* DE22 .... 25 G5
Alton Rd *BPR/DUF* DE56 .... 6 D3
Alts Nook Wy *BWSH/BRSTN* DE72 .. 66 B3
Alum Cl *DERBYSE* DE24 .... 54 B2
Alvaston St *DERBYSE* DE24 .... 54 A1
Alverton Cl *MCKLVR* DE3 .... 39 H5
Alward's Cl *DERBYSE* DE24 .... 53 H3
Ambaston La *BWSH/BRSTN* DE72 .. 55 G4
Amber Ct *BPR/DUF* DE56 .... 6 B1
Amberley Dr *DERBYSE* DE24 .... 52 A4
Amber Rd *DERBYW* DE22 .... 33 G2
Amber St *DERBYSE* DE24 .... 52 D2
Ambrose Ter *DERBY* DE1 .... 41 H1
Amen Aly *DERBY* DE1 .... 2 C3
Amesbury La *DERBYE* DE21 .... 35 F1
Amy St *DERBYW* DE22 .... 41 H2
Anderson St *DERBYSE* DE24 .... 53 G2
Andrew Cl *NORM/LIT* DE23 .... 50 B1
Andrews Dr *ILK* DE7 .... 21 F4
Anglers' La *DERBYE* DE21 .... 44 D4
Anglesey St *DERBYE* DE21 .... 35 E3
Anne Potter Cl
*BWSH/BRSTN* DE72 .... 45 H1
Anstey Ct *DERBYE* DE21 .... 35 H2
Anthony Crs *DERBYSE* DE24 .... 53 G3
Anthony Dr *DERBYSE* DE24 .... 53 G3
Apiary Ga *CDON/KEG* DE74 .... 73 E4
Appian Cl *BWSH/BRSTN* DE72 .... 45 H5
Appian Wy *DERBYSE* DE24 .... 54 C3
Applecross Ct *DERBYSE* DE24 .... 61 H1
Appledore Dr *DERBYE* DE21 .... 36 A2
Applegate Cl *DERBYE* DE21 .... 28 A5
Applemead Cl *DERBYE* DE21 .... 35 F1
Appleton Cl *DERBYE* DE21 .... 35 H4
Appleton Dr *BPR/DUF* DE56 .... 6 C1
Appletree Cl *BWSH/BRSTN* DE72 .... 45 H5
Applewood Cl *BPR/DUF* DE56 .... 6 C2
Arbor Cl *DERBYW* DE22 .... 2 B6
Arboretum St *NORM/LIT* DE23 .. 42 C3
*NORM/LIT* DE23 .... 42 C3
Archer St *DERBYSE* DE24 .... 43 F4
Arden Cl *NORM/LIT* DE23 .... 41 H4
Ardleigh Cl *MCKLVR* DE3 .... 50 A1
Argyle St *DERBYW* DE22 .... 42 A3
Argyll Cl *DERBYE* DE21 .... 45 E1
Arkwright Av *BPR/DUF* DE56 .... 6 D1
Arkwright St *DERBYSE* DE24 .... 52 D2
Arleston La *DERBYSE* DE24 .... 61 G3
Arleston St *NORM/LIT* DE23 .... 52 A2
Arlington Dr *DERBYSE* DE24 .... 53 G3
Arlington Rd *NORM/LIT* DE23 .... 41 G5
Armscote Cl *DERBYE* DE21 .... 36 A1
Arnhem Ter *DERBYE* DE21 .... 44 D3
Arnold St *DERBYW* DE22 .... 41 G1
Arran Cl *DERBYSE* DE24 .... 61 H1
Arridge Rd *DERBYE* DE21 .... 35 G4
Arthur Hind Cl *DERBYW* DE22 .... 34 A4
Arthur St *BWSH/BRSTN* DE72 .... 56 C2
*DERBY* DE1 .... 34 A4
Arundel Av *MCKLVR* DE3 .... 40 C4
Arundel Dr *DERBYE* DE21 .... 45 E1
Arundel St *DERBYW* DE22 .... 41 G3
Ascot Dr *DERBYSE* DE24 .... 53 E2
Ash Acre *BPR/DUF* DE56 .... 7 E3
Ashbourne Rd *ASHB* DE6 .... 22 B3
*ASHB* DE6 .... 31 F1
*BPR/DUF* DE56 .... 4 C4
*DERBYW* DE22 .... 32 A2
*DERBYW* DE22 .... 33 G5
Ashbrook Av *BWSH/BRSTN* DE72 .. 45 H4
Ashbrook Cl *DERBYW* DE22 .... 25 F5
Ashby Rd *MELB/CHEL* DE73 .... 75 H4
Ashby St *DERBYSE* DE24 .... 53 F3
Ash Cl *BWSH/BRSTN* DE72 .... 65 G5
*DERBYW* DE22 .... 25 G4
Ashcombe Gdns *DERBYE* DE21 .. 36 A2
Ashcroft Cl *DERBYSE* DE24 .... 53 G2
Ashe Pl *NORM/LIT* DE23 .... 42 A5
Ashfield Av *DERBYE* DE21 .... 35 F3
Ashford Ri *BPR/DUF* DE56 .... 6 C1
Ashgrove Ct *DERBYE* DE21 .... 36 A2
Ashleigh Dr *MELB/CHEL* DE73 .... 63 G2
Ashley St *DERBYW* DE22 .... 41 F1
Ashlyn Rd *DERBYE* DE21 .... 3 G4
Ashmeadow *BWSH/BRSTN* DE72 .. 45 G5
Ashop Rd *BPR/DUF* DE56 .... 7 E2
Ashopton Av *NORM/LIT* DE23 .... 52 A1
Ashover Cl *DERBYE* DE21 .... 35 G3
Ashover Rd *DERBYW* DE22 .... 33 G1
Ashton Cl *MCKLVR* DE3 .... 39 H3
Ashton Wy *BPR/DUF* DE56 .... 7 E3
Ashtree Av *DERBYSE* DE24 .... 52 C3
Ash Tree Cl *BPR/DUF* DE56 .... 11 H5
*ILK* DE7 .... 27 F4
Ash View Cl *RDERBYSW* DE65 .... 48 A5
Ashwater Cl *DERBYSE* DE24 .... 62 A2
Ashworth Av *DERBYE* DE21 .... 43 G1
Askerfield Av *DERBYW* DE22 .... 25 F4
Aspen Dr *DERBYE* DE21 .... 44 B2
Astlow Dr *BPR/DUF* DE56 .... 6 C1
Aston Cl *MELB/CHEL* DE73 .... 63 H4
Aston Hall Dr *BWSH/BRSTN* DE72 .. 65 F5
Aston La *BWSH/BRSTN* DE72 .... 65 H4
*MELB/CHEL* DE73 .... 64 A3
Aston Rd *NORM/LIT* DE23 .... 51 F4
Atchison Gdns *DERBYE* DE21 .... 36 A4
Athlone Cl *DERBYE* DE21 .... 35 E3
Athol Cl *DERBYSE* DE24 .... 51 H5
Atlow Rd *DERBYE* DE21 .... 35 F4
Attewell Cl *BWSH/BRSTN* DE72 .... 57 E2
Attlebridge Cl *DERBYE* DE21 .... 35 E3
Atworth Gv *NORM/LIT* DE23 .... 50 C2
Auburn Cl *ILK* DE7 .... 21 G5
Auckland Cl *MCKLVR* DE3 .... 40 C3
Audrey Dr *DERBYE* DE21 .... 35 H3
Augusta St *NORM/LIT* DE23 .... 42 C4
Aults Cl *RDERBYSW* DE65 .... 59 H2
Austen Av *NORM/LIT* DE23 .... 51 E1
Austin Sq *NORM/LIT* DE23 .... 52 A2
Autumn Gv *DERBYE* DE21 .... 43 G1
Avenue Rd *BPR/DUF* DE56 .... 11 H5
The Avenue *BWSH/BRSTN* DE72 .... 70 D2
*DERBY* DE1 .... 2 D6
*DERBYE* DE21 .... 43 G1
Averham Cl *DERBYE* DE21 .... 36 A2
Aviemore Wy *DERBYSE* DE24 .... 51 H5
Avocet Ct *DERBYSE* DE24 .... 51 G5
Avon Cl *DERBYSE* DE24 .... 61 G2
Avondale Rd *DERBYE* DE21 .... 36 C5
*NORM/LIT* DE23 .... 2 C7
*NORM/LIT* DE23 .... 42 B3
Avonmouyh Dr *DERBYSE* DE24 .... 53 F1
Avon St *DERBYSE* DE24 .... 53 F1
Aycliffe Gdns *DERBYSE* DE24 .... 53 G5
Aylesbury Av *DERBYE* DE21 .... 35 G4
Ayr Cl *DERBYE* DE21 .... 44 C2


## B


Babbacombe Cl *DERBYSE* DE24 .... 54 B2
Babington La *DERBY* DE1 .... 2 C6
Back La *CDON/KEG* DE74 .... 72 D1
*MELB/CHEL* DE73 .... 63 H2
Back Sitwell St *DERBY* DE1 .... 2 D5
Back Wyver La *BPR/DUF* DE56 .... 6 A2
Badger Cl *DERBYE* DE21 .... 37 E5
Bagot St *ILK* DE7 .... 21 H5
Bagshaw St *DERBYSE* DE24 .... 53 F1
Bailey St *NORM/LIT* DE23 .... 42 A3
Bainbridge St *NORM/LIT* DE23 .. 42 B3
Bains Dr *BWSH/BRSTN* DE72 .... 46 A5
Bakeacre La *RDERBYSW* DE65 .... 60 B1
Bakehouse La
*BWSH/BRSTN* DE72 .... 45 G1
Baker St *DERBYSE* DE24 .... 53 G1
Bakewell Cl *MCKLVR* DE3 .... 40 A3
Bakewell Dr *CDON/KEG* DE74 .... 72 D5
Bakewell St *DERBYW* DE22 .... 2 A5
Balaclava Rd *NORM/LIT* DE23 .... 52 B2
Balfour Rd *NORM/LIT* DE23 .... 52 B1
Ballards Wy *BWSH/BRSTN* DE72 .... 46 A5
Ballater Cl *DERBYSE* DE24 .... 51 H5
Balleny Cl *DERBYE* DE21 .... 35 G1
Ball La *BWSH/BRSTN* DE72 .... 55 F4
Balmoral Cl *HEANOR* DE75 .... 15 H1
*NORM/LIT* DE23 .... 41 E4
Balmoral Rd *BWSH/BRSTN* DE72 .... 45 H5
Bamburgh Cl *DERBYE* DE21 .... 44 C2
Bamford Av *NORM/LIT* DE23 .... 51 H1
Bancroft Dr *DERBYW* DE22 .... 25 F4
The Bancroft *RDERBYSW* DE65 .... 48 A5
Bangor St *DERBYE* DE21 .... 35 F3
Bank Ct *DERBYW* DE22 .... 33 H3
Bank Field Dr *DERBYE* DE21 .... 45 E2
Bankholmes Cl *DERBYSE* DE24 .. 61 H2
Banksburn Cl *HEANOR* DE75 .... 15 H1
Bank Side *DERBYW* DE22 .... 33 H1
Bank View Rd *DERBYW* DE22 .... 34 A3
Bannell's La *MCKLVR* DE3 .... 49 E1
Bannels Av *NORM/LIT* DE23 .... 51 E2
Banwell Cl *MCKLVR* DE3 .... 39 H3
Barcheston Cl *DERBYE* DE21 .... 36 A1
Barden Dr *DERBYW* DE22 .... 34 A1
Bardsey Ct *DERBYE* DE21 .... 28 A5
Bare La *BWSH/BRSTN* DE72 .... 45 H1
Barf Cl *MCKLVR* DE3 .... 40 B5
Bargate Cl *BPR/DUF* DE56 .... 12 D1
Bargate Rd *BPR/DUF* DE56 .... 6 C5
Barker Cl *ILK* DE7 .... 21 G4
Barley Cl *DERBYE* DE21 .... 18 D5
Barley Corn Cl *DERBYE* DE21 .... 36 B1
Barley Cft *BPR/DUF* DE56 .... 6 C5
*MELB/CHEL* DE73 .... 63 G3
Barlow St *DERBY* DE1 .... 42 D3
Barnard Rd *DERBYE* DE21 .... 35 E2
Barn Cl *CDON/KEG* DE74 .... 72 D4
*DERBYW* DE22 .... 25 F2
*RDERBYSW* DE65 .... 60 A2

Barnhill Gv *NORM/LIT* DE23 ........ 50 D2 1
Barnstaple Cl *DERBYE* DE21 ...... 35 H1 2
Barnwood Cl *MCKLVR* DE3 ........ 39 H4 1
Baron Cl *DERBYE* DE21 ............... 28 C5 1
Barrett St *DERBYSE* DE24.............. 53 H2
Barrie Dr *DERBYSE* DE24 ............... 52 A4
Barrons Ct *BWSH/BRSTN* DE72 .. 55 F4 1
Barron's Wy
*BWSH/BRSTN* DE72 .................. 45 H5 1
The Barroon *CDON/KEG* DE74 ........ 73 E4
Barrow La *MELB/CHEL* DE73 .......... 68 D1
Barton Knowle *BPR/DUF* DE56 .... 7 E3 1
Basildon Cl *DERBYSE* DE24.............. 53 G4
Baslow Dr *DERBYW* DE22 ............... 26 A5
Bassingham Cl *DERBYE* DE21 .... 36 A2 3
Bass St *DERBYW* DE22..................... 33 G5
Bateman St *DERBY* DE1 ................. 42 D4
Bath Rd *MCKLVR* DE3 ..................... 40 B4
Bath St *DERBY* DE1 ......................... 34 B4
Baverstock Cl *MELB/CHEL* DE73 .... 63 G1
Baxter Sq *NORM/LIT* DE23 ............ 52 A3
Bayleaf Crs *DERBYE* DE21 ......... 28 A5 3
Bayswater Cl *DERBYW* DE22 ........ 32 C5 1
Beackden Cl *BPR/DUF* DE56 ............ 7 F3
Beamwood Cl *DERBYE* DE21 ......... 35 G2
Beardmore Cl *DERBYE* DE21 ...... 35 G1 2
Beatty St *DERBYSE* DE24 ................ 53 G1
Beaufort Rd *DERBYSE* DE24 .......... 61 F2
Beaufort St *DERBYE* DE21 .............. 35 E3
Beaumaris Ct *DERBYE* DE21 .......... 45 E1
Beaumont Cl *MELB/CHEL* DE73 68 B2 1
Beaurepaire Crs *BPR/DUF* DE56 .. 6 C2 1
Beaureper Av *DERBYW* DE22 .... 25 H5 1
Becher St *NORM/LIT* DE23 ............. 42 B5
Beckenham Wy *DERBYW* DE22 ...... 33 E5
Becket St *DERBY* DE1 ........................ 2 B4
Becket Well La *DERBY* DE1 ............... 2 C4
Beckitt Cl *DERBYSE* DE24 ............ 53 H1 1
Becksitch La *BPR/DUF* DE56 ........... 6 A5
Bedford Cl *DERBYW* DE22 .......... 41 G3 1
Bedford St *DERBYW* DE22 .............. 41 G3
Beech Av *BWSH/BRSTN* DE72 ........ 45 H3
*DERBYSE* DE24 ................................ 54 A2
*DERBYW* DE22.................................. 16 D5
*MELB/CHEL* DE73 ........................... 76 A2
Beech Cl *BPR/DUF* DE56 ............ 14 A2 1
Beech Ct *DERBYE* DE21...................... 44 C1
Beechcroft *ILK* DE7 ......................... 27 E4
Beech Dr *DERBYW* DE22 .................. 34 A3
*RDERBYSW* DE65 ........................ 48 B5 1
*RDERBYSW* DE65 ............................ 60 B3
Beeches Av *DERBYE* DE21 ............... 44 C1
The Beeches *HEANOR* DE75 ............ 15 H2
Beech Gdns *DERBYSE* DE24 ............ 54 A2
Beechley Dr *DERBYE* DE21............... 36 A2
Beech Wk *NORM/LIT* DE23................ 41 G5
Beechwood Cl *BPR/DUF* DE56 ........ 5 H2
Beechwood Crs
*NORM/LIT* DE23 ....................... 41 F5 1
Beeley Cl *BPR/DUF* DE56 .................. 6 D1
*DERBYW* DE22................................. 33 G1
Belfield Rd *RDERBYSW* DE65 .......... 58 B1
Belfry Cl *MCKLVR* DE3 .................. 40 C5 1
Belgrave Cl *BPR/DUF* DE56 .......... 6 D2 1
Belgrave St *NORM/LIT* DE23 .......... 42 B3
Bell Av *BWSH/BRSTN* DE72.............. 65 F5
Belle Vue Av *RIPLEY* DE5 .................. 8 B1
Bellingham Ct *DERBYW* DE22 .... 33 F1 1
Bell La *ILK* DE7 ................................. 21 F1
Belmont Av *BWSH/BRSTN* DE72 .... 57 H1
Belmont Dr *BWSH/BRSTN* DE72 .... 45 G5
Belper La *BPR/DUF* DE56 .................. 5 H1
Belper Rd *BPR/DUF* DE56.................. 7 F5
*BPR/DUF* DE56 ................................ 12 D1
*DERBY* DE1 ..................................... 34 A3
*ILK* DE7 ........................................... 21 F4
Belsize Cl *DERBYW* DE22 ........... 32 C5 2
Belvedere Cl *MCKLVR* DE3 ............. 40 A3
Belvoir Cl *BWSH/BRSTN* DE72 ........ 57 F2
Belvoir St *NORM/LIT* DE23 .............. 42 A4
Bembridge Dr *DERBYSE* DE24......... 54 B4
Bemrose Rd *DERBYSE* DE24............. 53 F2
Benbow Av *MELB/CHEL* DE73 .... 75 H2 1
Bendall Gn *NORM/LIT* DE23 ............ 51 F4
Benmore Ct *DERBYE* DE21 ........ 28 A5 4
Bennett St *DERBYSE* DE24............... 53 E4
Bensley Cl *MELB/CHEL* DE73 .......... 63 H3
Benson St *DERBYSE* DE24 ............... 53 F2
Bentley Rd *CDON/KEG* DE74 .......... 72 C3
Bentley St *DERBYSE* DE24 ................ 53 F3
Beresford Dr *DERBYE* DE21 ...... 44 D2 1
Berkeley Cl *NORM/LIT* DE23............ 51 G2
Berkshire St *DERBYE* DE21.............. 35 E3
Bermuda Av *DERBYE* DE21 ........ 26 D2 1
Berry Park Cl *DERBYW* DE22 .......... 33 H2
Berwick Av *DERBYE* DE21 ................ 34 D4
Berwick Cl *DERBYSE* DE24 .............. 54 A4
Berwick Dr *DERBYSE* DE24............... 61 G1
Bessalone Dr *BPR/DUF* DE56............ 6 B2
Besthorpe Cl *DERBYE* DE21 ........... 36 A2
Bethulie Rd *NORM/LIT* DE23 .......... 52 B1
Beverley St *DERBYSE* DE24 ........ 43 E4 1
Bewdley Cl *MELB/CHEL* DE73 ........ 63 H1
Bicester Av *DERBYSE* DE24 ............. 61 F2
Bickley Moss *DERBYE* DE21 ........ 36 A2 6
Bideford Dr *NORM/LIT* DE23 .......... 51 G3
The Biggin *CDON/KEG* DE74 ...... 73 E4 1
Bingham St *DERBYSE* DE24 ............. 53 F3
Binscombe La *DERBYE* DE21 .......... 27 G5
Birch Cl *DERBYE* DE21....................... 37 F5
Birches Rd *DERBYW* DE22 .............. 25 G5
Birchfield Cl *MELB/CHEL* DE73 ....... 63 G2
Birchover Ri *DERBYE* DE21 ............. 35 G2
Birchover Wy *DERBYW* DE22.......... 33 G2
Birchview Cl *BPR/DUF* DE56 ........ 6 C5 1
Birchwood *HEANOR* DE75 ................ 9 H3
Birchwood Av *NORM/LIT* DE23 ...... 51 G3
Birdcage Wk *DERBYW* DE22 .......... 32 C5
Birdwood St *NORM/LIT* DE23 .... 42 A5 1
Birkdale Cl *MCKLVR* DE3 .......... 40 D4 1
Biscay Ct *DERBYE* DE21 ............. 36 B1 2
Bishops Ct *MELB/CHEL* DE73 ...... 76 A3 1
Bishop's Dr *DERBYE* DE21 ............... 35 H2
Blaby Cl *NORM/LIT* DE23.................. 51 G3
Blackberry Wy *BPR/DUF* DE56 ......... 7 G5
Blackbird Rw *BPR/DUF* DE56 ........ 12 D1
Blackmore St *NORM/LIT* DE23......... 52 A2
Blackmount Ct *DERBYSE* DE24 .. 61 G1 1
Blackthorn Cl *DERBYE* DE21 ...... 35 F1 1
*MELB/CHEL* DE73 ..................... 75 H2 2
Blackthorne Cl *BPR/DUF* DE56 .... 7 G5 1
Blackwell La *MELB/CHEL* DE73 ........ 76 A3
Blagreaves Av *NORM/LIT* DE23 ...... 51 F4
Blagreaves La *NORM/LIT* DE23 ....... 51 F2
Blakebrook Dr
*MELB/CHEL* DE73 ..................... 63 H1 1
Blakeley La *RDERBYSW* DE65.......... 58 A2
Blakelow Dr *RDERBYSW* DE65 .. 58 A1 1
Blakemore Av
*MELB/CHEL* DE73 ..................... 76 A2 1
Blakeney Ct *DERBYE* DE21 .............. 36 B2
Blanch Cft *MELB/CHEL* DE73 .......... 76 A3
Blandford Cl *DERBYSE* DE24 ...... 54 C3 1
Blankney Cl *DERBYSE* DE24 ............ 61 G2
Blencathra Dr *MCKLVR* DE3 ........... 50 B1
Blenheim Ct *BPR/DUF* DE56 ....... 7 E2 1
Blenheim Dr *DERBYW* DE22............ 25 F5
Blenheim Pde *DERBYW* DE22 .... 25 H4 1
Blind La *BWSH/BRSTN* DE72............ 57 G1
Blithfield Gdns
*MELB/CHEL* DE73 ..................... 63 H2 1
Bloomfield Cl *DERBY* DE1................. 42 C3
Bloomfield St *DERBY* DE1 ........... 3 G7 1
*DERBY* DE1 ................................ 42 D3 2
Bluebell Cl *DERBYSE* DE24 ............. 61 F2
Bluebird Ct *DERBYSE* DE24 ....... 51 G5 2
Blunt St *ILK* DE7 ........................ 21 F3 1
Blyth Pl *DERBYE* DE21 .............. 35 E2 1
Boden St *NORM/LIT* DE23................ 42 C4
Bodmin Cl *DERBYSE* DE24 ........ 61 G1 2
Bog La *MELB/CHEL* DE73 ................ 75 F5
Bold La *DERBY* DE1 ............................ 2 C3
Bonchurch Cl *DERBYSE* DE24 .... 54 B4 1
Bondgate *CDON/KEG* DE74 ............. 73 E4
Bonnie Prince Charlie Wk
*DERBYW* DE22................................ 32 B5
Bonnyrigg Dr *DERBYE* DE21 ...... 35 H1 3
Bonsall Av *NORM/LIT* DE23 ............ 51 G1
Bonsall Dr *MCKLVR* DE3 ................. 40 B3
Boothgate *BPR/DUF* DE56................. 7 F1
Booth St *DERBYSE* DE24.................. 53 G2
Border Crs *DERBYSE* DE24 ............. 54 A5
Borough St *CDON/KEG* DE74 .......... 73 E4
Borrowash By-pass
*DERBYE* DE21 ................................ 44 A3
Borrowash Rd *DERBYE* DE21.......... 45 E3
Borrowfield Rd *DERBYE* DE21........ 44 D3
Borrowfields
*BWSH/BRSTN* DE72 ................. 45 G5 1
Boscastle Rd *DERBYSE* DE24 .......... 54 A3
Boston Cl *DERBYE* DE21 ................. 36 B5
Boswell Sq *NORM/LIT* DE23 ........... 52 A2
Bosworth Av *NORM/LIT* DE23 .... 51 H3 1
Bosworth Rd *CDON/KEG* DE74 ....... 72 C4
Boulton Dr *DERBYSE* DE24............... 53 H3
Boulton La *DERBYSE* DE24............... 53 H3
Boundary Rd *DERBYW* DE22 .......... 41 H2
*RDERBYSW* DE65 ........................... 58 C4
Bourne Sq *BWSH/BRSTN* DE72 .. 57 H1 1
Bourne St *DERBY* DE1 ....................... 2 D6
Bowbridge Av *NORM/LIT* DE23 ...... 51 F4
Bower St *DERBYSE* DE24 ................. 53 G1
Bowland Cl *MCKLVR* DE3 ........... 40 B5 2
Bowlees Ct *NORM/LIT* DE23 ...... 50 B2 1
Bowler Dr *BPR/DUF* DE56 ......... 13 H3 1
Bowmer Rd *DERBYSE* DE24 ....... 43 F4 1
Bown Cl *BPR/DUF* DE56 ................. 13 H2
Boxmoor Cl *NORM/LIT* DE23 ...... 50 C2 2
Boyd Gv *MELB/CHEL* DE73 .............. 63 H4
Boyer St *DERBYW* DE22 .................. 41 H3
Boylestone Rd *NORM/LIT* DE23........ 51 F4
Brackens Av *DERBYSE* DE24........... 53 G3
Brackensdale Av *DERBYW* DE22 ..... 41 E1
Bracken's La *DERBYSE* DE24 ........... 53 G3
Brackley Dr *DERBYE* DE21 ............... 44 D1
Brackley Ga *ILK* DE7 ........................ 19 H3
Bracknell Dr *DERBYSE* DE24 .......... 53 G4
Bradbury Cl
*BWSH/BRSTN* DE72 ................. 45 H5 2
Bradgate Ct *NORM/LIT* DE23 .... 51 H3 2
Brading Cl *DERBYSE* DE24 .............. 54 C4
Bradley Dr *BPR/DUF* DE56 ................ 6 C3
Bradley St *DERBYW* DE22 ......... 33 H3 1
Bradmoor Gv
*MELB/CHEL* DE73 ..................... 64 A2 1
Bradshaw Cft *BPR/DUF* DE56 .......... 5 H1
Bradshaw Dr *BPR/DUF* DE56.......... 12 D4
Bradshaw Wy *DERBY* DE1 ................ 2 E6
Bradwell Cl *MCKLVR* DE3 ............... 40 B5
Bradwell Wy *BPR/DUF* DE56 ............ 6 C2
Braemar Cl *DERBYSE* DE24 ........ 61 G1 3
Brafield Cl *BPR/DUF* DE56 ................ 7 E3
Brailsford Rd *DERBYE* DE21............. 35 F3
Braintree Cl *DERBYE* DE21.............. 35 E1
Braithwell Cl *DERBYW* DE22 ...... 34 A1 1
Brambleberry Ct
*DERBYE* DE21 ........................... 28 A5 3
Bramble Ms *MCKLVR* DE3 ......... 40 A5 2
Bramble St *DERBY* DE1...................... 2 B4
Bramble Wy *BPR/DUF* DE56 ............ 7 G5
Bramfield Av *DERBYW* DE22 .......... 41 H3
Bramley Cl *DERBYE* DE21 .......... 28 B5 1
Brampton Cl *MCKLVR* DE3 ............. 39 H3
Brampton Ct *BPR/DUF* DE56 ........ 7 E3 2
Brandelhow Ct *DERBYE* DE21 .... 28 A5 6
Branksome Av *DERBYSE* DE24 ........ 54 B2
Brassington Rd *DERBYE* DE21 .. 35 G2 1
Brayfield Av *NORM/LIT* DE23.......... 51 G1
Brayfield Rd *NORM/LIT* DE23.......... 51 F1
Breach La *MELB/CHEL* DE73 ............ 75 F1
Breach Rd *RIPLEY* DE5 ...................... 9 E3
Breaston La *BWSH/BRSTN* DE72 .... 47 G2
Brecon Cl *DERBYE* DE21 .................. 36 D5
Breedon Av *NORM/LIT* DE23 .......... 51 G4
Breedon Hill Rd *NORM/LIT* DE23..... 42 A3
Brentford Dr *DERBYW* DE22 ........... 33 E5
Bretby Sq *NORM/LIT* DE23 .............. 51 F4
Bretton Av *NORM/LIT* DE23 ............ 41 F4
Bretton Rd *BPR/DUF* DE56 ........ 7 F2 1
Breydon Cl *DERBYSE* DE24.............. 53 E5
Briar Cl *BWSH/BRSTN* DE72 ............ 45 H5
*DERBYE* DE21 ................................ 44 A1
Briar Lea Cl *DERBYSE* DE24 ............ 52 A5
Briarsgate *DERBYW* DE22 ......... 33 G1 1
Briarwood Wy *NORM/LIT* DE23...... 51 F3
Brickkiln La *ILK* DE7......................... 20 A5
Brick Rw *DERBYW* DE22 .................. 34 B2
Brick St *DERBY* DE1 .................... 33 H5 1
Brickyard La *BPR/DUF* DE56 .......... 13 G1
The Brickyard *ILK* DE7 .................... 21 G4
Bridge Fld *BWSH/BRSTN* DE72 ....... 57 F2
Bridge Foot *BPR/DUF* DE56.............. 5 H2
Bridge Hl *BPR/DUF* DE56 ................. 5 H2
Bridgeness Rd *NORM/LIT* DE23...... 50 C3
Bridgeport Rd *DERBYE* DE21........... 36 B5
Bridge St *BPR/DUF* DE56 .................. 6 A3
*DERBY* DE1 ....................................... 2 A2
*DERBY* DE1 .............................. 33 H5 2
Bridge Vw *BPR/DUF* DE56 .............. 12 B3
Bridgwater Cl *DERBYSE* DE24 .... 54 B2 1
Bridle Cl *MELB/CHEL* DE73 ............. 63 H3
Brierfield Wy *MCKLVR* DE3............. 50 B1
Brigden Av *DERBYSE* DE24.............. 53 F2
Brighton Rd *DERBYSE* DE24............ 53 G1
Brightstone Cl *DERBYSE* DE24 .. 54 C4 1
Bright St *DERBYW* DE22 ............ 41 G1 1
Brisbane Rd *MCKLVR* DE3.............. 40 B2
Briset Cl *DERBYSE* DE24 ............ 61 H2 2
Bristol Dr *MCKLVR* DE3 .................. 40 B4
Broad Bank *DERBYW* DE22 ....... 33 H3 2
Broadfields Cl *DERBYW* DE22 .... 34 A3 1
Broad La *BWSH/BRSTN* DE72............ 55 E5
Broadleaf Cl *DERBYE* DE21 ....... 35 F1 2
Broadstone La *MELB/CHEL* DE73 .. 74 D5
Broadway *BPR/DUF* DE56 .............. 17 H4
*DERBYW* DE22................................. 33 H3
Broadway Park Cl
*DERBYW* DE22 ......................... 33 H3 3
Brockley *DERBYE* DE21...................... 44 D1
Bromley St *DERBYW* DE22 .............. 33 H4
Brompton Rd *DERBYW* DE22........... 32 C5
Bronte Pl *NORM/LIT* DE23 ............... 51 E1
Brook Cl *DERBYW* DE22 ................. 25 F4
*RDERBYSW* DE65 ........................... 60 A3
Brookfield *MELB/CHEL* DE73.......... 68 E
Brookfield Av *DERBYE* DE21 .......... 36 A
*NORM/LIT* DE23 ............................. 51 C
Brookfields *BPR/DUF* DE56 ........ 13 F3
Brookfields Dr *ILK* DE7 ................... 27 E
Brookhouse St *DERBYSE* DE24 .. 53 E4
Brooklands Dr *NORM/LIT* DE23...... 51 F
Brook Rd *BWSH/BRSTN* DE72 ........ 45 C
*BWSH/BRSTN* DE72 ........................ 55 E
Brook Side *BPR/DUF* DE56............... 6 A
Brookside Cl *DERBYW* DE22............ 33 H
Brookside Rd *ILK* DE7 ...................... 27 F
Brook St *DERBY* DE1 ........................ 2 A
*HEANOR* DE75 .................................. 9 C
Brookvale Av *RIPLEY* DE5.................. 7 H
Brookvale Ri *RIPLEY* DE5 .................. 7 H
Brookvale Rd *RIPLEY* DE5 ................ 7 H
Broom Cl *BPR/DUF* DE56 .................. 5 H
*BPR/DUF* DE56 ................................ 17 C
*DERBYSE* DE24 ................................ 61 C
*MELB/CHEL* DE73 ............................ 63 C
Broomhill Cl *MCKLVR* DE3 ......... 40 A3
Brough St *DERBYW* DE22 ................ 41 C
Broughton Av *NORM/LIT* DE23 ...... 41 C
Browning St *NORM/LIT* DE23 ........ 52 A
Brown's La *BPR/DUF* DE56 ............ 13 E
Brun La *ASHB* DE6 ........................... 31 C
Brunswick St *NORM/LIT* DE23 ........ 42 A
Brunswood Cl *DERBYE* DE21 .......... 44 D
Brunton Cl *MCKLVR* DE3 ................. 39 H
Bryony Cl *DERBYE* DE21 .................. 35 H
Buchanan St *DERBY* DE1 .............. 2 C1
Buchan St *DERBYSE* DE24 .............. 53 E
Buckford La *RDERBYSW* DE65 ......... 60 E
Buckhazels La *ASHB* DE6 ................. 23 F
Buckingham Av *DERBYE* DE21 .. 35 E3
Buckland Cl *DERBYW* DE22 ........ 33 H5
Buckminster Cl *DERBYE* DE21 ........ 35 C
Buller St *NORM/LIT* DE23 ................ 41 H
Bullpit La *BPR/DUF* DE56 ................ 18 E
Bunting Cl *MCKLVR* DE3 ............. 40 D3
Burbage Cl *BPR/DUF* DE56................ 7 E
Burbage Pl *DERBYSE* DE24.............. 53 C
Burdock Cl *DERBYE* DE21 ........... 35 F1
Burghley Cl *MELB/CHEL* DE73 ........ 63 C
Burghley Wy *NORM/LIT* DE23 ........ 50 E
Burleigh Dr *DERBYW* DE22.............. 34 A
Burley Dr *DERBYW* DE22.................. 25 H
Burley Hl *DERBYW* DE22.................. 26 E
Burley La *DERBYW* DE22.................. 25 C
Burlington Cl *BWSH/BRSTN* DE72 .. 57 C
Burlington Rd *DERBYW* DE22 .... 32 C5
Burlington Wy *MCKLVR* DE3 .......... 40 A
The Burma Rd *ASHB* DE6 ................ 22 A
Burnaby St *DERBYSE* DE24 ............. 53 C
Burnham Dr *MCKLVR* DE3 ............... 39 H
Burns Cl *NORM/LIT* DE23 ........... 51 E1
Burnside Cl *DERBYSE* DE24 ........ 61 G1
Burnside Dr *DERBYE* DE21 .............. 45 E
Burnside St *DERBYSE* DE24 ............ 53 H
Burton Rd *DERBY* DE1 ...................... 2 C
*NORM/LIT* DE23 .............................. 41 F
*RDERBYSW* DE65 ............................ 50 A
*RDERBYSW* DE65 ............................ 59 H
Buttermere Dr *DERBYW* DE22.......... 25 H
Butterwick Cl *NORM/LIT* DE23 .. 51 H4
Buttonoak Dr *MELB/CHEL* DE73 .... 63 H
The Butts *BPR/DUF* DE56.................. 6 E
Buxton Dr *DERBYE* DE21 ................. 18 D
*MCKLVR* DE3 .................................. 40 B
Buxton Rd *DERBYE* DE21................. 35 C
Byfield Cl *DERBYE* DE21 .................. 36 A
Byng Av *NORM/LIT* DE23 ................. 52 A
Byron St *NORM/LIT* DE23 ................ 42 A
Bywell La *BPR/DUF* DE56 ................. 13 C

## C

Cadgwith Dr *DERBYW* DE22............. 33 H
Cadwell Cl *DERBYSE* DE24 ............... 54 C
Caerhays Ct *DERBYSE* DE24 ...... 61 G1
Caernarvon Cl *DERBYE* DE21 ........... 45 E
Caesar St *DERBY* DE1 ...................... 34 C
Cairngorm Dr *DERBYSE* DE24 ......... 61 C
Cairns Cl *MCKLVR* DE3..................... 40 E
Calder Cl *DERBYW* DE22 .................. 25 H
Caldermill Dr *DERBYE* DE21............ 35 H
California Gdns *DERBYW* DE22 .. 41 F2
Calladine La *ILK* DE7 ....................... 14 C
Callow Hill Wy *NORM/LIT* DE23 ...... 50 C
Calver Cl *BPR/DUF* DE56.................... 6 C
*DERBYE* DE21 .................................. 27 F
Calverton Cl *DERBYSE* DE24............ 63 F
Calvert St *DERBY* DE1 ....................... 3 C
Calvin Cl *DERBYSE* DE24 ................. 53 H
Camberwell Av *DERBYW* DE22 ...... 32 D

amborne Cl DERBYE DE21 35 F2
ambridge St DERBYE DE21 44 D3
NORM/LIT DE23 42 B4
amden St DERBYW DE22 41 G2
amellia Cl MCKLVR DE3 40 A3
ameron Rd NORM/LIT DE23 52 A1
ampbell St BPR/DUF DE56 6 A4
DERBYSE DE24 53 E3
ampion Hl CDON/KEG DE74 72 D3
ampion St DERBYW DE22 41 G1
ampsie Ct DERBYSE DE24 61 G1 6
amp St DERBY DE1 34 B4
anada St BPR/DUF DE56 6 B5
anal Bank BWSH/BRSTN DE72 66 D3
anal St DERBY DE1 3 F6
anberra Cl MCKLVR DE3 40 B4
anon's Wk DERBYW DE22 34 A1 2
anterbury St DERBYE DE21 35 F2
antley Cl DERBYSE DE24 63 E1 1
ardales Cl RDERBYSW DE65 60 A2 1
ardean Cl DERBY DE1 34 C4 2
ardigan St DERBYE DE21 35 E4
ardinal Cl DERBYE DE21 35 G1
ardrona Cl DERBYE DE21 35 G1
arisbrooke Gdns
NORM/LIT DE23 51 F3 1
arlin Cl BWSH/BRSTN DE72 57 H1
arlisle Av NORM/LIT DE23 51 E1
arlton Av DERBYSE DE24 53 F5
arlton Dr DERBYSE DE24 53 F5
arlton Gdns DERBYSE DE24 53 F5
arlton Rd NORM/LIT DE23 41 G5
arlyle St DERBYSE DE24 52 A4
arnegie St NORM/LIT DE23 52 B1 1
arnforth Cl MCKLVR DE3 40 B5 3
arnoustie Cl MCKLVR DE3 40 C4 2
arol Crs DERBYE DE21 43 G2
aroline Cl DERBYSE DE24 54 B2
arr Flds ILK DE7 14 B3
arriers Rd RDERBYSW DE65 58 B5
arrington St DERBY DE1 3 F6
arron Cl DERBYSE DE24 51 H5
arrs Cl CDON/KEG DE74 72 D4 1
arsington Crs DERBYW DE22 33 G2
arsington Ms DERBYW DE22 33 G2
arson Rd DERBYE DE21 36 A5 1
arter St DERBYSE DE24 53 E3
ascade Gv NORM/LIT DE23 50 D2 2
asson Av DERBYSE DE24 53 H3
astings Rd NORM/LIT DE23 52 C1 1
astle Cl BWSH/BRSTN DE72 46 A4
astlecraig Ct DERBYSE DE24 61 H2 3
astle Cft DERBYSE DE24 54 C4
astle Hl BPR/DUF DE56 17 H1
CDON/KEG DE74 73 E3
RDERBYSW DE65 60 A3
astle La MELB/CHEL DE73 76 A3
astle Ms MELB/CHEL DE73 76 A3
astle Orch BPR/DUF DE56 17 H1
astleshaw Dr NORM/LIT DE23 50 B2
astle St DERBY DE1 2 E5
MELB/CHEL DE73 76 A3
astleton Av NORM/LIT DE23 52 A1
athedral Rd DERBY DE1 2 B2
athedral Vw NORM/LIT DE23 41 G4
atherine St NORM/LIT DE23 42 C4 3
atterick Dr MCKLVR DE3 39 H5
auseway DERBYW DE22 33 H1
avan Dr DERBYE DE21 44 A2
avendish Av DERBYW DE22 26 A5
DERBYW DE22 34 A1
avendish Cl BPR/DUF DE56 17 G3 1
BWSH/BRSTN DE72 66 D2
CDON/KEG DE74 72 D5 1
avendish Ct
BWSH/BRSTN DE72 66 D3 1
DERBY DE1 2 B3 1
avendish St DERBY DE1 2 B3 2
avendish Wy MCKLVR DE3 40 B4
aversfield Cl NORM/LIT DE23 50 D1 1
axton Ct NORM/LIT DE23 51 H2 1
axton St NORM/LIT DE23 51 H2
ecil St DERBYW DE22 41 G1
edar Cft BPR/DUF DE56 14 A3 1
edar Dr BWSH/BRSTN DE72 45 H2
edar Gv BPR/DUF DE56 6 B5
edar Rd CDON/KEG DE74 73 E5
edar St DERBYW DE22 33 H4
edarwood Ct DERBYE DE21 35 F1 4
elandine Cl DERBYE DE21 35 G1 3
elanese Rd DERBYE DE21 44 B3
emetery Hill Nottingham Rd
DERBYE DE21 3 K2
emetery Rd BPR/DUF DE56 6 B1
entenary Wy ASHB DE6 16 A3
BPR/DUF DE56 18 C3
entral Av BWSH/BRSTN DE72 45 G5
ILK DE7 21 G5
Centre Ct DERBY DE1 42 C3 2
Chaddesden La DERBYE DE21 43 G1
Chaddesden Park Rd
DERBYE DE21 35 G5
Chadfield Rd BPR/DUF DE56 11 H5
Chadwick Av DERBYSE DE24 53 F4
Chaffinch Cl DERBYE DE21 37 E5
Chain La MCKLVR DE3 40 D4
NORM/LIT DE23 40 D5
Chalfont Sq DERBYE DE21 36 A1
Chalkley Cl DERBYSE DE24 53 G2
Challis Av DERBYE DE21 36 A4
Chambers St DERBYSE DE24 53 F1
Champion Hl BPR/DUF DE56 17 H1
Chandlers Ford DERBYE DE21 35 G1
Chandos Pole St DERBYW DE22 33 G5 1
Chandres Ct DERBYW DE22 25 H4 2
Chandwick Ct DERBYSE DE24 61 G1 7
Chantry Cl MCKLVR DE3 39 H5 2
Chapel La DERBYE DE21 35 H4
DERBYE DE21 44 D1
MELB/CHEL DE73 63 H3 1
MELB/CHEL DE73 68 B1
Chapel Rw BWSH/BRSTN DE72 45 G4 1
Chapel St BPR/DUF DE56 6 A4
BPR/DUF DE56 12 D3
BPR/DUF DE56 13 H2
BPR/DUF DE56 18 A1 1
DERBY DE1 2 B2
DERBYE DE21 44 D1
MELB/CHEL DE73 74 B5
MELB/CHEL DE73 76 A3
Chapman Av DERBYSE DE24 54 A3
Chapter Cl DERBYE DE21 35 E1
Charing Ct DERBY DE1 34 C4 3
Charingworth Rd
DERBYE DE21 36 A1 3
Chariot Cl DERBYSE DE24 54 C4 2
Charlbury Cl NORM/LIT DE23 50 D1 2
Charles Av DERBYE DE21 36 C5
Charleston Rd DERBYE DE21 36 B5
Charlestown Dr DERBYW DE22 25 G4
Charlotte St NORM/LIT DE23 42 B4
Charnwood Av BPR/DUF DE56 6 A3
BWSH/BRSTN DE72 45 H4
CDON/KEG DE74 73 F4
NORM/LIT DE23 51 G4
Charnwood St DERBY DE1 2 C7
Charterhouse Cl DERBYE DE21 27 G5 1
Charterstone La
DERBYW DE22 25 H4 3
Chartwell Dr DERBYE DE21 3 H3
The Chase BPR/DUF DE56 14 A2
DERBYE DE21 19 E3
DERBYSE DE24 52 A5
Chatham Ct BPR/DUF DE56 7 E3 3
Chatham St NORM/LIT DE23 52 B1
Chatsworth Crs DERBYW DE22 34 A1
Chatsworth Dr DERBYE DE21 19 E3
MCKLVR DE3 40 B3
Chatsworth St NORM/LIT DE23 41 H5
Chatteris Dr DERBYE DE21 35 E2
Cheadle Cl NORM/LIT DE23 41 E5
Cheam Cl DERBYW DE22 32 B5
Cheapside BPR/DUF DE56 6 A4 1
DERBY DE1 2 B3
Chedworth Dr DERBYSE DE24 54 C3 2
Chellaston La BWSH/BRSTN DE72 64 D4
MELB/CHEL DE73 64 B3
Chellaston Park Ct
MELB/CHEL DE73 63 G3 1
Chellaston Rd DERBYSE DE24 53 F5 1
Chelmarsh Cl
MELB/CHEL DE73 63 H1 2
Chelmorton Pl DERBYE DE21 35 G3 2
Chelmsford Cl MCKLVR DE3 39 H3 2
Chelsea Cl DERBYW DE22 32 B5
Chelwood Rd MELB/CHEL DE73 63 G2
Chequers La DERBYE DE21 3 J3
Chequers Rd DERBYE DE21 3 H3
Cheribough Rd CDON/KEG DE74 72 D5
Cheriton Gdns NORM/LIT DE23 50 B2 2
Cherrybrook Dr DERBYE DE21 28 A5
Cherry Cl BWSH/BRSTN DE72 57 H1
Cherry Tree Av BPR/DUF DE56 6 B1
Cherry Tree Ms DERBYE DE21 44 A2 2
Chertsey Rd MCKLVR DE3 39 H4
Chesapeake Rd DERBYE DE21 36 A5
Cheshire St DERBYSE DE24 53 E4
Chester Av DERBYW DE22 26 C3
Chesterfield Rd BPR/DUF DE56 6 B2
Chesterford Ct NORM/LIT DE23 50 C3 2
Chester Green Rd DERBY DE1 34 B4
Chesterton Av NORM/LIT DE23 51 H2
Chesterton Rd DERBYE DE21 36 D5
Chestnut Av BPR/DUF DE56 6 B5
BPR/DUF DE56 12 D3
MCKLVR DE3 40 B3
MELB/CHEL DE73 63 G1
NORM/LIT DE23 42 B4 1
Chestnut Cl BPR/DUF DE56 17 H3
ILK DE7 14 B3
Chestnut Gv BWSH/BRSTN DE72 45 H3
RDERBYSW DE65 48 A5
Chevely Ct DERBYE DE21 35 E3 3
Cheverton Cl DERBYSE DE24 54 C4 3
Chevin Av BWSH/BRSTN DE72 45 H4
MCKLVR DE3 40 C4
Chevin Bank BPR/DUF DE56 11 G4
Chevin Pl DERBYW DE22 34 A4
Chevin Rd BPR/DUF DE56 5 G3
BPR/DUF DE56 11 H5
DERBYW DE22 34 A4
Chevin V BPR/DUF DE56 11 H5
Cheviot St DERBYW DE22 41 F1
Cheyenne Gdns DERBYE DE21 44 A1
Chilson Dr MCKLVR DE3 39 H3
Chime Cl DERBYE DE21 35 F1
Chingford Ct DERBYW DE22 33 E5 1
Chinley Rd DERBYE DE21 35 H2
Chiswick Cl DERBYW DE22 32 C5
Church Cl MELB/CHEL DE73 63 H3 2
Churchdown Cl DERBYE DE21 36 A1 4
Church Hl RDERBYSW DE65 48 A4
Churchill Cl BWSH/BRSTN DE72 57 G1
Church La ASHB DE6 30 D1
BPR/DUF DE56 6 A3
CDON/KEG DE74 73 G3
DERBYE DE21 26 D1
DERBYE DE21 35 H5 1
DERBYW DE22 32 C3
DERBYW DE22 34 B1
ILK DE7 14 C4
ILK DE7 27 F4
ILK DE7 28 D2
MELB/CHEL DE73 68 B2
Church La North
DERBYW DE22 26 A5 1
Church Ms DERBYE DE21 44 C2 2
Church Rd DERBYW DE22 25 F2
Church Sq MELB/CHEL DE73 76 A4 1
Church St BPR/DUF DE56 12 D4
BPR/DUF DE56 13 G2
BWSH/BRSTN DE72 45 H2
DERBYE DE21 13 G5
DERBYE DE21 44 C2
DERBYSE DE24 54 B2
MELB/CHEL DE73 76 A3
NORM/LIT DE23 41 F5
NORM/LIT DE23 42 B4
RIPLEY DE5 14 B1
Church Vw BWSH/BRSTN DE72 57 H2
HEANOR DE75 9 G3
Church Wk BPR/DUF DE56 18 A3
The Circle DERBYSE DE24 51 H4 2
City Rd DERBY DE1 34 B4
Clapgun St CDON/KEG DE74 73 E4
Clarence Rd NORM/LIT DE23 41 H5
Clarke Av HEANOR DE75 9 H4 1
Clarkes La BWSH/BRSTN DE72 65 G4
Clarke St DERBY DE1 3 F1
Clay St BWSH/BRSTN DE72 56 D2
Clayton Gv HEANOR DE75 9 H3
Clement Rd ILK DE7 14 B3 1
Cleveland Av BWSH/BRSTN DE72 56 C2
DERBYE DE21 44 A1
Clifton Dr MCKLVR DE3 40 B3
Clifton Rd DERBYW DE22 25 G5
Clifton St DERBY DE1 42 D3
Clinton St DERBYE DE21 3 K2
Clipstone Gdns DERBYE DE21 36 A1
Cloisters Ct DERBYE DE21 35 G1 4
The Close DERBYW DE22 34 A1
NORM/LIT DE23 41 G4
Cloudwood Cl NORM/LIT DE23 41 E5
Clover Cl DERBYE DE21 45 E1
Clover Ct BWSH/BRSTN DE72 66 B2
Cloverdale Dr DERBYSE DE24 62 A2
Cloverslade RDERBYSW DE65 59 H3 1
Cloves Hl ILK DE7 20 B3
Club La MELB/CHEL DE73 68 B2
Cluster Rd BPR/DUF DE56 6 A3
Clusters Ct BPR/DUF DE56 6 A3 2
Coach Dr DERBYW DE22 25 F1
Cobden St DERBYW DE22 41 G1
Cobham Cl DERBYSE DE24 61 G1
Cobthorn Dr DERBYW DE22 25 F4
Cockayne St North
DERBYSE DE24 53 F3
Cockayne St South
DERBYSE DE24 53 F3
Cockshut La MELB/CHEL DE73 75 G3
Cod Beck Cl DERBYSE DE24 54 B3 1
Codnor-denby La RIPLEY DE5 9 F2
Coke St DERBYW DE22 41 G1 2
Cole La BWSH/BRSTN DE72 45 H2
BWSH/BRSTN DE72 46 A4
Coleman St DERBYSE DE24 53 F2
Coleraine Cl DERBYE DE21 44 A2
Coleridge St NORM/LIT DE23 52 A2 1
College Ms DERBY DE1 41 H1
Collier La BWSH/BRSTN DE72 45 H2
Collingham Gdns DERBYW DE22 40 D1
Collis Cl DERBYSE DE24 53 F2
Collumbell Av
BWSH/BRSTN DE72 45 H1
Colombo St NORM/LIT DE23 42 C5
Coltsfoot Dr DERBYSE DE24 62 A2
Columbine Cl DERBYE DE21 35 H2 2
Colvile St DERBYW DE22 33 G5
Colwell Dr DERBYSE DE24 54 C4
Colwyn Av NORM/LIT DE23 41 G5
Colyear St DERBY DE1 2 C4
Comfrey Cl NORM/LIT DE23 50 C3 2
Commerce St DERBYSE DE24 53 G1
MELB/CHEL DE73 75 H3
Common La ILK DE7 29 F1
Common Piece La
RDERBYSW DE65 60 B3
The Common DERBYW DE22 17 F5
Compton Av BWSH/BRSTN DE72 65 F4
Compton Cl DERBYSE DE24 54 B3 2
Coniston Av DERBYE DE21 36 D5
Coniston Crs DERBYE DE21 35 E1
Connaught Rd DERBYW DE22 41 F2
Consett Cl DERBYE DE21 35 E2
Consort Gdns DERBYE DE21 28 B5 2
Constable Av DERBYW DE22 41 F3
Constable Dr NORM/LIT DE23 41 E4
Constable La NORM/LIT DE23 41 F4
Conway Av BWSH/BRSTN DE72 46 A4
Cook Cl BPR/DUF DE56 7 F2
Cookham Cl MCKLVR DE3 39 H4
Cooks Av CDON/KEG DE74 72 D4
Co-operative St NORM/LIT DE23 42 A4
Coopers Cl BWSH/BRSTN DE72 46 A5 2
Cooper St DERBYW DE22 33 F5 1
Copeland St DERBY DE1 2 E5
Copes Wy DERBYE DE21 35 H3
Copperleaf Cl DERBYW DE22 2 A6
Copper Yd RIPLEY DE5 9 E5
Coppice Cl BPR/DUF DE56 13 H2 1
DERBYW DE22 34 A2
Copse Gv NORM/LIT DE23 50 D2 3
Corbel Cl DERBYE DE21 35 F1
Corbridge Gv NORM/LIT DE23 50 D2 4
Corby Cl DERBYSE DE24 53 G4 1
Corden Av MCKLVR DE3 40 D4
Corden St NORM/LIT DE23 42 B4
Cordville Cl DERBYE DE21 44 A1 1
Cordwell Cl CDON/KEG DE74 72 C4
Corfe Cl NORM/LIT DE23 51 G3 2
Coriander Gdns
NORM/LIT DE23 51 G5 3
Corinium Cl DERBYSE DE24 54 C4
Cornflower Dr DERBYE DE21 35 H1
Cornhill DERBYW DE22 26 A4
Corn Market DERBY DE1 2 D3
Cornmill Cl DERBYSE DE24 54 C4 4
Cornwall Rd DERBYE DE21 3 K1
DERBYE DE21 35 E4
Coronation Av BPR/DUF DE56 6 B2
DERBYSE DE24 54 B4
Coronation Cl MELB/CHEL DE73 75 H2
Coronation Rd ILK DE7 29 G2
Coronation St NORM/LIT DE23 52 C1 2
Coronet Ct DERBYE DE21 28 C5 2
Corporation St DERBY DE1 2 D3
Cotswold Cl NORM/LIT DE23 51 F1
Cottisford Cl NORM/LIT DE23 50 D1
Cotton Brook Rd
NORM/LIT DE23 52 C1
Cotton La DERBYSE DE24 52 C1
Countisbury Dr DERBYE DE21 35 H1
Courtland Dr DERBYSE DE24 53 H3
Courtland Gdns DERBYSE DE24 54 A3
Courtland Rd RDERBYSW DE65 58 B1 1
Courtney Wy BPR/DUF DE56 7 E2 2
The Court DERBYSE DE24 54 A3 1
The Covert DERBYE DE21 44 D2
Cowdray Cl DERBYSE DE24 61 G2 1
Cowley St DERBYW DE22 33 H4
Cowlishaw Cl BWSH/BRSTN DE72 66 B3
Cowper St DERBYSE DE24 52 B4
Cowsley Rd DERBYE DE21 35 E4
Coxbench Rd DERBYE DE21 19 F1
Cox Green Ct NORM/LIT DE23 50 C2
Coxon St DERBYE DE21 44 D1
Crabtree Cl CDON/KEG DE74 72 D5
DERBYW DE22 25 F4
Crab Tree Hl DERBYE DE21 18 D5
Crabtree Hill Keddleston Rd
DERBYW DE22 25 F5
Craddock Av DERBYE DE21 44 D3

**Craiglee Ct** *DERBYSE* DE24 **61** G1 8
**Cranberry Gv** *NORM/LIT* DE23 **50** C3 3
**Cranhill Cl** *NORM/LIT* DE23 **50** C3 4
**Cranmer Rd** *DERBYE* DE21 **3** G3
**Crawley Rd** *DERBYSE* DE24 **53** G4
**Crayford Rd** *DERBYSE* DE24 **53** H4
**Crecy Cl** *NORM/LIT* DE23 **41** F3
**The Crescent** *BWSH/BRSTN* DE72 **57** F2
*DERBYE* DE21 **43** G1
*DERBYSE* DE24 **53** F3
*ILK* DE7 **14** B3
*ILK* DE7 **21** G4
**Cressbrook Wy** *DERBYE* DE21 **28** A5 7
**The Crest** *DERBYW* DE22 **33** H1
**Crewe St** *NORM/LIT* DE23 **42** A5
**Crewton Wy** *DERBYSE* DE24 **53** G2
**Crich Av** *NORM/LIT* DE23 **41** E4
**Crich La** *BPR/DUF* DE56 **6** B1
**Cricklewood Rd** *DERBYW* DE22 **33** E5
**Cringle Ms** *DERBYE* DE21 **35** F1
**Croft Cl** *BWSH/BRSTN* DE72 **45** H2
*DERBYE* DE21 **37** E5
**Croft End** *DERBYE* DE21 **18** D5
**Crofters Ct** *DERBYE* DE21 **35** F1 5
**Croft La** *DERBYE* DE21 **27** E5
**The Croft** *BPR/DUF* DE56 **12** D1
*BWSH/BRSTN* DE72 **56** D3
*ILK* DE7 **20** B4
*MELB/CHEL* DE73 **75** H2 3
*NORM/LIT* DE23 **51** G1
**Cromarty Cl** *DERBYSE* DE24 **51** H5
**Cromer Cl** *MCKLVR* DE3 **39** H5
**Cromford Dr** *MCKLVR* DE3 **40** A2
**Cromford Rd** *DERBYE* DE21 **35** H3
**Crompton St** *DERBY* DE1 **2** B5
**Cromwell Av** *RDERBYSW* DE65 **60** A2
**Cromwell Rd** *NORM/LIT* DE23 **42** A4
**Cropton Cl** *DERBYSE* DE24 **54** B3
**Crosby St** *DERBYW* DE22 **41** G2
**Cross Cl** *NORM/LIT* DE23 **51** F1
**Crossdale Gv** *DERBYE* DE21 **28** B5 3
**Crosshill** *RIPLEY* DE5 **9** G1
**Cross St** *DERBYW* DE22 **33** G5
**Crown Hill Wy** *ILK* DE7 **21** G5 1
**Crownland Dr**
*MELB/CHEL* DE73 **63** H2 2
**Crown Ms** *DERBYW* DE22 **41** H3
**Crown St** *BPR/DUF* DE56 **17** H1
*DERBYW* DE22 **41** H3
**Crown Ter** *BPR/DUF* DE56 **6** A3 3
**Crowshaw St** *DERBYSE* DE24 **52** C1 3
*DERBYSE* DE24 **52** D1 1
**Cuckmere Cl** *DERBYW* DE22 **26** C3
**Culworth Cl** *BPR/DUF* DE56 **7** E3 4
**Cumberhills Rd** *DERBYW* DE22 **17** E4
**Cumberland Av** *DERBYE* DE21 **35** F5
**Cumberland Crs**
*BWSH/BRSTN* DE72 **45** G5
**Cummings St** *NORM/LIT* DE23 **42** B4
**The Cunnery** *ASHB* DE6 **31** E1
**Curborough Dr** *DERBYSE* DE24 **54** B3
**Curlew Cl** *DERBYSE* DE24 **51** G5 4
**Curzon Cl** *DERBYW* DE22 **25** F4
**Curzon La** *BPR/DUF* DE56 **17** G2
*DERBYSE* DE24 **53** H1
**Curzon Rd** *DERBYE* DE21 **35** G4
**Curzon St** *DERBY* DE1 **2** B4
*DERBYW* DE22 **2** A4
**Cuttlebrook Cl**
*NORM/LIT* DE23 **51** H3 3


## D


**Dahlia Dr** *DERBYE* DE21 **28** B5
**Dairy House Rd** *NORM/LIT* DE23 **42** B5
**Dale Cl** *BWSH/BRSTN* DE72 **57** G1
**Dale Ct** *BPR/DUF* DE56 **13** G2 1
**Dale Park Av** *BPR/DUF* DE56 **13** H2
**Dale Rd** *DERBYE* DE21 **37** F5
*DERBYE* DE21 **45** F1
*DERBYSE* DE24 **54** B2
*ILK* DE7 **29** H4
*NORM/LIT* DE23 **42** A4
**Dale View Gdns** *BPR/DUF* DE56 **13** G2
**Dalkeith Av** *DERBYSE* DE24 **53** G4
**Dalley La** *BPR/DUF* DE56 **5** F1
**Dalness Ct** *DERBYSE* DE24 **61** G1 9
**Dalton Av** *DERBYW* DE22 **41** F3
**Danebridge Crs** *DERBYE* DE21 **35** H2
**Danesby Crs** *RIPLEY* DE5 **13** G1
**Danesby Ri** *RIPLEY* DE5 **13** H1
**Darby St** *NORM/LIT* DE23 **42** A4
**Dark La** *BPR/DUF* DE56 **12** B4
**Darley Abbey Dr**
*DERBYW* DE22 **34** B1 2
**Darley Gv** *DERBY* DE1 **34** B4
*DERBYW* DE22 **34** B2
**Darley La** *DERBY* DE1 **2** C1
**Darley Park Dr** *DERBYW* DE22 **34** A2
**Darley Park Rd** *DERBYW* DE22 **34** A2
**Darley St** *DERBYW* DE22 **34** B2
**Darsway** *CDON/KEG* DE74 **72** D3
**Dartford Pl** *DERBYSE* DE24 **53** H4
**Darwin Av** *DERBYSE* DE24 **53** E5
**Darwin Rd** *MCKLVR* DE3 **40** B3
**Dashwood St** *NORM/LIT* DE23 **42** B3 4
**Datchet Cl** *NORM/LIT* DE23 **50** D1
**Davenport Rd** *DERBYSE* DE24 **52** D1
**Daventry Cl** *MCKLVR* DE3 **39** H3
**David's Cl** *MELB/CHEL* DE73 **63** F3
**Dawlish Ct** *DERBYSE* DE24 **54** B2
**Dawsmere Cl** *DERBYE* DE21 **35** E2 2
**Daylesford Cl** *NORM/LIT* DE23 **50** D1 3
**Days La** *BPR/DUF* DE56 **6** A4
**Dayton Cl** *DERBYE* DE21 **44** B1
**Deacon Cl** *DERBYE* DE21 **35** F1 6
**Deadman's La** *DERBYSE* DE24 **43** E4
**Dean Cl** *NORM/LIT* DE23 **40** D4
**Deans Dr** *BWSH/BRSTN* DE72 **45** G4
**Dean St** *DERBYW* DE22 **41** H3
**Deborah Dr** *DERBYE* DE21 **35** H4
**Dee Cl** *DERBYSE* DE24 **61** H1
**Dee La** *RDERBYSW* DE65 **49** E2
**Deep Dale La** *DERBYSE* DE24 **61** H2
**Deepdale Rd** *BPR/DUF* DE56 **6** C2
*DERBYE* DE21 **45** E3
**Deer Park Vw** *DERBYE* DE21 **37** E5
**Degge St** *DERBY* DE1 **2** C5
**Deincourt Cl** *DERBYE* DE21 **37** F5
**Delamere Cl** *BWSH/BRSTN* DE72 **57** G1
*DERBYE* DE21 **35** H2 3
**Delven La** *CDON/KEG* DE74 **72** D4 2
**Denarth Av** *DERBYSE* DE24 **63** F1
**Denbigh St** *DERBYE* DE21 **35** F4
**Denby Common** *RIPLEY* DE5 **9** E5
**Denby La** *RIPLEY* DE5 **14** A1
**Denison Gdns** *DERBYE* DE21 **36** A5
**Dennis Cl** *NORM/LIT* DE23 **50** B2
**Denstone Dr** *DERBYSE* DE24 **53** H5
**Denver Rd** *MCKLVR* DE3 **40** A3
**Depedale Av** *BWSH/BRSTN* DE72 **45** H4
**Depot St** *NORM/LIT* DE23 **42** B4
**Derby La** *NORM/LIT* DE23 **52** A1
**Derby Rd** *BPR/DUF* DE56 **12** A5
*BPR/DUF* DE56 **13** F3 2
*BPR/DUF* DE56 **18** A4
*BWSH/BRSTN* DE72 **45** F4
*BWSH/BRSTN* DE72 **47** E2
*BWSH/BRSTN* DE72 **56** B1
*BWSH/BRSTN* DE72 **65** F1
*DERBYE* DE21 **13** E5
*DERBYE* DE21 **19** E4
*DERBYE* DE21 **28** D5
*DERBYE* DE21 **44** A2
*MELB/CHEL* DE73 **63** G2
*MELB/CHEL* DE73 **75** H2
*RIPLEY* DE5 **8** D1
**Derrington Leys** *DERBYSE* DE24 **54** C3
**Derventio Cl** *DERBY* DE1 **34** B4 1
**Derwent Av** *BPR/DUF* DE56 **12** A2
*BWSH/BRSTN* DE72 **45** H3
*DERBYW* DE22 **26** B4
**Derwent Cl** *DERBYW* DE22 **26** B4 1
**Derwent Ct** *BPR/DUF* DE56 **6** C3 1
**Derwent Dr** *DERBYSE* DE24 **61** G2
**Derwent Ri** *DERBYE* DE21 **45** E2
**Derwent Rd** *DERBYE* DE21 **44** C3 1
**Derwent St** *BPR/DUF* DE56 **5** H4
*BWSH/BRSTN* DE72 **56** D2
*DERBY* DE1 **2** E3
**Derwent V** *BPR/DUF* DE56 **6** A5 1
**Derwent Vw** *BPR/DUF* DE56 **6** A2
**Devas Gdns** *DERBYE* DE21 **44** C1
**Devon Cl** *DERBYE* DE21 **3** K1
**Devonshire Av**
*BWSH/BRSTN* DE72 **45** H4
*DERBYW* DE22 **26** A5
**Devonshire Dr** *BPR/DUF* DE56 **17** G3
*MCKLVR* DE3 **40** B3
**Dewchurch Dr** *NORM/LIT* DE23 **51** E4
**Dexter St** *NORM/LIT* DE23 **42** D4
**Diamond Dr** *DERBYE* DE21 **27** G5
**Dickens Sq** *NORM/LIT* DE23 **52** A2
**Dickinson St** *DERBYSE* DE24 **43** E4
**Diseworth Cl**
*MELB/CHEL* DE73 **63** H2 3
**Dix Av** *ILK* DE7 **15** E4
**Dobholes La** *ILK* DE7 **14** D4
**Dodburn Ct** *DERBYSE* DE24 **51** G5
**Dog La** *MELB/CHEL* DE73 **76** D4
**Doles La** *RDERBYSW* DE65 **59** H1
**Dolphin Cl** *DERBYE* DE21 **37** F5
**Donald Hawley Wy**
*BPR/DUF* DE56 **18** A2
**Donington Cl** *NORM/LIT* DE23 **51** H4 3
**Donington Dr** *NORM/LIT* DE23 **51** H4
**Donington La**
*BWSH/BRSTN* DE72 **67** F4
*CDON/KEG* DE74 **67** F5
**Dorchester Av** *DERBYE* DE21 **35** F4
**Dorking Rd** *DERBYW* DE22 **33** E5
**Dorrien Av** *NORM/LIT* DE23 **52** A2
**Dorset St** *DERBYE* DE21 **3** J1
**Douglas Av** *HEANOR* DE75 **9** H5
**Douglas St** *DERBY* DE1 **42** D4
*NORM/LIT* DE23 **42** C4
**Dove Cl** *BPR/DUF* DE56 **13** H2 2
*MCKLVR* DE3 **40** D3 2
**Dovecote Dr** *BWSH/BRSTN* DE72 **45** F4
**The Dovecote** *DERBYE* DE21 **13** G4
**Dovedale Av** *DERBYSE* DE24 **54** B2
**Dovedale Cl** *RIPLEY* DE5 **8** C1
**Dovedale Crs** *BPR/DUF* DE56 **6** C2
**Dovedale Ri** *DERBYW* DE22 **33** G2
**Dovedale Rd** *DERBYE* DE21 **44** D3
**Dover St** *NORM/LIT* DE23 **42** B5 2
**Dower Cl** *DERBYW* DE22 **34** B2 2
**Downham Cl** *MCKLVR* DE3 **40** B5 4
**Downing Cl** *DERBYW* DE22 **32** C5 4
**Downing Rd** *DERBYE* DE21 **3** K4
**Drage St** *DERBY* DE1 **34** C4
**Draycott Cl** *HEANOR* DE75 **9** H3 1
**Draycott Dr** *MCKLVR* DE3 **39** H3
**Draycott Rd** *BWSH/BRSTN* DE72 **45** H5
*BWSH/BRSTN* DE72 **57** F2
**Drayton Av** *DERBYW* DE22 **32** C5 5
**Dresden Cl** *MCKLVR* DE3 **39** H4
**Drewry Ct** *DERBYW* DE22 **2** A4
**Drewry La** *DERBYW* DE22 **41** H2
**Dreyfus Cl** *DERBYE* DE21 **45** E1 1
**The Drive** *BPR/DUF* DE56 **4** C4
**Drury Av** *DERBYE* DE21 **44** C2
**Dryden St** *NORM/LIT* DE23 **52** A3
**Drysdale Rd** *MCKLVR* DE3 **40** A3
**Duesbury Cl** *DERBYSE* DE24 **53** F2
**Duffield Bank** *BPR/DUF* DE56 **18** B1
**Duffield Rd** *BPR/DUF* DE56 **18** C4
*DERBYW* DE22 **26** B3
*DERBYW* DE22 **34** A2
**Dukeries La** *DERBYE* DE21 **36** A1
**Duke St** *DERBY* DE1 **2** D1
**Duluth Av** *DERBYE* DE21 **35** H4
**Dulverton Av** *DERBYSE* DE24 **61** F2 1
**Dulwich Rd** *DERBYW* DE22 **32** B5
**Dumbles La** *RIPLEY* DE5 **9** E5
**Dunbar Cl** *DERBYSE* DE24 **61** H2
**Duncan Cl** *BPR/DUF* DE56 **6** C1
**Duncan Rd** *NORM/LIT* DE23 **52** A1
**Dunedin Cl** *MCKLVR* DE3 **40** B3
**Dunkery Ct** *DERBYE* DE21 **35** H1 4
**Dunkirk** *DERBYW* DE22 **2** B5 2
**Dunnicliffe La** *MELB/CHEL* DE73 **75** H3
**Dunoon Cl** *DERBYSE* DE24 **61** H1 2
**Dunsmore Dr** *DERBYE* DE21 **35** F1
**Dunstall Park Rd** *DERBYSE* DE24 **53** E1
**Dunvegan Cl** *DERBYSE* DE24 **61** G2 2
**Durham Av** *DERBYE* DE21 **35** F5
**Durley Cl** *DERBYSE* DE24 **54** B2 2
**Durward Cl** *DERBYSE* DE24 **52** D2 3


## E


**Ealing Cl** *DERBYW* DE22 **32** D5 2
**Eardley Cl** *DERBYE* DE21 **44** A1
**Earls Crs** *DERBYE* DE21 **36** A1
**Earlswood Cl**
*BWSH/BRSTN* DE72 **57** G1 1
**Earlswood Dr** *MCKLVR* DE3 **40** C2
**East Av** *MCKLVR* DE3 **40** A3
**Eastbrae Rd** *NORM/LIT* DE23 **51** H2
**East Cl** *DERBYW* DE22 **33** H1
**East Crs** *BPR/DUF* DE56 **12** D2 1
**East Croft Av** *NORM/LIT* DE23 **51** G4
**East Lawn** *RDERBYSW* DE65 **60** A2
**Eastleigh Dr** *MCKLVR* DE3 **40** B4
**East Service Rd** *DERBYE* DE21 **44** A4
**East St** *DERBY* DE1 **2** D4 1
**Eastway** *CDON/KEG* DE74 **73** E4
**Eastwood Av** *NORM/LIT* DE23 **41** F4 1
**Eastwood Dr** *NORM/LIT* DE23 **41** F4
**Eaton Av** *DERBYW* DE22 **26** B3
**Eaton Bank** *BPR/DUF* DE56 **18** B3
**Eaton Cl** *DERBYW* DE22 **26** B3
**Eaton Ct** *BPR/DUF* DE56 **17** H3
*DERBY* DE1 **33** H5
**Eaton Rd** *CDON/KEG* DE74 **73** E4
**Ecclesbourne Av** *BPR/DUF* DE56 **18** A2
**Ecclesbourne Cl** *BPR/DUF* DE56 **17** H2
**Edale Av** *DERBYSE* DE24 **54** A2
*MCKLVR* DE3 **40** A4
*NORM/LIT* DE23 **41** H
**Edale Cl** *DERBYW* DE22 **33** C
**Edale Dr** *DERBYE* DE21 **45** E
**Eden Rd** *DERBYE* DE21 **44** A2
**Edensor Dr** *BPR/DUF* DE56 **6** D
**Edensor Sq** *DERBYW* DE22 **2** A6
**Eden St** *DERBYSE* DE24 **54** A
**Edgbaston Ct** *NORM/LIT* DE23 **51** F1
**Edge Hl** *MELB/CHEL* DE73 **63** C
**Edgelaw Ct** *DERBYSE* DE24 **61** G1
**Edgware Rd** *DERBYW* DE22 **32** C
**Edith Wood Cl** *DERBYSE* DE24 **54** A
**Edmund Rd** *DERBYE* DE21 **45** E
**Ednaston Av** *NORM/LIT* DE23 **51** C
**Edward Av** *DERBYE* DE21 **43** H
**Edwards Crs** *BPR/DUF* DE56 **13** H
**Edward St** *BPR/DUF* DE56 **6** E
*DERBY* DE1 **2** E
**Edwinstowe Rd** *DERBYE* DE21 **35** H
**Eggesford Rd** *DERBYSE* DE24 **61** C
**Eggington Rd** *RDERBYSW* DE65 **58** A
**Egmanton Cl** *DERBYE* DE21 **36** A2
**Egreaves Av** *HEANOR* DE75 **9** H
**Eland Cl** *DERBYE* DE21 **37** F
**Elgin Av** *NORM/LIT* DE23 **40** D5
**Eliot Rd** *NORM/LIT* DE23 **51** E
**Elizabeth Cl** *DERBYE* DE21 **44** A
**Elkstone Cl** *DERBYE* DE21 **36** A1
**Ellastone Gdns** *DERBYSE* DE24 **54** A
**Ellendale Rd** *DERBYE* DE21 **36** A
**Ellesmere Av** *DERBYSE* DE24 **43** E
**Ellison Av** *BWSH/BRSTN* DE72 **65** F
**Elm Av** *BPR/DUF* DE56 **6** C5
**Elm Gv** *DERBYE* DE21 **44** A
*DERBYW* DE22 **25** C
**Elms Av** *NORM/LIT* DE23 **41** E
**Elms Dr** *NORM/LIT* DE23 **41** E
**Elms Gv** *RDERBYSW* DE65 **58** E
**Elms St** *DERBY* DE1 **34** A
**Elm St** *BWSH/BRSTN* DE72 **45** C
**Elm Tree Av** *BPR/DUF* DE56 **13** H
**Elmtree Av** *DERBYSE* DE24 **52** C2
**Elmwood Dr** *DERBYE* DE21 **34** D
**Elton Rd** *DERBYSE* DE24 **52** C
**Elvaston La** *BWSH/BRSTN* DE72 **54** D
*DERBYSE* DE24 **54** A
**Elvaston St** *BWSH/BRSTN* DE72 **57** E
**Embankment Cl** *DERBYW* DE22 **32** C4
**Emerald Cl** *DERBYE* DE21 **35** G
**Emerson Sq** *NORM/LIT* DE23 **52** A
**Empress Rd** *NORM/LIT* DE23 **42** A
**Endsleigh Gdns** *DERBYW* DE22 **32** C5
**Enfield Rd** *DERBYW* DE22 **33** E
**Ennis Cl** *DERBYE* DE21 **36** B
**Enoch Stone Dr** *DERBYE* DE21 **44** A2
**Epping Cl** *DERBYW* DE22 **32** B5
**Epworth Dr** *DERBYSE* DE24 **53** H
**Essex St** *DERBYE* DE21 **3** J
**Eton St** *DERBYSE* DE24 **43** F
**Etruria Gdns** *DERBY* DE1 **34** B4
**Etta's Wy** *RDERBYSW* DE65 **48** A
**Ettrick Dr** *DERBYSE* DE24 **61** H
**Etwall La** *RDERBYSW* DE65 **48** C
**Etwall Rd** *MCKLVR* DE3 **39** H
*MCKLVR* DE3 **49** F
*RDERBYSW* DE65 **59** F
**Etwall St** *DERBYW* DE22 **41** G
**Euston Dr** *DERBY* DE1 **34** C4
**Evans Av** *DERBYW* DE22 **26** B
**Evanston Gdns** *DERBYE* DE21 **36** A
**Evelyn Gv** *DERBYE* DE21 **43** H
**Evergreen Cl** *DERBYE* DE21 **27** H5
**Evesham Cl** *DERBYE* DE21 **35** F2
**Excelsior Av** *DERBYSE* DE24 **53** G
**Exchange St** *DERBY* DE1 **2** D
**Exeter Pl** *DERBY* DE1 **2** E
**The Eyrie** *DERBYSE* DE24 **61** H2


## F


**Fairbourne Dr** *MCKLVR* DE3 **40** A
**Fairdene** *NORM/LIT* DE23 **42** A4
**Faires Cl** *BWSH/BRSTN* DE72 **46** A5
**Faire St** *DERBYW* DE22 **41** H
**Fairfax Rd** *NORM/LIT* DE23 **42** A
**Fairfield Av**
*BWSH/BRSTN* DE72 **45** H3
**Fairfield Rd** *ILK* DE7 **14** B
*NORM/LIT* DE23 **41** H
**Fairford Gdns** *NORM/LIT* DE23 **50** D3
**Fairisle Cl** *DERBYE* DE21 **28** B5
**Fairlawns** *BPR/DUF* DE56 **17** G
**Fairview Cl** *BPR/DUF* DE56 **14** A
*NORM/LIT* DE23 **50** D
**Fairview Gra** *BPR/DUF* DE56 **14** A3
**Fairway Cl** *DERBYW* DE22 **33** G

airway Crs DERBYW DE22 33 G1
airwood Dr DERBYSE DE24 54 C3
alcons Ri BPR/DUF DE56 6 D2
alcon Wy DERBYSE DE24 61 H2
allow Rd DERBYE DE21 37 E5
almouth Rd DERBYSE DE24 54 B4
ar Cft BWSH/BRSTN DE72 57 G1
ar La BWSH/BRSTN DE72 46 A1
ar Laund BPR/DUF DE56 6 C1
arley Rd NORM/LIT DE23 41 G4
arm Cl BPR/DUF DE56 6 D3
BPR/DUF DE56 13 H2 3
arm Dr DERBYSE DE24 53 H4
armhouse Rd DERBYSE DE24 61 H2
armlands La NORM/LIT DE23 51 E3
arm St DERBYW DE22 2 A7 1
arnah Green Rd BPR/DUF DE56 5 G4
arnborough Gdns
DERBYW DE22 26 C4
arncombe La DERBYE DE21 27 G5 2
arneworth Rd MCKLVR DE3 39 H4
arnham Cl MCKLVR DE3 39 H4
arningham Cl DERBYE DE21 45 E1 2
arnway DERBYW DE22 33 H2
arrier Gdns NORM/LIT DE23 50 D2 5
arringdon Cl DERBYW DE22 32 C5 7
aversham Cl DERBYSE DE24 53 G4
ellow Lands Wy
MELB/CHEL DE73 63 H2
ellside BPR/DUF DE56 6 B3
DERBYE DE21 45 E1
enchurch Wk DERBYW DE22 33 E5
enton Rd MCKLVR DE3 39 H4
enwick St DERBYSE DE24 53 E2
ernhill Ct MELB/CHEL DE73 63 H1
ernwood Cl NORM/LIT DE23 51 F1 2
errers Cl CDON/KEG DE74 72 D4
errers Crs BPR/DUF DE56 17 G2
errers Wy DERBYW DE22 33 H1
estival Av BWSH/BRSTN DE72 57 F2
ield Cl BWSH/BRSTN DE72 45 G3
ield Ct BPR/DUF DE56 13 H3
ield Crs DERBYSE DE24 53 H4
ield Dr DERBYSE DE24 53 H4
ieldfare Ct NORM/LIT DE23 50 D3 3
ieldgate Dr DERBYE DE21 35 G1
ield Head Wy DERBYE DE21 28 A5 3
ield La BPR/DUF DE56 6 A3
DERBYE DE21 35 H4
DERBYSE DE24 54 A3
ieldon Cl ASHB DE6 31 E1 1
ield Ri NORM/LIT DE23 51 F2
ield Rw BPR/DUF DE56 6 A3
ieldsway Dr DERBYE DE21 35 E1
ife St DERBYSE DE24 53 F1
incham Cl DERBYE DE21 35 E2 3
inch Crs MCKLVR DE3 49 H1
inchley Av DERBYW DE22 32 C5
indern Cl BPR/DUF DE56 6 C1
DERBYW DE22 33 G2
indern La RDERBYSW DE65 49 F4
RDERBYSW DE65 59 H5
indern St DERBYW DE22 41 G1 3
inmere Cl NORM/LIT DE23 50 D1
inningley Dr DERBYW DE22 33 H1 1
insbury Av DERBYW DE22 33 E5
irestone BPR/DUF DE56 11 G2
irfield Av BWSH/BRSTN DE72 57 H1
irs Crs DERBYW DE22 25 H3
irtree Gv DERBYE DE21 36 A1
isher La BPR/DUF DE56 17 H1
isher St DERBYSE DE24 53 F3 1
iskerton Wy DERBYE DE21 36 A3
lagshaw La ASHB DE6 22 D3
lamstead Av HEANOR DE75 9 G3
lamstead La RIPLEY DE5 14 C1
lamstead St DERBYSE DE24 53 E3
he Flat BPR/DUF DE56 13 G2
laxholme Av BPR/DUF DE56 18 A4 1
leet Crs BPR/DUF DE56 6 A4 2
leet Pk BPR/DUF DE56 6 B4
leet St NORM/LIT DE23 42 B4
he Fleet BPR/DUF DE56 6 A5
lint St DERBYSE DE24 53 E3
lood St BWSH/BRSTN DE72 45 H2
olkestone Dr DERBYSE DE24 53 H4
olly Rd DERBYW DE22 34 C2
ord Av HEANOR DE75 9 H3
ord La DERBYE DE21 26 D3
DERBYW DE22 26 C3
ord St BPR/DUF DE56 6 A3
DERBY DE1 2 B3
ordwells Cl NORM/LIT DE23 50 D1 4
oremark Av NORM/LIT DE23 51 H1
orest Cl BPR/DUF DE56 6 C2
orester St DERBY DE1 2 B5
orman St DERBY DE1 2 B4
DERBYW DE22 2 A4
Forrester Av
BWSH/BRSTN DE72 71 E2 1
Forty Foot La MELB/CHEL DE73 76 D4
Forum Cl DERBYSE DE24 54 C4 2
Fosbrook Dr CDON/KEG DE74 72 C3
Fosse Cl BWSH/BRSTN DE72 45 H5
Foundry La BPR/DUF DE56 12 A3
Fountains Cl DERBYW DE22 26 B4 2
Fowler Av DERBYE DE21 44 C2
Fowler St BWSH/BRSTN DE72 57 E2
DERBYW DE22 33 H5 4
Fox Cl DERBYSE DE24 61 G2
Foxdell Wy MELB/CHEL DE73 64 A2
Foxes Wk DERBYW DE22 25 H4 4
Foxfields Dr DERBYE DE21 35 F1
Foxglove Dr DERBYE DE21 27 G5
Foxlands Av DERBYW DE22 34 A1
Foxley Ct DERBYE DE21 35 H1 3
Fox Rd CDON/KEG DE74 72 C3
Fox St DERBY DE1 2 E1
Foyle Av DERBYE DE21 43 H2
Frampton Gdns
NORM/LIT DE23 50 C3 5
Franchise St DERBYW DE22 41 H2
Francis St DERBYE DE21 3 J2
Franklyn Dr DERBYSE DE24 53 H3
Frazer Cl DERBYE DE21 36 D5
Frederick Av DERBYSE DE24 53 G3
Frederick St DERBYW DE22 33 G5 2
Freehold St DERBYW DE22 41 H2
Freeman Av NORM/LIT DE23 51 H3
Freemantle Rd MCKLVR DE3 40 B3 1
Freesia Cl MCKLVR DE3 40 B5 3
French La DERBYE DE21 13 G5
French St NORM/LIT DE23 41 H4
Fresco Dr NORM/LIT DE23 50 C2
Friar Ga DERBY DE1 2 B3
Friar Gate Ct DERBY DE1 2 A3
Friars Cl DERBYW DE22 34 A1 3
Friary Av DERBYSE DE24 53 F4
Friary St DERBY DE1 2 A4
Frizams La MELB/CHEL DE73 60 C5
Froggatt Cl DERBYW DE22 26 B3
Fulbrook Rd NORM/LIT DE23 50 D2
Fulham Rd DERBYW DE22 40 D1
Full St DERBY DE1 2 C2
Fulmar Cl MCKLVR DE3 40 D3
Furnace La HEANOR DE75 9 H3
Furrows Cl DERBYE DE21 28 B5 3


## G


Gable Ct MCKLVR DE3 50 B1 1
Gainsborough Cl
DERBYE DE21 36 A2 3
Gairloch Cl DERBYSE DE24 61 G2
Galway Av DERBYE DE21 44 A2
Garden Crs CDON/KEG DE74 73 E4
Garden St DERBY DE1 2 B1
Garfield Av BWSH/BRSTN DE72 56 D2
Garfield Cl NORM/LIT DE23 51 F3 2
Garrick St DERBYSE DE24 53 H2
Garry Cl DERBYSE DE24 61 G2
Garth Crs DERBYSE DE24 54 A3 2
Garthorpe Ct DERBYE DE21 35 G1 5
Gary Cl NORM/LIT DE23 51 G4
Gascoigne Dr DERBYE DE21 44 C2
Gaskell Av NORM/LIT DE23 51 H2
Gasny Av CDON/KEG DE74 73 E2
Gatcombe Cl DERBYE DE21 35 H1
Gayton Av NORM/LIT DE23 51 G3
Gayton Thorpe Cl
NORM/LIT DE23 50 C2 3
Gema Cl DERBYW DE22 26 B4
George St BPR/DUF DE56 6 A3
DERBY DE1 2 B3
MELB/CHEL DE73 75 H3
Gerard Cl DERBYE DE21 37 E5 2
Gerard Ct DERBY DE1 2 B5
Gerard Gv RDERBYSW DE65 48 B5 2
Gerard St DERBY DE1 2 B6
Gertrude Rd BWSH/BRSTN DE72 56 D2
DERBYE DE21 35 H3
Gibfield La BPR/DUF DE56 6 A5 2
Gilbert Cl DERBYE DE21 44 C2
Gilbert Crs BPR/DUF DE56 17 H3
Gilbert St DERBYSE DE24 54 A4
Gilderdale Wy DERBYE DE21 28 A5
Gillamoor Ct DERBYSE DE24 54 C3 3
Gisborne Cl MCKLVR DE3 40 B2
Gisborne Crs DERBYW DE22 26 A4
Gisborne Gn DERBY DE1 33 H5 5
Gladstone Cl MELB/CHEL DE73 63 G1
Gladstone Rd DERBYE DE21 44 D1
Gladstone St NORM/LIT DE23 41 H5
Glamis Cl DERBYE DE21 36 A1
Glastonbury Rd DERBYSE DE24 54 B2
Gleadmoss La DERBYE DE21 35 H2 4
Glebe Av ILK DE7 15 E4
Glebe Crs ILK DE7 29 G2
Glebe Ri NORM/LIT DE23 41 F5
Glen Av BPR/DUF DE56 12 D3
Glencroft Dr DERBYSE DE24 61 G1
Glendale Dr DERBYE DE21 45 E1
Glendon Rd DERBYSE DE24 61 G1
Glendon St ILK DE7 21 F4
Gleneagles Cl MCKLVR DE3 40 C4 3
Glenfield Crs MCKLVR DE3 39 H4
Glengarry Wy DERBYSE DE24 51 G5
Glenmore Dr DERBYSE DE24 51 G5 5
Glenmoy Cl NORM/LIT DE23 51 G2
Glenn Wy BWSH/BRSTN DE72 66 B3
Glenorchy Ct DERBYE DE21 28 A5 3
Glen Vw BPR/DUF DE56 6 A5
Glenwood Rd MELB/CHEL DE73 63 H4
Glossop St DERBYSE DE24 52 C2
Gloster St DERBYSE DE24 43 F4
Goathland Rd DERBYSE DE24 61 G2
Goldcrest Dr DERBYE DE21 37 E5
Golden Va ILK DE7 14 A4
Gold La DERBYW DE22 32 B3
Goldstone Ct DERBYE DE21 44 D2 2
Golf La BPR/DUF DE56 11 H5
Goodale St NORM/LIT DE23 42 B5
Goodrington Rd DERBYE DE21 28 B5 6
Goodsmoor Rd DERBYSE DE24 51 H4
Goods Rd BPR/DUF DE56 5 H5
Goods Yd BPR/DUF DE56 12 A1 1
Goodwin's La BPR/DUF DE56 11 F1
Goodwood Dr DERBYSE DE24 54 B3
Gordon Rd BWSH/BRSTN DE72 45 G5
NORM/LIT DE23 42 A3
Gorse Cl NORM/LIT DE23 51 E3
Gorsey Cl BPR/DUF DE56 5 H1 1
Gorsty Leys RDERBYSW DE65 60 A3 1
Gosforth Rd DERBYSE DE24 53 F2
Gower St DERBY DE1 2 C5
Grafham Cl MELB/CHEL DE73 63 H2
Grafton St NORM/LIT DE23 41 H4
Grammer St RIPLEY DE5 9 F3
Grampian Wy DERBYSE DE24 61 G1
Grandfield St HEANOR DE75 9 H3
Grandstand Rd DERBYE DE21 3 H1
Grange Av BWSH/BRSTN DE72 57 G1
NORM/LIT DE23 51 H2
Grange Cl MELB/CHEL DE73 76 A2
Grange Dr CDON/KEG DE74 72 D4
Grange Farm Cl CDON/KEG DE74 73 F2
Grange Rd DERBYSE DE24 54 A4
Grange St NORM/LIT DE23 42 C4
The Grange HEANOR DE75 15 H2
Grangewood Dr BPR/DUF DE56 12 B3
Grant Av DERBYE DE21 44 A1 2
Grantham Av DERBYE DE21 35 F2
Granville Cl BPR/DUF DE56 17 H2
Granville St DERBY DE1 41 H1
Grasmere Av DERBYE DE21 36 D5
Grasmere Crs DERBYSE DE24 51 H5
Grassthorpe Cl DERBYE DE21 36 A2 3
Grassy La MCKLVR DE3 49 F2
Gravel Pit La DERBYE DE21 44 D2
Grayling St NORM/LIT DE23 42 C4
Great Northern Rd DERBY DE1 41 H1
Greatorex Av DERBYSE DE24 53 F4
Greenacres NORM/LIT DE23 51 E1 2
Green Av MELB/CHEL DE73 63 H3
Greenbank DERBYE DE21 44 C2 3
Greenburn Cl NORM/LIT DE23 51 F3
Greenfields Av
NORM/LIT DE23 51 E2 1
Greenfinch Cl DERBYE DE21 37 E5 3
Greenland Av DERBYW DE22 41 E1
Green La BPR/DUF DE56 6 A3
BWSH/BRSTN DE72 45 H1
DERBY DE1 2 C5
DERBYSE DE24 54 B1
MELB/CHEL DE73 68 B3
MELB/CHEL DE73 76 D5
RDERBYSW DE65 49 E5
Green Pk DERBYW DE22 32 D5 3
Greenside Ct MCKLVR DE3 39 H4
The Green ASHB DE6 30 B2
BWSH/BRSTN DE72 65 G5 1
CDON/KEG DE74 72 D4
DERBYW DE22 33 G2
MCKLVR DE3 40 A5
RDERBYSW DE65 60 A3
Green Wy RDERBYSW DE65 60 A2 2
Greenway Cl BWSH/BRSTN DE72 45 G3
The Greenway DERBYSE DE24 54 C4 6
Greenwich Dr North
DERBYW DE22 41 E1
Greenwich Dr South
DERBYW DE22 40 D1
Greenwood Av DERBYE DE21 35 G3
Greenwood Cl DERBYSE DE24 53 E4 2
Gregory Av BWSH/BRSTN DE72 57 F1
Gregorys Wy BPR/DUF DE56 6 D2
Grendon Cl BPR/DUF DE56 6 C1 2
Grenfell Av NORM/LIT DE23 51 H3
Gresham Rd DERBYSE DE24 52 D1
Grey St DERBYW DE22 2 B6
Griffin Cl DERBYSE DE24 53 G2
Grimshaw Av DERBYSE DE24 54 A2
Grindlow Rd DERBYE DE21 35 H3
Groome Av HEANOR DE75 9 H3 2
Grosvenor Dr NORM/LIT DE23 50 D3
Grosvenor St DERBYSE DE24 42 D5
Grovebury Dr NORM/LIT DE23 51 F4
Grove Cl BWSH/BRSTN DE72 55 E5
Grove Pk RDERBYSW DE65 58 A2
Groves Nook MELB/CHEL DE73 63 F3 1
Grove St NORM/LIT DE23 42 B3
The Grove MCKLVR DE3 40 B4
Gunhills La BPR/DUF DE56 10 B4
Gurney Av NORM/LIT DE23 51 G3
Gypsy La BWSH/BRSTN DE72 56 B1
Haddon Cl DERBYW DE22 25 G5
Haddon Dr DERBYE DE21 45 E2
DERBYW DE22 25 G5
MCKLVR DE3 40 B3
Haddon St NORM/LIT DE23 41 H5
Haig St DERBYSE DE24 53 G1
Hailsham Cl MCKLVR DE3 40 A3 2
Haines Cl DERBYSE DE24 52 A5
Hallam Flds CDON/KEG DE74 73 E5
Hall Dyke DERBYE DE21 44 D1
Hall Farm Cl CDON/KEG DE74 72 D4
Hall Farm Rd BPR/DUF DE56 17 H3
Hallgate Cl DERBYE DE21 28 B5
Hall Leys La MELB/CHEL DE73 76 C1
Hall Pk MELB/CHEL DE73 68 B2
Hall Park Cl NORM/LIT DE23 41 E5
Hall St DERBYSE DE24 53 H2
Halstock Dr DERBYSE DE24 54 B1
Hambledon Dr DERBYSE DE24 61 G2 3
Hamblin Crs DERBYSE DE24 52 A5
Hamilton Cl MCKLVR DE3 40 C3 1
Hamilton Rd DERBYE DE21 37 E5
NORM/LIT DE23 42 A4
Hampden St NORM/LIT DE23 52 B1 2
Hampshire Rd DERBYE DE21 34 D3
Hampstead Dr DERBYW DE22 32 D5
Hampton Cl DERBYE DE21 45 E1
Hanbury Rd DERBYE DE21 35 F5
Handel St DERBYSE DE24 52 D1
Handford St DERBYW DE22 41 G1
Handyside St DERBY DE1 2 C1
Hanger Bank BWSH/BRSTN DE72 65 G4
Hanover Sq DERBYW DE22 32 D5
Hanslynn BWSH/BRSTN DE72 55 E5 1
Hanwell Wy DERBYW DE22 33 E5
Harcourt Pl CDON/KEG DE74 73 E3
Harcourt St DERBY DE1 2 B6
Hardacre Cl MELB/CHEL DE73 75 H2 4
Hardhurst Rd DERBYSE DE24 54 A4
Hardwick Av DERBYW DE22 25 G5
Hardwick Dr MCKLVR DE3 40 B4
Hardwick St DERBYSE DE24 52 D1
Harebell Cl DERBYE DE21 27 H5
Harepit Cl DERBYSE DE24 53 H4 1
Harewood Cl BPR/DUF DE56 7 E2 3
Harewood Rd DERBYW DE22 25 G5
Hargrave Av
BWSH/BRSTN DE72 45 H1 2
Harlech Cl DERBYE DE21 45 F1 1
Harlesden Av DERBYW DE22 32 D4
Harlow Cl DERBYSE DE24 53 G5 1
Harpswell Cl DERBYW DE22 33 H1 2
Harpur Av NORM/LIT DE23 51 E2
Harrier Rd BPR/DUF DE56 6 D2
Harrier Wy DERBYSE DE24 61 H1
Harriet St NORM/LIT DE23 42 B3
Harringay Gdns DERBYW DE22 33 F5 2
Harrington Av
BWSH/BRSTN DE72 45 H4
Harrington Rd NORM/LIT DE23 41 F5 2
Harrington St
BWSH/BRSTN DE72 57 E2 1
DERBYSE DE24 53 F3 2
NORM/LIT DE23 52 B1
Harrison St DERBYW DE22 41 H3 1
Harrogate Crs DERBYE DE21 35 E2
Harrow St DERBYSE DE24 43 F4
Hartington St NORM/LIT DE23 2 D7
Hartington Wy MCKLVR DE3 40 A4
Hartland Dr NORM/LIT DE23 51 G3
Hartshorne Rd NORM/LIT DE23 51 F4
Harvest Wy DERBYE DE21 28 B5
Harvey Rd CDON/KEG DE74 73 E5
DERBYSE DE24 53 H2
Hasgill Cl DERBYE DE21 28 B5 7

Haslam's La DERBYW DE22 34 B1
Haslemere Ct NORM/LIT DE23 42 C4 4
Hassop Rd DERBYE DE21 35 H3
Hastings St CDON/KEG DE74 73 E5
NORM/LIT DE23 42 B5
Hatchmere Cl DERBYE DE21 35 H2
Hatfield Rd DERBYSE DE24 53 G4
Hathern Cl NORM/LIT DE23 51 H4
Hathersage Av NORM/LIT DE23 51 H1
Hatton Ct MELB/CHEL DE73 75 H3 1
Haulton Dr CDON/KEG DE74 72 D3
Havelock Rd NORM/LIT DE23 52 A1
Haven Baulk Av NORM/LIT DE23 50 B2
Haven Baulk La MCKLVR DE3 50 A2
Haven Ct DERBYSE DE24 54 C3
Hawke St DERBYW DE22 41 F1
Hawksdale Cl
MELB/CHEL DE73 63 H2 4
Hawkshead Av DERBYE DE21 35 E2
Hawthorn Av DERBYSE DE24 53 H2 1
Hawthorn Crs
RDERBYSW DE65 60 A2 3
Hawthorne Av
BWSH/BRSTN DE72 45 G3
Hawthorne Cl BPR/DUF DE56 7 G5 2
Hawthorn Rd CDON/KEG DE74 73 E2
The Hawthorns DERBYE DE21 19 E5 1
Hawthorn St DERBYSE DE24 52 D1
Hawtrey Gdns DERBYSE DE24 53 H3 1
Haydn Rd DERBYE DE21 35 G3
Haydock Park Rd DERBYSE DE24 53 F1
Hayes Av BWSH/BRSTN DE72 57 E2
NORM/LIT DE23 51 G1
The Hayes RDERBYSW DE65 59 H3
Hayes Wood Rd ILK DE7 21 G4
Hayfield Cl BPR/DUF DE56 6 C2 2
Hayley Cft BPR/DUF DE56 18 A4
Haywood Cl DERBYSE DE24 53 H4 2
Hazel Av NORM/LIT DE23 51 G3
Hazel Cl RDERBYSW DE65 60 B2 1
Hazeldene Cl BPR/DUF DE56 11 H5
Hazel Dr DERBYE DE21 37 F5
Hazel Gv BPR/DUF DE56 17 H2 1
Hazelrigg Cl CDON/KEG DE74 72 C3
Hazelwood Hl BPR/DUF DE56 11 E2
Hazelwood Rd BPR/DUF DE56 11 F3
DERBYE DE21 35 G3 3
Headingley Ct NORM/LIT DE23 51 F1 3
Heage La RDERBYSW DE65 48 B2
Heanor Rd ILK DE7 15 F3
RIPLEY DE5 9 F4
Heath Av NORM/LIT DE23 41 F4
Heathcote Cl DERBYSE DE24 54 B4 2
Heath Ct DERBYSE DE24 61 H1 3
Heather Cl DERBYSE DE24 61 G2 4
Heather Crs NORM/LIT DE23 51 F3
Heathermead Cl DERBYE DE21 35 G2
Heath La RDERBYSW DE65 60 A3
Hebden Cl NORM/LIT DE23 50 C3
Hebrides Cl DERBYSE DE24 61 G1 11
Hedgebank Ct DERBYE DE21 28 B5 8
Hedgerow Gdns DERBYE DE21 28 B5 9
Hedingham Wy MCKLVR DE3 49 H1
Heigham Cl DERBYSE DE24 63 E1
Helston Cl DERBYSE DE24 54 A3 3
Hemington Hl CDON/KEG DE74 73 F3
Hemington La CDON/KEG DE74 73 H2
Hemlock Cl DERBYE DE21 27 H5
Hendon Wy DERBYW DE22 33 E5
Henry St DERBY DE1 2 B1
Hereford Rd DERBYE DE21 35 E3
Hermitage Av BWSH/BRSTN DE72 45 H4
Hermitage Ct DERBYE DE21 36 A2
Heronswood Dr DERBYE DE21 36 C5 1
Heron Wy MCKLVR DE3 40 D4
Heydon Cl BPR/DUF DE56 6 C1 3
Heyworth St DERBYW DE22 33 F5
Hickling Cl DERBYSE DE24 63 E1 2
High Bank RIPLEY DE5 9 E5
Highbury Cl DERBYW DE22 32 C5 3
Highfield Cl HEANOR DE75 9 G2
Highfield Gdns DERBYW DE22 34 A3
Highfield La DERBYE DE21 43 F1
Highfield Rd BPR/DUF DE56 6 A5
BPR/DUF DE56 13 G2
DERBYE DE21 26 D1
DERBYW DE22 34 A4
NORM/LIT DE23 51 F2 1
High Gv BPR/DUF DE56 7 E3
Highgrove Dr MELB/CHEL DE73 63 G2
High Pavement BPR/DUF DE56 6 B4 1
High St BPR/DUF DE56 6 B3
BPR/DUF DE56 13 H2
CDON/KEG DE74 72 D5
HEANOR DE75 9 H3
MELB/CHEL DE73 63 H3 3
MELB/CHEL DE73 75 H3
Highwood Av BPR/DUF DE56 12 C1
High Wood Bank BPR/DUF DE56 12 D1
Hilary Cl BPR/DUF DE56 7 F2
Hilderstone Cl DERBYSE DE24 54 C3
Hill Brow DERBY DE1 2 C5
Hill Cl DERBYE DE21 44 D2
ILK DE7 21 F4
Hillcrest Dr BPR/DUF DE56 13 H2
Hillcreste Dr MELB/CHEL DE73 63 G1 1
Hill Crest Rd DERBYE DE21 35 E4
Hill Croft Dr BWSH/BRSTN DE72 45 H2
Hill Cross Av NORM/LIT DE23 51 F2
Hill Cross Dr NORM/LIT DE23 51 E2
Hill Rise Cl NORM/LIT DE23 51 G2
Hillside RDERBYSW DE65 60 A2
Hillside Av DERBYE DE21 43 H1
Hillside Crs DERBYE DE21 44 D2
Hillside Ri BPR/DUF DE56 6 A5
Hillside Rd DERBYE DE21 44 D2
Hills Rd BWSH/BRSTN DE72 57 E1
Hillsway MELB/CHEL DE73 63 G1
NORM/LIT DE23 41 E5
The Hill DERBYW DE22 34 B2 3
Hill Top DERBYE DE21 35 E1
Hilltop La BPR/DUF DE56 7 F5
Hill Vw BPR/DUF DE56 17 G2 1
Hill View Cl ILK DE7 14 A3 3
Hill View Gv DERBYE DE21 44 D1 1
Hilton Cl MCKLVR DE3 40 A5
Hilton Rd RDERBYSW DE65 48 A5
Hind Av BWSH/BRSTN DE72 57 F2
Hindscarth Crs MCKLVR DE3 40 B5 6
Hobart Cl MCKLVR DE3 40 C4
Hob Hl BPR/DUF DE56 11 E2
Hobkirk Dr DERBYSE DE24 61 H2
Hodge Beck Cl DERBYSE DE24 54 B3
Hodthorpe Cl DERBYE DE21 35 H2 3
Holborn Dr DERBYW DE22 32 D4
Holbrook Rd BPR/DUF DE56 6 A5
DERBYSE DE24 54 A3
Holbrook Vw BPR/DUF DE56 13 H2 4
Holcombe St NORM/LIT DE23 42 C5
Holden Av BWSH/BRSTN DE72 65 F4
Holderness Cl DERBYSE DE24 61 G2
Hollies Rd DERBYW DE22 25 G5
Hollington Cl DERBYE DE21 35 F4 1
Hollis St DERBYSE DE24 53 H1
Holloway Rd BPR/DUF DE56 17 G1
DERBYSE DE24 53 G3
Hollow Brooks DERBYE DE21 26 D1 1
Hollowood Av NORM/LIT DE23 51 F1
The Hollow CDON/KEG DE74 73 E3
MCKLVR DE3 40 A5
NORM/LIT DE23 41 E5
Hollybrook Wy NORM/LIT DE23 50 C3
Holly Bush La BPR/DUF DE56 12 B4 1
Holly Cl BWSH/BRSTN DE72 56 D2
Holly Ct MCKLVR DE3 40 A5 3
Holly House La BPR/DUF DE56 5 F3
Hollymoor Dr MELB/CHEL DE73 63 F2
Holm Av DERBYE DE21 26 C1
Holme La DERBYE DE21 44 B4
Holmesfield Dr MCKLVR DE3 40 C4 4
Holmes Rd BWSH/BRSTN DE72 57 G1
Holmes St NORM/LIT DE23 42 B4
Holmfield NORM/LIT DE23 51 H2
Holmoak Cl DERBYE DE21 28 A5 10
Holt Av DERBYSE DE24 54 B3
Holtlands Dr DERBYSE DE24 53 G4
Holyhead Dr DERBYE DE21 36 A1
Holyrood Cl DERBYE DE21 45 E1
Homefarm Cl BWSH/BRSTN DE72 45 H1
Home Farm Dr DERBYW DE22 26 B4
Honeycroft Cl BPR/DUF DE56 6 C5 3
Hope Av MCKLVR DE3 40 A4
Hope St DERBY DE1 2 E5
MELB/CHEL DE73 75 G3
Hopetoun St NORM/LIT DE23 52 B1
Hopping Hl BPR/DUF DE56 12 A2
Hopton Cl DERBYE DE21 35 H2
Hopwell Rd BWSH/BRSTN DE72 46 D5
Hornbeam Cl DERBYE DE21 35 F1 7
Horncastle Rd DERBYE DE21 35 E2
Hornsea Rd DERBYE DE21 35 E2
The Horse Shoes
CDON/KEG DE74 73 F3
Horsley Crs BPR/DUF DE56 12 D3 1
Horsley La DERBYE DE21 19 F1
Horsley Rd DERBYE DE21 13 G4
Horton St NORM/LIT DE23 42 D4
Horwood Av NORM/LIT DE23 41 G4
Hospital La MCKLVR DE3 49 G2
Houghton Ct DERBYE DE21 35 G1
Hoult St DERBYW DE22 41 G2
Hounslow Rd DERBYW DE22 33 E5
Hoveton Cl DERBYSE DE24 63 E1
Howard St NORM/LIT DE23 42 A4
Howden Cl MCKLVR DE3 39 H5
Howe St DERBYW DE22 41 G1
Howth Cl DERBYE DE21 43 H2
Hoylake Ct MCKLVR DE3 39 H3
Hoylake Dr MCKLVR DE3 39 H3
Hoyland Ct BPR/DUF DE56 7 F2 2
Hubert Shaw Cl
DERBYSE DE24 53 F5 2
Hucklow Ct DERBYE DE21 28 A5 11
Hulland St DERBY DE1 3 G7
Hulland Vw DERBYW DE22 33 G2
Humber Cl DERBYSE DE24 54 B3 3
Humbleton Dr DERBYW DE22 40 D1
Hunter Dr BPR/DUF DE56 13 G2
Hunter Rd BPR/DUF DE56 7 E2
Hunters Cft DERBYSE DE24 61 H2 3
Huntingdon Ct MELB/CHEL DE73 76 A2
Huntingdon Dr CDON/KEG DE74 72 D3
Huntingdon Gn DERBYE DE21 3 H2
Huntley Av DERBYE DE21 37 F5
Hurst Dr ILK DE7 29 H2
Hutton St DERBYSE DE24 53 F3
Hyde Park Rd DERBYW DE22 32 D5

## I

Ibsley Cl DERBYSE DE24 54 B3
Ilford Rd DERBYW DE22 40 D1
Ilkeston Rd ILK DE7 20 D3
Imperial Ct DERBYW DE22 25 G3
Industrial St NORM/LIT DE23 42 B4 2
Ingham Dr MCKLVR DE3 50 A1
Ingleby Av NORM/LIT DE23 52 A2
Ingleby La MELB/CHEL DE73 74 B5
Ingle Cl DERBYE DE21 44 D1
Ingledew Cl DERBYE DE21 35 F2
Ingle's Channel BPR/DUF DE56 6 B3 1
Inglewood Av MCKLVR DE3 40 A2
Ingliston Cl DERBYSE DE24 54 C3 4
Inn La DERBYW DE22 25 E2
Instow Dr NORM/LIT DE23 51 G4
Inveraray Cl DERBYSE DE24 61 G1
Invernia Cl NORM/LIT DE23 51 H4 4
Iona Cl DERBYSE DE24 51 H5
Iron Ga DERBY DE1 2 C3
Irvine Cl DERBYSE DE24 61 G1
Irving Pl DERBYSE DE24 53 G2
Islay Rd DERBYSE DE24 51 H5
Isleworth Dr DERBYW DE22 32 C5
Ismay Rd DERBYE DE21 35 G5
Ivybridge Cl DERBYE DE21 28 B5 10
Ivy Sq NORM/LIT DE23 42 D4 1

## J

Jacksdale Cl DERBYW DE22 33 G2
Jackson Av MCKLVR DE3 40 D4
Jacksons La BPR/DUF DE56 11 H3
RDERBYSW DE65 58 B2
Jackson St DERBYW DE22 41 H2 1
James Cl DERBY DE1 41 H1
Jardine Ct BWSH/BRSTN DE72 57 E2 2
Jarvey's La DERBYW DE22 32 B3
Jarvis Rd DERBYSE DE24 61 H2
Jasmine Cl DERBYE DE21 44 A1
Jawbone La MELB/CHEL DE73 76 B2
Jedburgh Cl DERBYSE DE24 61 H2 6
Jefferson Pl DERBYSE DE24 53 G2 2
Jemison Cl NORM/LIT DE23 50 B2 3
Jenny's Ct BPR/DUF DE56 6 D2 2
Jesop Dr DERBYSE DE24 61 H2 7
Jodrell Av BPR/DUF DE56 7 E3
John Berrysford Cl DERBYE DE21 43 G1
John F Kennedy Gdns
DERBYE DE21 36 B5 1
John Lombe Dr DERBY DE1 34 B4
John O'gaunts Wy BPR/DUF DE56 7 E2
John Port Cl RDERBYSW DE65 48 B5 3
Johnson Av DERBYSE DE24 53 F2
John St DERBY DE1 3 F6
Joseph St BPR/DUF DE56 6 A3
NORM/LIT DE23 42 B5
Jubalton Cl DERBYSE DE24 53 F3 3
Jubilee Cl MELB/CHEL DE73 76 A3
Jubilee Ct BPR/DUF DE56 6 B5
Jubilee Rd DERBYSE DE24 53 F5
Junction St DERBY DE1 41 H2 2
Jury St DERBY DE1 2 B3

## K

Kean Pl DERBYSE DE24 53 G2
Keats Av NORM/LIT DE23 40 D5
Keble Cl DERBY DE1 42 C3
Kedleston Cl DERBYW DE22 33
Kedleston Old Rd
DERBYW DE22 33 G3
Kedleston Rd DERBY DE1 34 A4
DERBYW DE22 24
DERBYW DE22 33
Kedleston St DERBY DE1 2
Kegworth Av NORM/LIT DE23 51 F3
Keldholme La DERBYSE DE24 54 B2
Kelmoor Rd DERBYSE DE24 54
Kelvedon Dr NORM/LIT DE23 50 D3
Kemble Pl DERBYSE DE24 53 G2
Kempton Park Rd
DERBYSE DE24 53
Kendon Av NORM/LIT DE23 51
Kendray Cl BPR/DUF DE56 7 E2
Kenilworth Av NORM/LIT DE23 52
Kennedy Cl DERBYE DE21 35 H4
Kensal Ri DERBYW DE22 33
Kensington Av HEANOR DE75 15
Kensington St DERBYW DE22 2
Kentish Ct DERBY DE1 34 C4
Kent St DERBYE DE21 35
Kernel Cl NORM/LIT DE23 50
Kerry Dr ILK DE7 15
Kerry St DERBYE DE21 35
Kerry's Yd BPR/DUF DE56 13 G2
Kershope Dr DERBYE DE21 28 A5
Kestrels Cft DERBYSE DE24 61
Keswick Av NORM/LIT DE23 51
Kevin Cl DERBYE DE21 36
Kew Gdns DERBYW DE22 41 E1
Keyhaven Cl DERBYE DE21 35
Keynsham Cl DERBYSE DE24 53
Keys St DERBY DE1 2
Kibworth Cl DERBYE DE21 36 A3
Kilburn La BPR/DUF DE56 7
Kilburn Rd BPR/DUF DE56 6 D3
Kildare Rd DERBYE DE21 44
Killingworth Av
DERBYSE DE24 52 A5
Killis La BPR/DUF DE56 13
Kiln Cft RDERBYSW DE65 48
Kilnsey Ct NORM/LIT DE23 50
Kimberley Rd BWSH/BRSTN DE72 45
King Alfred St DERBYW DE22 2
Kingfisher Cl MCKLVR DE3 49 G2
Kingsbury Rd DERBYW DE22 32
Kingsclere Av DERBYE DE21 36
Kings Cl HEANOR DE75 15 H1
Kings Cft DERBYW DE22 26
Kings Dr MCKLVR DE3 41
Kingsland Cl DERBYE DE21 35 G1
Kingsley Rd DERBYW DE22 25
Kingsley St DERBYSE DE24 52
King's Mead Cl DERBY DE1 2
King's Mill La BWSH/BRSTN DE72 71
Kingsmuir Rd MCKLVR DE3 39
Kingston St DERBY DE1 34
King St BPR/DUF DE56 6
BPR/DUF DE56 17
DERBY DE1 2
Kingsway DERBYW DE22 33
Kingsway Crs BPR/DUF DE56 13 H2
Kingsway Park Cl DERBYW DE22 41
Kingswood Av BPR/DUF DE56 6 D1
Kinross Av DERBYE DE21 34
Kintyre Dr DERBYSE DE24 61
Kipling Dr MCKLVR DE3 40
Kirk Dale Av DERBYE DE21 45
Kirkfield Dr BWSH/BRSTN DE72 57
Kirkistown Cl DERBYSE DE24 54 B3
Kirkland Cl CDON/KEG DE74 72
Kirkland Wy DERBYSE DE24 61
Kirk Leys Av North DERBYE DE21 44
Kirk Leys Av South DERBYE DE21 44
Kirkman Rd HEANOR DE75 9
Kirk's La BPR/DUF DE56 6
Kirkstead Cl DERBYE DE21 36
Kirk St DERBY DE1 34
Kitchener Av NORM/LIT DE23 52
Knightsbridge DERBYW DE22 32
Knights Cl DERBYSE DE24 61
Knoll Cl NORM/LIT DE23 50
Knowl Av BPR/DUF DE56 5
Kyle Gv DERBYE DE21 28 A5
Kynance Cl DERBYSE DE24 54 B4

## L

Laburnum Crs DERBYW DE22 25
Laburnum Gv DERBYW DE22 40
Ladbroke Gdns DERBYSE DE24 32
Ladybank Rd MCKLVR DE3 39
Ladybower Rd DERBYE DE21 45

dycroft Paddock
DERBYW DE22 25 H4 5
dy La RIPLEY DE5 14 C1
dy Lea Hl DERBYE DE21 13 H5
dy Lea Rd ILK DE7 13 H4
dy Mantle Cl
MELB/CHEL DE73 63 F2 1
dysmith Rd
BWSH/BRSTN DE72 45 G4
dywood Av BPR/DUF DE56 6 C2
ke Av HEANOR DE75 9 H3
ke Dr NORM/LIT DE23 52 A1
keside Dr NORM/LIT DE23 50 C2
mbhouse La BPR/DUF DE56 4 B2
mbley Dr DERBYW DE22 33 F1
mbourn Cl DERBYW DE22 26 B5 1
mbourn Dr DERBYW DE22 26 C3
mbrook Cl MCKLVR DE3 39 H4
mpad Cl MELB/CHEL DE73 75 H2 5
mpeter Cl DERBYE DE21 36 A1 6
nark St DERBYE DE21 35 F4
ncaster Wk DERBYE DE21 37 F5 1
nder La BPR/DUF DE56 6 B3
ngdale Dr DERBYE DE21 35 E1
ngford Rd MCKLVR DE3 40 A3
ngley Rd DERBYE DE21 44 D3
ngley St DERBYW DE22 41 G1
ng Rd DERBYSE DE24 53 G3
ngsett Dr MELB/CHEL DE73 63 H2
nscombe Park Rd
DERBYW DE22 33 H2 1
nsdowne Av DERBYSE DE24 53 G4 2
nsing Gdns DERBYE DE21 36 A5 2
pwing Cl DERBYSE DE24 61 H2
rch Cl DERBYW DE22 25 G5
rch Rd BPR/DUF DE56 14 A3
rges St DERBY DE1 41 H1 1
rk Cl NORM/LIT DE23 51 F3
rkhill Crs DERBYSE DE24 52 A5 2
rkspur Ct DERBYE DE21 27 H5 2
shley Gdns DERBYE DE21 35 G1
thbury Cl DERBYE DE21 35 E2
thkill Av DERBYSE DE24 54 B2
thkill Dr RIPLEY DE5 8 C1
thkill Rd DERBYE DE21 35 G3
timer Cl NORM/LIT DE23 50 B2 4
timer St DERBYSE DE24 53 E3
trigg Cl MCKLVR DE3 40 B5 7
uder Cl DERBYSE DE24 61 H2
unceston Rd DERBYSE DE24 54 A4
und Av BPR/DUF DE56 6 C1
und Cl BPR/DUF DE56 6 C2 3
und Hl BPR/DUF DE56 6 B2
und Nook BPR/DUF DE56 6 B2
urel Crs ILK DE7 15 E5
urie Pl DERBYSE DE24 53 F2
vender Rw DERBYW DE22 34 A2
verstoke Ct DERBYW DE22 41 H2 3
wn Av DERBYW DE22 33 G1
RDERBYSW DE65 48 B4
wn Heads Av NORM/LIT DE23 41 F4
wnlea Cl NORM/LIT DE23 51 H4
wnside DERBYE DE21 45 E1
e Lawns BWSH/BRSTN DE72 65 G4 1
wnswood Cl
NORM/LIT DE23 51 F1 4
wrence Av BWSH/BRSTN DE72 57 G1
DERBYE DE21 36 A4
wrence St NORM/LIT DE23 52 A1 1
a Cl DERBYW DE22 25 H5
acroft Rd NORM/LIT DE23 42 C5
a Dr DERBYE DE21 35 G5 1
MCKLVR DE3 40 B3
afenden Cl DERBYW DE22 34 B1 3
afgreen Cl NORM/LIT DE23 51 F3
ake St DERBYW DE22 41 G1 4
amington Cl NORM/LIT DE23 41 G5
ander Cl NORM/LIT DE23 51 G2 1
aper St DERBY DE1 33 H5
as Gn BWSH/BRSTN DE72 65 F4
awood Gdns DERBYE DE21 28 A5
che Cft BPR/DUF DE56 7 E3
dbury Cha DERBYSE DE24 61 G2
eds Pl DERBY DE1 3 G6
e Farm Cl MELB/CHEL DE73 63 G3 2
e Lees DERBYSE DE24 54 C4
eway DERBYE DE21 44 C2
icester St DERBYW DE22 41 H3
man St DERBYW DE22 41 H3
niscar Av HEANOR DE75 9 H3
ns Rd DERBYW DE22 33 F1
nton Av DERBYE DE21 35 G5
ominster Dr DERBYE DE21 36 B1 3
onard Cl NORM/LIT DE23 2 D7
onard St NORM/LIT DE23 2 E7
opold St DERBY DE1 2 D6
slie Cl NORM/LIT DE23 50 B1
ven Cl DERBYSE DE24 62 A2
Leveret Cl MELB/CHEL DE73 64 A2 2
Lewis St NORM/LIT DE23 42 A5
Lewiston Rd DERBYE DE21 44 A1
Lexington Rd DERBYE DE21 44 A1
Leyland St DERBYW DE22 33 H4
Leys Ct BPR/DUF DE56 7 E3 5
Leys Field Gdns
MELB/CHEL DE73 63 H2
The Leys DERBYE DE21 19 E3
Leytonstone Dr DERBYW DE22 40 D1
Lichfield Dr DERBYSE DE24 53 H2
Lidgate Cl MCKLVR DE3 39 H5
Lilac Av DERBYW DE22 40 D1
Lilac Cl DERBYSE DE24 53 H3
Lilley St DERBYSE DE24 54 A3
Lime Av BPR/DUF DE56 17 H1
DERBY DE1 2 B7
DERBYE DE21 35 E1
Lime Crs BPR/DUF DE56 6 C5 4
Limedale Av DERBYE DE21 28 A5
Lime Gv BWSH/BRSTN DE72 56 C2
DERBYE DE21 44 A1
Lime La DERBYE DE21 27 H5
ILK DE7 28 C3
Limerick Rd DERBYE DE21 44 A2
Limes Av MCKLVR DE3 40 A5
Lime Wk NORM/LIT DE23 41 G5
Linacres Dr MELB/CHEL DE73 63 H2
Lincoln Av DERBYSE DE24 53 H1
Lincoln Gn MELB/CHEL DE73 63 G2 1
Linden Cl BPR/DUF DE56 14 A2
Lindford Cl DERBYE DE21 27 G5
Lindisfarne Cl DERBYSE DE24 61 G1 12
Lindon Dr DERBYSE DE24 54 B3
Lindrick Cl MCKLVR DE3 40 C5 2
Lindsey Cl DERBYE DE21 35 F5
Lingfield Ri MCKLVR DE3 39 H3 3
Links Cl DERBYSE DE24 52 A5
Linnet Cl DERBYE DE21 37 E5 4
Linnet Hl MCKLVR DE3 49 H2
Liskeard Dr DERBYW DE22 25 G4
Lismore Ct DERBYSE DE24 61 G1 13
Liston Dr DERBYW DE22 34 A3 2
Litchurch La DERBYSE DE24 42 D4
Litchurch St DERBY DE1 3 F7 1
NORM/LIT DE23 2 E7
Little Bridge St DERBY DE1 2 A2
Littledale Cl DERBYE DE21 28 B5 11
Little Longstone Cl
MCKLVR DE3 40 C4 5
Little Meadow Rd
MELB/CHEL DE73 63 H2
Littleover Crs NORM/LIT DE23 51 G1
Littleover La NORM/LIT DE23 51 G1
Little Woodbury Dr
NORM/LIT DE23 50 C3 6
Litton Cl BPR/DUF DE56 6 C2 4
Litton Dr DERBYE DE21 45 E3
Liverpool St DERBYE DE21 35 F3 1
Liversage Pl DERBY DE1 2 E6
Liversage Rd DERBY DE1 2 E6
Liversage St DERBY DE1 2 E5
Livingstone Rd NORM/LIT DE23 41 H5
Lochinvar Cl DERBYE DE21 45 E2
Lockington Cl
MELB/CHEL DE73 63 G2 2
Lockington Rd CDON/KEG DE74 73 G2
Locko Rd DERBYE DE21 36 D4
Lockwood Rd DERBYW DE22 25 G4
Lodge Cl BPR/DUF DE56 17 H2 2
RDERBYSW DE65 48 B5
Lodge Dr BPR/DUF DE56 5 H2
Lodge La ASHB DE6 23 F4
DERBY DE1 2 B2
DERBYE DE21 44 C3
DERBYW DE22 23 H2
Lodge St BWSH/BRSTN DE72 56 D2
Lodge Wy MCKLVR DE3 40 A4
Lombard St DERBYW DE22 32 C5 9
Lomond Av DERBYSE DE24 62 A2
London Rd BWSH/BRSTN DE72 66 C3
DERBY DE1 2 D5
DERBYSE DE24 43 G5
NORM/LIT DE23 42 D3
Long Bridge La DERBYSE DE24 53 E1
Long Cft BWSH/BRSTN DE72 65 F4
Longford Cl DERBYW DE22 33 G1
Longford St DERBYW DE22 33 G3
Longlands La RDERBYSW DE65 59 H3
Longley La DERBYE DE21 36 C5
Longmoor La BWSH/BRSTN DE72 47 H5
Long Rw BPR/DUF DE56 6 A3
BWSH/BRSTN DE72 67 E2
Longstock Cl DERBYE DE21 35 F2 2
Longstone Ri BPR/DUF DE56 6 C1 4
Longthorpe Cl NORM/LIT DE23 50 D2 6
Longwalls La BPR/DUF DE56 5 F1
Lonsdale Pl DERBYW DE22 41 G2
Loom Cl BPR/DUF DE56 6 D2
Lord St DERBYSE DE24 53 E3
Lorne St DERBYW DE22 42 A3 4
Lorraine Cl DERBYSE DE24 63 F1 1
Loscoe-denby La RIPLEY DE5 9 G3
Loscoe Gra HEANOR DE75 9 H4
Loscoe Rd DERBYE DE21 35 H2
Lothian Pl CDON/KEG DE74 72 D4 3
DERBYE DE21 35 E4
Lothlorien Cl NORM/LIT DE23 51 E2 2
Loudon St NORM/LIT DE23 42 B3
Loudoun Pl CDON/KEG DE74 72 D3 1
Lousie Greaves La DERBYE DE21 36 D5
Louvain Rd NORM/LIT DE23 41 F3
Lower Dale Rd NORM/LIT DE23 42 A4
Lower Eley St DERBY DE1 2 B7
Lower Gn RDERBYSW DE65 60 A3
Lower Hall Cl BPR/DUF DE56 12 D4 1
Lower Rd DERBYW DE22 32 B3
Lowes La MELB/CHEL DE73 63 E3
Lowe St DERBYSE DE24 53 F2
Lowlands Rd BPR/DUF DE56 6 C3
Loxley Cl DERBYE DE21 36 A1
Loxton Ct MCKLVR DE3 39 H3
Loyne Cl DERBYSE DE24 62 A2
Luccombe Dr DERBYSE DE24 54 C4
Lucerne Rd DERBYE DE21 28 B5
Ludgate Wk DERBYW DE22 40 B1
Ludlow Cl DERBYE DE21 45 E1 3
Lulworth Cl NORM/LIT DE23 51 G3 3
Lumb La BPR/DUF DE56 5 F5
Lundie Cl DERBYSE DE24 61 G2
Lupin Cl DERBYE DE21 28 B5 12
Lychgate Cl DERBYE DE21 35 E1 1
Lydstep Cl DERBYE DE21 36 B1
Lyndhurst Gv DERBYE DE21 43 H1
Lyndhurst St NORM/LIT DE23 42 B4 3
Lynton St DERBYW DE22 41 H2
Lynwood Rd DERBYSE DE24 52 A5
Lytham Cl DERBYE DE21 35 E2 4
Lyttelton St DERBYW DE22 41 E1


## M


Macaulay St DERBYSE DE24 52 B4
Mackenzie St DERBYW DE22 33 F5
Macklin St DERBY DE1 2 B4
Mackworth Rd DERBYW DE22 33 H5
Macready Pl DERBYSE DE24 53 G2 4
Madeley Ct MCKLVR DE3 40 A5 4
Madeley St NORM/LIT DE23 42 B4
Madison Av DERBYE DE21 35 F4
Maidstone Dr DERBYSE DE24 53 G4
Maidwell Cl BPR/DUF DE56 6 C2
Main Av DERBYW DE22 26 A3
Maine Dr DERBYE DE21 35 H5
Main Rd BWSH/BRSTN DE72 55 F3
ILK DE7 21 E2
Main St BWSH/BRSTN DE72 56 A3
BWSH/BRSTN DE72 57 G2
BWSH/BRSTN DE72 70 D3
CDON/KEG DE74 73 G3
ILK DE7 14 A3
MELB/CHEL DE73 74 C5
MELB/CHEL DE73 76 B1
MELB/CHEL DE73 76 D4
RDERBYSW DE65 48 A5
RDERBYSW DE65 60 A3
Makeney Rd BPR/DUF DE56 12 D3
BPR/DUF DE56 18 A3
Malcolm Gv NORM/LIT DE23 50 B1 2
Malcolm St NORM/LIT DE23 42 C4
Malham Rd NORM/LIT DE23 50 C3 7
Malin Cl DERBYSE DE24 54 A4
Mallard Wk MCKLVR DE3 49 H2
Maltby Cl DERBYW DE22 34 A1 4
The Maltings
BWSH/BRSTN DE72 66 D3 2
Malton Pl DERBYE DE21 35 E2
Malvern Cl MCKLVR DE3 40 A3 3
Malvern Wy DERBYE DE21 35 E2
Manchester St DERBYW DE22 33 G5
Manifold Dr DERBYSE DE24 54 A1
Manor Av DERBYW DE22 41 F3
Manor Ct BWSH/BRSTN DE72 57 G1
Manor Farm Rd
BWSH/BRSTN DE72 65 G4
Manorleigh BWSH/BRSTN DE72 57 H1
Manor Pk BWSH/BRSTN DE72 45 F5
Manor Park Wy DERBYW DE22 41 E3 1
Manor Rd BPR/DUF DE56 6 A4
BWSH/BRSTN DE72 45 F5
MELB/CHEL DE73 63 G3
NORM/LIT DE23 41 F4 2
Mansfield Rd DERBY DE1 2 D1
DERBYE DE21 27 F5 2
Mansfields Cft
RDERBYSW DE65 48 A5 2
Mansfield St DERBY DE1 34 B4
Maple Av NORM/LIT DE23 51 G3
Maplebeck Ct DERBY DE1 2 D1
DERBY DE1 34 B4 3
Maple Dr BPR/DUF DE56 6 C5
DERBYSE DE24 53 H3
MELB/CHEL DE73 63 G2
Maple Gv DERBYW DE22 25 G3
Mapleton Av DERBYE DE21 35 G2
Mapleton Rd BWSH/BRSTN DE72 56 C1
Marchington Cl DERBYW DE22 33 H2
Maree Cl DERBYSE DE24 51 H5
Marfleet Cl MCKLVR DE3 39 H3
Margaret Av DERBYE DE21 43 F1
Margaret St DERBY DE1 34 B4 4
Margreave Rd DERBYE DE21 35 G4
Marigold Cl DERBYE DE21 28 A5
Marina Dr DERBYE DE21 44 C1
DERBYSE DE24 53 F4
Marina Rd HEANOR DE75 15 G2
Marjorie Rd DERBYE DE21 35 F3
Markeaton La DERBYW DE22 33 E3
Markeaton St DERBYW DE22 33 H5
Market Head BPR/DUF DE56 6 A4
Market Pl BPR/DUF DE56 6 B4 2
MELB/CHEL DE73 76 A3 2
RIPLEY DE5 9 G1
Market St BWSH/BRSTN DE72 56 D2
Markham Ct DERBYE DE21 35 G1 7
Mark's Cl NORM/LIT DE23 51 G3
Marlborough Dr BPR/DUF DE56 6 D2
Marlborough Rd
BWSH/BRSTN DE72 57 G2
DERBYSE DE24 52 C2
Marsden Cl BPR/DUF DE56 17 H2 3
Marsden St DERBYSE DE24 53 F2 1
Marshaw Cl MCKLVR DE3 40 B5
Marshgreen Cl DERBYSE DE24 54 C4 7
Marsh La BPR/DUF DE56 6 C2
Marsh Lane Crs BPR/DUF DE56 6 C3 2
Marston Cl BPR/DUF DE56 6 D1
NORM/LIT DE23 51 G4
Martindale Ct BPR/DUF DE56 7 E2 5
Martin Dr DERBYE DE21 35 H3
Maryland Rd DERBYE DE21 36 A5
Marylebone Crs DERBYW DE22 40 C1
Masefield Av NORM/LIT DE23 51 H2
Matlock Rd BPR/DUF DE56 6 A2
DERBYE DE21 35 G2
Matthew St DERBYSE DE24 53 G3
Matthew Wy NORM/LIT DE23 50 B2 5
Max Rd DERBYE DE21 35 F3
Maxwell Av DERBYW DE22 33 G3
Mayfair Crs DERBYW DE22 32 B5
Mayfield Av BPR/DUF DE56 13 H2
Mayfield Rd DERBYE DE21 35 F4
Maylands BWSH/BRSTN DE72 45 G5 2
Maylands Av BWSH/BRSTN DE72 57 H1
Maypole La NORM/LIT DE23 50 B2
May St DERBYW DE22 2 A7
Maytree Cl DERBYE DE21 28 B5 13
Mcneil Gv BWSH/BRSTN DE72 56 D2 1
Mead Cl DERBYSE DE24 52 A5
Meadow Cl BWSH/BRSTN DE72 56 D2
BWSH/BRSTN DE72 57 H2
DERBYE DE21 44 D2
ILK DE7 14 C4
RDERBYSW DE65 60 A2 4
Meadow Ct BPR/DUF DE56 6 A3
BPR/DUF DE56 13 H3 2
BWSH/BRSTN DE72 56 A3
Meadow Crs CDON/KEG DE74 73 E5
Meadowgrass Cl NORM/LIT DE23 51 E3
Meadow La DERBY DE1 3 F3
DERBYE DE21 43 G1
DERBYSE DE24 43 G5
Meadowlark Gv DERBYE DE21 35 H2
Meadow Nook DERBYSE DE24 54 B4
Meadow Rd DERBY DE1 2 E3
Meadow V BPR/DUF DE56 17 G2
Meadow View Cl
DERBYE DE21 28 A5 14
Meadow Wy MELB/CHEL DE73 63 G3
Mear Dr BWSH/BRSTN DE72 45 G5
Meath Av DERBYE DE21 44 A2
Medina Cl DERBYSE DE24 54 C4
Medway Dr DERBYW DE22 26 B3
Meerbrook Cl DERBYE DE21 35 H2
Megaloughton La DERBYE DE21 44 B3
Melbourn Cl BPR/DUF DE56 17 H3
Melbourne Cl BPR/DUF DE56 6 B5 1
DERBYW DE22 33 G2
MCKLVR DE3 40 C3
Melbourne La MELB/CHEL DE73 74 D5
Melbourne St DERBY DE1 2 D7
Melbreak Cl MCKLVR DE3 40 B5 3

Melfort Cl *DERBYSE* DE24 62 A2
Mellor's La *BPR/DUF* DE56 12 D4
Mellor St *DERBYSE* DE24 53 F3
Melrose Cl *DERBYSE* DE24 61 H2
Melton Av *MELB/CHEL* DE73 75 H2
*NORM/LIT* DE23 51 F3
Melville Ct *RDERBYSW* DE65 58 A1 2
Memorial Rd *DERBYW* DE22 33 F1
Mendip Ct *DERBYE* DE21 35 F1
Menin Rd *DERBYW* DE22 33 F1
Mercaston La *DERBYW* DE22 23 H1
Mercaston Rd *DERBYE* DE21 35 G3
Merchant Av *DERBYE* DE21 44 C2
Merchant St *DERBYW* DE22 33 H5
Mercian Ms *DERBYE* DE21 44 C2 4
Mere Beck *BWSH/BRSTN* DE72 56 A3
Merlin Gn *DERBYSE* DE24 51 G5 6
Merlin Wy *MCKLVR* DE3 49 G2
Merridale Rd *NORM/LIT* DE23 51 F2
Merrill Wy *DERBYSE* DE24 52 D4
Merrybower Cl *DERBYSE* DE24 61 F1 1
Merthyr Ct *DERBYE* DE21 36 A1 7
Metcalfe Cl *DERBYSE* DE24 54 A1
Meynell Ct *DERBYW* DE22 33 F1
Meynell St *NORM/LIT* DE23 42 A4
Michelle Cl *DERBYSE* DE24 61 F1 2
Michigan Cl *DERBYE* DE21 44 B1
Micklecroft Gdns
*NORM/LIT* DE23 50 B2 6
Mickleross Cl *MCKLVR* DE3 40 A2 1
Middlebeck Cl *MELB/CHEL* DE73 63 G3
Middleton Av *NORM/LIT* DE23 41 F4
*RIPLEY* DE5 9 G2
Middleton Dr *NORM/LIT* DE23 41 F4 3
Midland Pl *DERBY* DE1 3 G6
Midland Rd *DERBY* DE1 3 F7
Midshires Wy *BPR/DUF* DE56 5 F1
*ILK* DE7 29 E2
Midway *DERBYW* DE22 33 H1 3
Milbank Cl *DERBYW* DE22 32 B5 2
Milburn Gdns *DERBYE* DE21 28 A5 15
Milbury Cl *DERBYE* DE21 35 G1
Mile Ash La *DERBYW* DE22 34 A2
Milford Rd *BPR/DUF* DE56 17 H1
Milford St *DERBY* DE1 34 A4
Millbank Av *BPR/DUF* DE56 6 C5 5
Mill Cl *BPR/DUF* DE56 13 H2 6
*BWSH/BRSTN* DE72 45 H5
*RDERBYSW* DE65 60 A2
Mill Cft *MCKLVR* DE3 40 A2
Milldale Cl *RIPLEY* DE5 8 C1 1
Milldale Ct *BPR/DUF* DE56 6 C4 1
Milldale Rd *DERBYE* DE21 45 E3
Millersdale Cl *BPR/DUF* DE56 6 C2
Millfield *BWSH/BRSTN* DE72 67 E2
Mill Hl *DERBYSE* DE24 54 B5
Mill Hill La *BWSH/BRSTN* DE72 47 H5
*NORM/LIT* DE23 42 A3
Mill Hill Rd *NORM/LIT* DE23 42 A3 6
Millhouse Ct
*BWSH/BRSTN* DE72 57 E2 3
Mill La *BPR/DUF* DE56 6 C4
*MCKLVR* DE3 40 A2
Mill Meadow Wy
*RDERBYSW* DE65 48 A5
Mill Moor Cl *MELB/CHEL* DE73 63 F2 2
Millom Pl *DERBYE* DE21 35 E2
Mills Cl *BWSH/BRSTN* DE72 56 D2
Mill St *BPR/DUF* DE56 6 A3
*DERBY* DE1 33 H5
Milner Av *BWSH/BRSTN* DE72 56 D2
Milton Rd *MCKLVR* DE3 39 H3
Milton St *DERBYW* DE22 41 G2
Milward Rd *HEANOR* DE75 9 H5
Mimosa Crs *NORM/LIT* DE23 51 H4
Minster Rd *DERBYE* DE21 35 F1
Minton Rd *CDON/KEG* DE74 72 C3
Misterton Cl *DERBYW* DE22 33 H1 4
The Moat *CDON/KEG* DE74 73 E3 1
Moira Cl *DERBYE* DE21 35 H4 2
Moira Dl *CDON/KEG* DE74 73 F4
Moira St *MELB/CHEL* DE73 75 H3 2
Molineux St *NORM/LIT* DE23 42 C4
Monarch Dr *DERBYE* DE21 28 C5
Moncrieff Crs *DERBYE* DE21 35 H3
Mondello Dr *DERBYSE* DE24 54 B3
Monks Cl *DERBYSE* DE24 61 F2
Monk St *DERBYW* DE22 2 A5
Monmouth St *DERBYE* DE21 3 J1
Monsal Dr *DERBYE* DE21 45 E3
Monteith Pl *CDON/KEG* DE74 73 E3 2
Montford Ms *CDON/KEG* DE74 73 E3 3
Montpelier *DERBYW* DE22 25 G1
Montrose Cl *DERBYSE* DE24 51 H5
Monyash Cl *DERBYE* DE21 35 H3
Monyash Wy *BPR/DUF* DE56 6 C2
Moor Dr *DERBYSE* DE24 53 H4
Moor End *DERBYE* DE21 44 D1 2
Moore St *NORM/LIT* DE23 42 B3
Moorfield Rd *BPR/DUF* DE56 12 D3
Moorgate *DERBYW* DE22 32 B5 3
Moorhead Av *DERBYSE* DE24 53 G4 3
Moorland Rd *MCKLVR* DE3 40 A3
Moor La *ASHB* DE6 31 E1
*BWSH/BRSTN* DE72 37 H4
*BWSH/BRSTN* DE72 65 G4
*DERBYE* DE21 19 E4
*DERBYSE* DE24 52 D3
*DERBYSE* DE24 62 C3
*MELB/CHEL* DE73 62 C5
Moorpool Crs *BPR/DUF* DE56 12 D3 2
Moor Ri *BPR/DUF* DE56 12 D2
Moor Rd *ILK* DE7 27 G2
Moorside Crs *DERBYSE* DE24 52 A5
Moorside La *BPR/DUF* DE56 12 D2
Moor St *DERBYE* DE21 44 D1
Moorway *ILK* DE7 27 F4
Moorway Cft *NORM/LIT* DE23 51 E2 3
Moorway La *NORM/LIT* DE23 50 D4
Morefern Dr *DERBYE* DE21 35 G1
Morledge *DERBY* DE1 2 D4
Morleston St *NORM/LIT* DE23 42 C3 4
Morley Almshouses La *ILK* DE7 28 A1
Morley Cl *BPR/DUF* DE56 7 F1
Morley Gdns *DERBYE* DE21 36 A3
Morley La *ILK* DE7 19 G5
*ILK* DE7 29 G2
Morley Rd *DERBYE* DE21 35 H4
Morley St *DERBYW* DE22 33 F5
Morlich Dr *DERBYSE* DE24 51 G5
Morningside Cl *DERBYSE* DE24 53 E5 1
Mornington Crs *DERBYW* DE22 33 E5 2
Morpeth Gdns *DERBYE* DE21 35 E1 2
Morrell Wood Dr
*BPR/DUF* DE56 7 F2 3
Mortimer St *DERBYSE* DE24 52 C2
Mosedale Cl *DERBYSE* DE24 53 G1 1
Moses La *ILK* DE7 28 D1
Moss St *DERBYW* DE22 41 H3
Mostyn Av *NORM/LIT* DE23 41 G5
Mottistone Cl *DERBYSE* DE24 54 C4 3
Moult Av *DERBYE* DE21 44 D2
Moulton Cl *BPR/DUF* DE56 7 E2 6
Mountbatten Cl
*DERBYSE* DE24 53 F5 3
Mount Carmel St
*NORM/LIT* DE23 42 A3 7
Mountfield Wy *DERBYSE* DE24 54 C5 1
Mountford Cl *DERBYE* DE21 36 A1 3
Mount Pleasant
*CDON/KEG* DE74 73 E4 2
Mount Pleasant Dr
*BPR/DUF* DE56 5 H2
Mount St *DERBY* DE1 2 C7
Mowbray Gdns
*DERBYSE* DE24 52 D1 2
Mowbray St *DERBYSE* DE24 52 D1
Moy Av *DERBYSE* DE24 62 A2
Moyne Gdns *MELB/CHEL* DE73 63 H4
Muirfield Dr *MCKLVR* DE3 40 C5
Mulberries Ct *DERBYW* DE22 25 H4 6
Mulberry Cl *BPR/DUF* DE56 6 C4 2
Mulberry Ms *RIPLEY* DE5 8 B1 1
Mull Ct *DERBYSE* DE24 61 G1 14
Mullion Pl *DERBYSE* DE24 54 A4
Mundy Cl *DERBY* DE1 33 H5
Mundy St *DERBY* DE1 33 H5
Murray Rd *MCKLVR* DE3 40 C2
Murray St *DERBYSE* DE24 53 G1 2
Muswell Rd *DERBYW* DE22 40 B1
Myers Cl *DERBYSE* DE24 52 A5

## N

Nailers Wy *BPR/DUF* DE56 6 D2
Nairn Av *DERBYE* DE21 35 E4
Nairn Cl *DERBYSE* DE24 61 G1
Namur Cl *DERBYW* DE22 41 F3
Napier Cl *MCKLVR* DE3 40 B2 1
Napier St *DERBYW* DE22 41 F1 1
Naseby Rd *BPR/DUF* DE56 7 E3
Nearwood Dr *DERBYE* DE21 27 F5 3
Neilson St *DERBYSE* DE24 53 G2
Nelson Cl *MCKLVR* DE3 40 B3
Nelson St *DERBY* DE1 3 G7 2
Nesfield Cl *DERBYSE* DE24 54 B2
Ness Wk *DERBYW* DE22 25 H5
Nether Cl *BPR/DUF* DE56 11 G5
Netherclose St
*NORM/LIT* DE23 42 B5 3
Netherfield La *CDON/KEG* DE74 67 H5
Nether La *BPR/DUF* DE56 10 D2
*BPR/DUF* DE56 13 E4
Netherside Dr *MELB/CHEL* DE73 63 H2
Netherwood Ct *DERBYW* DE22 25 F5 1
Nettlefold Crs *MELB/CHEL* DE73 76 A1
Nevinson Av *NORM/LIT* DE23 51 G3
Nevinson Dr *NORM/LIT* DE23 51 G2
Nevis Cl *DERBYSE* DE24 61 G2
Newark Rd *DERBYE* DE21 35 E1
Newbold Av *BWSH/BRSTN* DE72 45 H5
Newbold Cl *MELB/CHEL* DE73 63 G2 3
Newbold Dr *CDON/KEG* DE74 73 E2
Newborough Rd
*DERBYSE* DE24 54 B3 3
New Breck Rd *BPR/DUF* DE56 6 B4
Newbridge Crs *DERBYSE* DE24 53 F5
Newbury St *DERBYSE* DE24 53 F1 1
Newdigate St *ILK* DE7 21 H5
*NORM/LIT* DE23 52 A1
Newgate Cl *MELB/CHEL* DE73 64 A2 3
Newhaven Rd *DERBYE* DE21 36 A5
New Inn La *DERBYE* DE21 26 D1
Newland St *DERBY* DE1 2 B4
Newlyn Dr *NORM/LIT* DE23 52 A1 2
Newmarket Ct *DERBYSE* DE24 43 F5
Newmarket Dr *DERBYSE* DE24 53 F1
New Mount Cl *NORM/LIT* DE23 51 G4 1
Newport Ct *DERBYSE* DE24 54 B4
Newquay Pl *DERBYSE* DE24 54 B4 4
New Rd *BPR/DUF* DE56 6 A4
*DERBYW* DE22 34 B2
Newstead Av *DERBYE* DE21 35 G5 2
New St *BWSH/BRSTN* DE72 45 H2
*BWSH/BRSTN* DE72 56 D2
*DERBY* DE1 3 F5
*DERBYE* DE21 18 D5 1
Newton's Wk *DERBYW* DE22 33 H3
New Zealand La *BPR/DUF* DE56 17 H3
New Zealand Sq
*DERBYW* DE22 41 F1 2
Nicholas Cl *DERBYE* DE21 36 D5
Nicola Gdns *NORM/LIT* DE23 51 G5
Nightingale Rd *DERBYSE* DE24 52 D2
Noel St *DERBYW* DE22 33 G5 3
The Nook *BPR/DUF* DE56 12 D3 3
*HEANOR* DE75 9 H3 3
*MELB/CHEL* DE73 68 B1
Nooning La *BWSH/BRSTN* DE72 56 B2
Norbury Cl *DERBYW* DE22 33 G2
Norbury Crs *NORM/LIT* DE23 51 F4 1
Norbury Wy *BPR/DUF* DE56 6 D1 2
Norfolk St *NORM/LIT* DE23 42 C4
Norman Av *NORM/LIT* DE23 51 H2
Normanton La *NORM/LIT* DE23 41 F5
*NORM/LIT* DE23 51 F1
Normanton Rd *DERBY* DE1 2 C6
*NORM/LIT* DE23 42 B4
Northacre Rd *DERBYE* DE21 36 A1
North Av *DERBYW* DE22 26 B5
*MCKLVR* DE3 40 B3
North Cl *MCKLVR* DE3 40 B3
Northfield *BPR/DUF* DE56 7 G5
*DERBYSE* DE24 61 G1 15
North La *BPR/DUF* DE56 5 G5
*BPR/DUF* DE56 11 H3
Northmead Dr *DERBYW* DE22 41 E3
North Pde *DERBY* DE1 34 B4 3
North Rw *DERBYW* DE22 34 B2 4
North St *DERBY* DE1 34 A4
*MELB/CHEL* DE73 75 H3
*NORM/LIT* DE23 41 F4
Northumberland St
*NORM/LIT* DE23 42 A4 2
Northwood Av *DERBYE* DE21 35 F4
Norwich St *DERBYE* DE21 35 E4
Norwood Cl *DERBYW* DE22 40 D1 1
Nottingham Rd *BPR/DUF* DE56 6 B4 3
*BWSH/BRSTN* DE72 45 G5
*DERBY* DE1 2 D2
*DERBYE* DE21 3 H2
*DERBYE* DE21 35 G5
*DERBYE* DE21 45 E3
Nunsfield Dr *DERBYSE* DE24 54 A2
Nun's St *DERBY* DE1 33 H5
Nursery Cl *BWSH/BRSTN* DE72 45 G4
Nutwood Cl *DERBYW* DE22 26 B5 2

## O

Oadby Ri *NORM/LIT* DE23 51 H3 4
Oak Cl *BPR/DUF* DE56 17 H3
*BWSH/BRSTN* DE72 45 H1
*DERBYW* DE22 25 H4
Oak Crs *NORM/LIT* DE23 51 E1
Oakdale Gdns *DERBYE* DE21 28 A5 16
Oak Dr *DERBYSE* DE24 53 H3
*MCKLVR* DE3 40 B3
Oakfield Ct *ILK* DE7 21 F3 2
Oakham Cl *DERBYE* DE21 35 E2 3
Oakhurst Cl *BPR/DUF* DE56 5
Oaklands Av *NORM/LIT* DE23 51
Oaklands Cl *RIPLEY* DE5 14 C1
Oaklands Rd *RDERBYSW* DE65 48
Oaklands Wy *MELB/CHEL* DE73 76
Oakleigh Av *DERBYE* DE21 35
Oakover Dr *DERBYW* DE22 25
Oakridge *DERBYE* DE21 36
Oak Rd *BWSH/BRSTN* DE72 55
Oakside Wy *DERBYE* DE21 28
The Oaks *DERBYE* DE21 18 D5
Oak St *NORM/LIT* DE23 42
Oaktree Av *DERBYSE* DE24 52
Oak Tree Ct *BWSH/BRSTN* DE72 45
Oakwood Cl *DERBYSE* DE24 61 G2
Oakwood Dr *DERBYE* DE21 36
Offerton Av *NORM/LIT* DE23 51
Old Barn Cl *DERBYE* DE21 18 D5
Oldbury Cl *DERBYE* DE21 35
Old Chester Rd *DERBY* DE1 34 B3
Old Church Cl *DERBYW* DE22 25
Old Gate Av
*BWSH/BRSTN* DE72 70 D2
Old Hall Av *BPR/DUF* DE56 17
*DERBYSE* DE24 54
*NORM/LIT* DE23 41
Old Hall Rd *NORM/LIT* DE23 41
Old La *DERBYW* DE22 34
Old Mansfield Rd *DERBYE* DE21 34
Old Mill Cl *BPR/DUF* DE56 17
Old Pit La *ILK* DE7 15
Old School Ms
*BWSH/BRSTN* DE72 65 G4
Old Vicarage Cl
*NORM/LIT* DE23 41 F5
Old Vicarage La *DERBYW* DE22 25 F3
Olive St *DERBYW* DE22 41
Olivier St *NORM/LIT* DE23 42
Olton Rd *MCKLVR* DE3 39
Onslow Rd *MCKLVR* DE3 40
Opal Cl *DERBYE* DE21 35
Openwoodgate *BPR/DUF* DE56 6
Openwood Rd *BPR/DUF* DE56 7
Orchard Av *CDON/KEG* DE74 72
Orchard Cl *BPR/DUF* DE56 12
*BWSH/BRSTN* DE72 45
*BWSH/BRSTN* DE72 57
*DERBYSE* DE24 54 B5
*ILK* DE7 27 E4
*MELB/CHEL* DE73 75 H3
*NORM/LIT* DE23 51
Orchard Ct *DERBYE* DE21 44
The Orchards *DERBYW* DE22 25 G5
Orchard St *DERBY* DE1 2 B2
*MCKLVR* DE3 40
The Orchard *BPR/DUF* DE56 6 B3
*ILK* DE7 14 C4
Orchard Wy *MELB/CHEL* DE73 63
Ordish Av *DERBYE* DE21 43
Oregon Wy *DERBYE* DE21 44
Orkney Cl *DERBYSE* DE24 61
Orly Av *CDON/KEG* DE74 72
Ormskirk Ri *DERBYE* DE21 45
Orton Wy *BPR/DUF* DE56 6
Osmaston Park Rd
*DERBYSE* DE24 52
Osmaston Rd *DERBY* DE1 2
*DERBYSE* DE24 42
*DERBYSE* DE24 53
*NORM/LIT* DE23 2
Osprey Cl *DERBYSE* DE24 61
Osterly Gn *DERBYW* DE22 40
Oswestry Cl *DERBYE* DE21 28 A5
Otterburn Dr *DERBYW* DE22 33
Otter St *DERBY* DE1 34
Oulton Cl *DERBYSE* DE24 53
Outram Wy *DERBYSE* DE24 61
Oval Ct *NORM/LIT* DE23 51
Overdale Rd *NORM/LIT* DE23 41
Over La *BPR/DUF* DE56 4
*BPR/DUF* DE56 7
Overstone Cl *BPR/DUF* DE56 7 E3
Owlers La *DERBYW* DE22 41
Owlswick Cl *NORM/LIT* DE23 50
Oxenhope Cl *NORM/LIT* DE23 50 B2
Oxford St *DERBY* DE1 3
*DERBYE* DE21 44
Oxwich Ct *DERBYE* DE21 36 A1

## P

Pack Horse Rd *MELB/CHEL* DE73 76
Paddock Cl *CDON/KEG* DE74 72
Paddock Cft *DERBYE* DE21 35 G1
The Paddock *BPR/DUF* DE56 12
*BWSH/BRSTN* DE72 45

DERBYSE DE24 54 C5 2
adley Cl DERBYW DE22 26 B3 1
adstow Cl DERBYSE DE24 61 G1 16
adstow Rd DERBYSE DE24 54 B4
alatine Gv NORM/LIT DE23 50 C2
alladium Dr NORM/LIT DE23 50 D3 5
all Ml ILK DE7 27 F4
alm Cl NORM/LIT DE23 40 D5
almerston Ct
MELB/CHEL DE73 76 A3 3
almerston St NORM/LIT DE23 41 H5
arcel Ter DERBYW DE22 41 G1
ares Wy BWSH/BRSTN DE72 45 H1
ark Av CDON/KEG DE74 72 C4
ILK DE7 29 H2 1
ark Cl BPR/DUF DE56 13 H2
DERBYE DE21 18 C5
ark Dr NORM/LIT DE23 41 F5
arker Cl DERBY DE1 2 A1
arker St DERBY DE1 34 A4
ark Farm Dr DERBYW DE22 33 G1
arkfields Dr DERBYW DE22 33 H3 4
ark Gv DERBYW DE22 33 H3
ark Hall Rd RIPLEY DE5 7 H4
ark Hill Dr NORM/LIT DE23 52 A2
arklands Dr
MELB/CHEL DE73 63 H4 1
ark La BWSH/BRSTN DE72 70 D3 1
CDON/KEG DE74 72 A4
DERBYW DE22 26 A4
NORM/LIT DE23 41 F5
ark Leys Ct DERBYE DE21 44 D2
ark Rd BPR/DUF DE56 6 B5
BPR/DUF DE56 17 H2
DERBYE DE21 44 C1
MCKLVR DE3 40 A4
ark Side BPR/DUF DE56 6 B4
arkside Rd DERBYE DE21 43 H1
arkstone Ct MCKLVR DE3 39 H4
ark St DERBY DE1 3 G6
ark Vw BWSH/BRSTN DE72 65 G5
DERBYE DE21 18 D5
ark View Cl DERBYW DE22 26 A4
arkway MELB/CHEL DE73 63 G3
ark Wy RDERBYSW DE65 48 B4
arliament Cl DERBYW DE22 41 H2
arliament St DERBYW DE22 41 H2
arsons Gv RIPLEY DE5 8 C5
artridge Wy MCKLVR DE3 40 D3
astures Av NORM/LIT DE23 50 C2
astures Hl NORM/LIT DE23 50 D1
he Pastures BPR/DUF DE56 17 H1
aterson Av DERBYE DE21 35 H5
atmore Sq NORM/LIT DE23 52 A2 2
avilion Rd NORM/LIT DE23 51 F1
axton Cl MCKLVR DE3 39 H5
ayne St DERBYW DE22 33 G5 4
each St DERBYW DE22 41 G1
eakdale Cl RIPLEY DE5 8 C1 2
eak Dr DERBYSE DE24 52 B2
earl Cl DERBYE DE21 35 H1
eartree Cl CDON/KEG DE74 72 D4 4
ear Tree Crs NORM/LIT DE23 52 B1
ear Tree Rd NORM/LIT DE23 42 B5
ear Tree St NORM/LIT DE23 52 B1
eatburn Av HEANOR DE75 15 H1
eckham Gdns DERBYW DE22 40 D1 2
eebles Cl DERBYSE DE24 61 H2 3
eel St DERBYW DE22 33 G5
eers Cl DERBYE DE21 36 A1
eet St DERBYW DE22 41 H2
egwell Cl NORM/LIT DE23 51 G2
elham St DERBYW DE22 2 A6
embroke St DERBYE DE21 35 E3 4
DERBYE DE21 35 E4 1
enalton Cl DERBYSE DE24 53 F3
endennis Cl DERBYSE DE24 54 A3 4
endlebury Dr MCKLVR DE3 40 B5
endleside Wy NORM/LIT DE23 50 B2
enge Rd DERBYW DE22 32 D4 1
enhaligan's Cl
MELB/CHEL DE73 63 G3 3
eniston Ri MELB/CHEL DE73 75 H4
enn La MELB/CHEL DE73 75 H3
enn St BPR/DUF DE56 6 B3
ennycross Cl NORM/LIT DE23 50 D2 2
enny Long La DERBYW DE22 33 H3
enrhyn Av NORM/LIT DE23 51 G1
enrith Pl DERBYE DE21 35 E1 3
entewen Cl DERBYW DE22 33 H1
entland Cl DERBYE DE21 35 H1
enzance Rd DERBYSE DE24 54 A4 1
ercy St DERBYW DE22 41 H3
eregrine Cl DERBYSE DE24 51 G5 7
erth Cl MCKLVR DE3 40 B2
erth St DERBYE DE21 35 E2
eterborough St
DERBYE DE21 35 F3 2
Peterlee Pl DERBYSE DE24 53 H3
Petersham Dr DERBYSE DE24 54 B3
Petty Close La ASHB DE6 30 B1
Peveril Av BWSH/BRSTN DE72 45 H4
Peveril St DERBYSE DE24 53 E3
Pheasant Field Dr
DERBYE DE21 37 F5 2
Philips Cft BPR/DUF DE56 17 H1
Phoenix St DERBY DE1 2 D2
Pickering Ri DERBYE DE21 34 D2
Pilgrims Wy DERBYSE DE24 61 F2
Pilsley Cl BPR/DUF DE56 6 D1 3
Pimlico DERBYW DE22 33 E5 3
Pimm's Rd ASHB DE6 31 F3
Pinchom's Hill Rd BPR/DUF DE56 6 C4
Pine Cl DERBYE DE21 44 A2
ILK DE7 15 E5
RDERBYSW DE65 48 A5
Pinecroft Ct DERBYE DE21 36 A2
The Pines BWSH/BRSTN DE72 57 E2
Pinewood Rd BPR/DUF DE56 5 H1
The Pinfold BPR/DUF DE56 6 D2 3
BWSH/BRSTN DE72 55 E5
Pingle DERBYW DE22 25 H4
Pingle Crs BPR/DUF DE56 6 A2
Pingle La BPR/DUF DE56 6 A2
The Pingle DERBYE DE21 44 D2
Pingreaves Dr
MELB/CHEL DE73 63 H2 5
Pippin Hl RIPLEY DE5 14 D1
Pit Close La MELB/CHEL DE73 63 H3 4
Pittar St DERBYW DE22 2 A7
Plackett Cl BWSH/BRSTN DE72 57 G1
Plains La BPR/DUF DE56 5 E3
Plantain Gdns NORM/LIT DE23 51 F4 2
Platts Av HEANOR DE75 15 H1 3
Plimsoll St DERBYW DE22 33 F5 3
Ploughfield Cl NORM/LIT DE23 51 E3 1
Plough Ga DERBYW DE22 34 A1 5
Pole's Rd ASHB DE6 31 F3
Pollards Oaks
BWSH/BRSTN DE72 45 G5 3
Pond Rd BPR/DUF DE56 12 D3
Ponsonby Ter DERBY DE1 41 H1
Pontefract St DERBYSE DE24 53 E2
Pontypool Cl DERBYE DE21 36 A1 10
Pool Cl DERBYSE DE24 54 B5
Poole St DERBYSE DE24 53 F3 4
Pool Rd MELB/CHEL DE73 76 B4
Poplar Av DERBYE DE21 44 D1
Poplar Cl DERBYSE DE24 54 A2 1
Poplar Nook DERBYW DE22 26 B4 3
Poplar Rw DERBYW DE22 34 B2 5
Porter Rd NORM/LIT DE23 41 H4
Porter's La DERBYE DE21 27 G5
RDERBYSW DE65 60 A2
Porthcawl Pl DERBYE DE21 36 B1 4
Portico Rd NORM/LIT DE23 50 D3
Portland Cl MCKLVR DE3 40 A4
Portland St NORM/LIT DE23 52 B1
RDERBYSW DE65 48 A5
Portman Cha DERBYSE DE24 61 G2
Portreath Dr DERBYW DE22 25 H5
Port Wy DERBYE DE21 19 E1
Portway Cl DERBYW DE22 26 B4 4
Posy La BWSH/BRSTN DE72 65 F5
Potter St DERBYE DE21 44 C2
MELB/CHEL DE73 76 A3
Pottery Cl BPR/DUF DE56 6 D2
Pottery La RIPLEY DE5 8 B4
Powell St NORM/LIT DE23 41 H4
Poynter Cl HEANOR DE75 15 H1 3
Poyser Av DERBYE DE21 35 H4
Poyser La ASHB DE6 31 F2
Prescot Cl MCKLVR DE3 39 H5
Prestbury Cl DERBYE DE21 36 A2 10
Pride Pkwy DERBYSE DE24 3 J6
Priestland Av DERBYE DE21 44 C2
Primary Cl BPR/DUF DE56 6 B3 3
Prime Pkwy DERBY DE1 2 E1
Primrose Cl DERBYE DE21 27 G5
Primrose Dr ILK DE7 20 B5
Primula Wy NORM/LIT DE23 51 G5
Prince Charles Av DERBYW DE22 33 E4
DERBYW DE22 40 C1
Princes Dr NORM/LIT DE23 41 E4
Princess Dr BWSH/BRSTN DE72 45 F5
Princes St NORM/LIT DE23 42 B5
Priors Barn Cl
BWSH/BRSTN DE72 45 H4
Priorway Av BWSH/BRSTN DE72 45 H4
Priorway Gdns
BWSH/BRSTN DE72 45 H5 3
Priory Cl MELB/CHEL DE73 63 H3
Priory Gdns DERBYE DE21 27 G5
Pritchett Dr NORM/LIT DE23 50 B1
Prospect Dr BPR/DUF DE56 6 A5
Prospect Rd RIPLEY DE5 13 H1
Provident St NORM/LIT DE23 42 B4 4
Pulborough Gdns
NORM/LIT DE23 50 D3 6
Pullman Rd DERBYE DE21 43 G2
Purchase Av HEANOR DE75 9 H5
Putney Cl DERBYW DE22 40 B1
Pybus St DERBYW DE22 33 G5
Pykestone Cl DERBYE DE21 35 G1
Pytchley Cl BPR/DUF DE56 7 E3 7

# Q

Quantock Cl DERBYSE DE24 61 G2
Quarndon Hts DERBYW DE22 33 F1 2
Quarndon Vw DERBYW DE22 33 F1 3
Quarn Dr DERBYW DE22 25 F5
Quarn St DERBY DE1 33 H5
Quarn Wy DERBY DE1 2 A1
Quarry Rd BPR/DUF DE56 6 A5 3
ILK DE7 20 A4
Queen Mary Ct DERBYW DE22 34 A4
Queens Av ILK DE7 29 H2 2
Queensbury Cha
NORM/LIT DE23 50 D2 3
Queen's Dr BPR/DUF DE56 5 H2
NORM/LIT DE23 41 F4
Queensferry Gdns
DERBYSE DE24 53 E5
Queensland Cl MCKLVR DE3 40 B2 2
Queen St BPR/DUF DE56 6 B4
DERBY DE1 2 C2
Queensway CDON/KEG DE74 72 C3
DERBYW DE22 33 G4
MELB/CHEL DE73 76 A2
Quick Cl MELB/CHEL DE73 75 H3 4
Quick Hill Rd DERBYSE DE24 61 F2
Quillings Wy
BWSH/BRSTN DE72 46 A5 4
Quorn Ri NORM/LIT DE23 51 H3

# R

Rabown Av NORM/LIT DE23 51 G1
Radbourne La ASHB DE6 39 H1
DERBYW DE22 32 C4
Radbourne St DERBYW DE22 33 F5
Radcliffe Av DERBYE DE21 35 G4
Radcliffe Dr DERBYW DE22 41 G3
Radford Rd ILK DE7 15 E4
Radford St DERBYSE DE24 53 G2
Radnor St DERBYE DE21 35 E4
Radstock Gdns DERBYE DE21 35 F1 8
Radstone Cl DERBYE DE21 36 A1 11
Raglan Av DERBYW DE22 41 F1 3
Railway Ter DERBY DE1 3 G6
Rainham Gdns DERBYSE DE24 53 H4
Rainier Dr DERBYE DE21 35 H5 2
Raleigh St DERBYW DE22 41 F1 4
Ramblers Dr DERBYE DE21 28 B5
Ramsdean Cl DERBYE DE21 35 E3
Randolph Rd NORM/LIT DE23 52 A1
Ranelagh Gdns DERBYW DE22 33 E4 1
Rangemore Cl MCKLVR DE3 40 B2
Rannoch Cl DERBYE DE21 45 E1 4
DERBYW DE22 25 H5
Ranworth Cl DERBYSE DE24 63 E1
Raven Oak Cl BPR/DUF DE56 6 B5
Ravenscourt Rd DERBYW DE22 33 E5
Ravenscroft Dr DERBYE DE21 35 G5
Ravensdale Rd DERBYW DE22 25 F5
Raven St DERBYW DE22 41 H3
Rawdon Cl CDON/KEG DE74 72 D3 2
Rawdon St NORM/LIT DE23 42 A4
Rawlinson Av NORM/LIT DE23 52 B2
Rawson Gn BPR/DUF DE56 13 G1
Raynesway DERBYE DE21 44 A2
DERBYSE DE24 54 A2 2
Raynesway Park Dr
DERBYE DE21 43 H5
Reader St DERBYE DE21 44 D1
Rectory Gdns BWSH/BRSTN DE72 65 F5
Rectory La ILK DE7 27 E3
Rectory Rd BWSH/BRSTN DE72 57 H1
Reculver Cl NORM/LIT DE23 51 G2
Redbury Cl DERBY DE1 41 H2 4
Redcar Gdns DERBYE DE21 35 E2
Redhill Ct BPR/DUF DE56 6 C5 3
Redland Cl DERBYSE DE24 52 A5 3
Red La BPR/DUF DE56 12 C4
Redmires Dr MELB/CHEL DE73 63 H2
Redruth Pl DERBYSE DE24 54 B4 3
Redshaw St DERBYW DE22 33 H4
Redstart Cl DERBYE DE21 37 E5
Redway Cft MELB/CHEL DE73 75 H2 6
Redwing Cft NORM/LIT DE23 51 G2 2
Redwood Rd DERBYSE DE24 61 H1
Reeves Rd NORM/LIT DE23 42 C5
Regency Cl NORM/LIT DE23 51 G2
Regent St DERBY DE1 3 F7 2
Reginald Rd North DERBYE DE21 35 G4
Reginald Rd South DERBYE DE21 35 G5
Reginald St NORM/LIT DE23 42 C4
Regis Cl DERBYE DE21 36 A1
Reigate Dr DERBYW DE22 32 C4
Renals St NORM/LIT DE23 42 B3 7
Renfrew St DERBYE DE21 35 F4
Repton Av NORM/LIT DE23 51 H1
Retford Cl DERBYE DE21 35 E1 4
Ribblesdale Cl DERBYW DE22 33 F1 4
Richardson Dr ILK DE7 15 E4 1
Richardson St DERBYW DE22 33 G5 3
Richmond Av NORM/LIT DE23 51 F1 5
Richmond Cl NORM/LIT DE23 50 D2 2
Richmond Dr BPR/DUF DE56 11 G5 1
Richmond Rd DERBYE DE21 35 G5 3
NORM/LIT DE23 42 B5
Riddings DERBYW DE22 25 H4
Riddings La ASHB DE6 30 A1
Riddings St DERBYW DE22 2 A7
Ridgeway MELB/CHEL DE73 63 H4
Ridgeway Av NORM/LIT DE23 51 F3
Ridgewood Ct DERBYE DE21 35 F1 2
Riding Bank MELB/CHEL DE73 75 F3
The Ridings BWSH/BRSTN DE72 37 H5
Rigga La BPR/DUF DE56 18 B4
Rigsby Ct MCKLVR DE3 39 H3
Rimsdale Cl DERBYSE DE24 61 H1
Ripon Crs DERBYE DE21 35 F3
The Rise DERBYW DE22 33 H1
Risley La BWSH/BRSTN DE72 47 G4
Rivenhall Cl NORM/LIT DE23 50 C2 4
Riverside Rd DERBYSE DE24 3 J6
River St DERBY DE1 2 C1
River Vw BPR/DUF DE56 12 A3
Robert St DERBY DE1 2 E2
Robin Croft Rd DERBYW DE22 25 H4
Robinia Cl DERBYE DE21 28 B5 14
Robin Rd DERBYW DE22 34 A4
Robinscross
BWSH/BRSTN DE72 45 G5 4
Robinson's Hl MELB/CHEL DE73 75 G4
Robson Cl DERBYSE DE24 53 H2
Roby Lea CDON/KEG DE74 72 C3
Rochester Cl DERBYSE DE24 53 H4
Rochley Cl DERBYE DE21 27 G5
Rockbourne Cl DERBYSE DE24 54 C3
The Rockety DERBYE DE21 19 F1
Rockhouse Rd DERBYSE DE24 53 H3
Rockingham Cl DERBYW DE22 26 B4
Rodsley Crs NORM/LIT DE23 51 G4 2
Roe Farm La DERBYE DE21 35 F4
Roehampton Dr DERBYW DE22 32 D4
Roe Wk NORM/LIT DE23 42 B5 4
Roman Rd DERBY DE1 34 C4
Roman Wy BWSH/BRSTN DE72 45 H5
Romsley Cl MCKLVR DE3 40 A2 2
Rona Cl DERBYSE DE24 51 H5
Ronald Cl NORM/LIT DE23 50 B2
Roosevelt Av DERBYE DE21 36 A5
The Ropewalk ILK DE7 21 G4
Rosamond's Ride
NORM/LIT DE23 51 G1
Rose Av BWSH/BRSTN DE72 45 H5
Roseberry Ct DERBYE DE21 36 A2 11
Rosedale Av DERBYSE DE24 53 H3 2
Roseheath Cl NORM/LIT DE23 51 H4 5
Rose Hill St NORM/LIT DE23 42 B4
Rose La MELB/CHEL DE73 74 B5
Rosemary Dr DERBYSE DE24 53 H4
Rosemoor La DERBYE DE21 36 A2
Rosemount Ct DERBYW DE22 25 F5 2
Rosengrave St DERBY DE1 2 B6
Rosette Ct DERBYE DE21 28 B5 13
Rosewood Cl DERBYSE DE24 54 B2 4
Rossington Dr NORM/LIT DE23 50 C3
Rosslyn Gdns DERBYSE DE24 53 H3
Rothbury Pl DERBYE DE21 35 F2
Rothesay Cl DERBYSE DE24 51 H5
Rothwell La BPR/DUF DE56 6 C3 3
Rothwell Rd MCKLVR DE3 40 A3
Rough Heanor Rd MCKLVR DE3 40 D3
Roughton Cl MCKLVR DE3 50 A1 1
Routh Av CDON/KEG DE74 73 E5 1
Rowan Cl DERBYE DE21 44 A1
DERBYSE DE24 61 G1 17
Rowan Dr BPR/DUF DE56 14 A2
Rowan Park Cl NORM/LIT DE23 51 G2
Rowditch Av DERBYW DE22 41 G3
Rowditch Pl DERBYW DE22 41 G2
Rowena Cl DERBYSE DE24 53 G2
Rowland St DERBYSE DE24 53 F3 3
Rowley Gdns NORM/LIT DE23 51 F2 2

Rowley La *NORM/LIT* DE23 ........... **51** F2
Rowsley Av *NORM/LIT* DE23 ........... **51** G1
Roxburgh Av *DERBYE* DE21 ........ **35** F4 2
Royal Cl *BWSH/BRSTN* DE72........... **45** G5
Royal Ga *BPR/DUF* DE56.................. **7** E4
Royal Gv *DERBYE* DE21 ............. **28** C5 3
Royal Hill Rd *DERBYE* DE21 ........... **36** C5
Royal Wy *DERBYSE* DE24 ............... **43** F3
Roydon Cl *MCKLVR* DE3 ................. **39** H2
Royston Dr *BPR/DUF* DE56 ............. **7** E2
Rudyard Av *DERBYE* DE21 .............. **44** D1
Ruffstone Cl *BPR/DUF* DE56 .......... **12** D3
Rupert Rd *DERBYE* DE21 ................ **35** H4
Rushcliffe Av *DERBYE* DE21........... **35** G5
Rushcliffe Gdns *DERBYE* DE21 .. **35** G5 4
Rushdale Av *NORM/LIT* DE23.......... **51** G3
Rushup Cl *DERBYW* DE22 ............ **26** B3 2
Ruskin Rd *DERBYW* DE22 ................ **34** A4
Ruskin Wy *NORM/LIT* DE23 ............ **51** E1
Russell St *DERBYSE* DE24 ............... **42** D5
Russet Cl *DERBYE* DE21 .................. **36** A2
Rutherford Ri *DERBYE* DE21 ...... **35** G1 9
Rutland Av *BWSH/BRSTN* DE72...... **45** H4
Rutland Dr *MCKLVR* DE3 ........... **40** A3 4
Rutland St *NORM/LIT* DE23 ............ **42** B5
Ryal Cl *BWSH/BRSTN* DE72............. **45** H1
Ryan Cl *DERBYSE* DE24 ............. **61** H1 4
Rycroft Rd *CDON/KEG* DE74 .......... **67** G5
Rydal Cl *DERBYW* DE22.................... **25** H4
Rye Butts *MELB/CHEL* DE73 ...... **63** F3 2
Rye Cl *DERBYE* DE21 ........................ **27** F5
Ryedale Gdns *NORM/LIT* DE23 ...... **51** F5
Ryegrass Cl *BPR/DUF* DE56 .......... **7** E3 8
Ryegrass Rd *DERBYE* DE21 ............ **36** B1
Rykneld Cl *NORM/LIT* DE23 ........... **50** B3
Rykneld Dr *NORM/LIT* DE23............ **50** B2
Rykneld Rd *NORM/LIT* DE23 .......... **50** B4
Rykneld Wy *NORM/LIT* DE23 .......... **50** B3
Ryknield Hl *RIPLEY* DE5 .................... **8** A5
Ryknield Rd *BPR/DUF* DE56............. **14** A3
Rymill Dr *DERBYE* DE21 .................. **35** G2


## S


Sacheverel St *DERBY* DE1 ................ **2** C6
Sackville St *NORM/LIT* DE23............ **52** A1
Sadler Ga *DERBY* DE1 ........................ **2** C3
Saffron Dr *DERBYE* DE21 ................ **35** H2
St Agnes Av *DERBYW* DE22 ............ **25** G4
St Albans Rd *DERBYW* DE22............ **41** F3
St Alkmund's Cl
*BPR/DUF* DE56 .......................... **17** H1 1
St Alkmunds Wy
*BPR/DUF* DE56 .......................... **17** H1 2
*DERBY* DE1 ........................................ **2** D2
St Andrews Vw *DERBYE* DE21........ **35** F3
St Anne's La *CDON/KEG* DE74 .... **73** E4 3
St Augustine St *NORM/LIT* DE23.... **42** A5
St Bride's Wk *DERBYW* DE22 ...... **33** E5 4
St Chad's Rd *NORM/LIT* DE23 ........ **41** H4
St Clare's Cl *NORM/LIT* DE23 .......... **41** G4
St Cuthbert's Rd *DERBYW* DE22 .... **41** F3
St David's Cl *DERBYW* DE22............ **41** G3
St Edmund's Cl *DERBYW* DE22 ...... **26** A4
St Edward's Rd *CDON/KEG* DE74.... **73** E5
St George's Pl *BPR/DUF* DE56 ...... **6** A3 4
St Giles Rd *NORM/LIT* DE23 ............ **42** A5
St Helen's St *DERBY* DE1 ................. **2** B2
St Hugh's Cl *DERBYW* DE22 ........ **34** A1 6
St James Cl *BPR/DUF* DE56 .......... **7** E3 9
St James' Rd *NORM/LIT* DE23 ........ **42** A5
St James's St *DERBY* DE1 .................. **2** C4
St James' St *NORM/LIT* DE23.......... **42** B5
St John's Av *DERBYE* DE21.............. **44** A1
St John's Cl *DERBYW* DE22 ........ **25** H5 2
St John's Dr *BPR/DUF* DE56 ...... **13** H2 7
St John's Rd *BPR/DUF* DE56 ........ **6** B3 4
*ILK* DE7............................................... **15** E5
St Mark's Rd *DERBYE* DE21 ............ **35** E4
St Mary's Av
*BWSH/BRSTN* DE72 ................. **56** D2 2
St Mary's Cl *DERBYSE* DE24 ........ **53** H3 3
St Mary's Ct *DERBY* DE1..................... **2** C1
St Mary's Ga *DERBY* DE1.................... **2** C3
St Marys Wharf Rd *DERBY* DE1...... **34** C4
St Matthew's Wk
*DERBYW* DE22 ........................... **34** A1 7
St Mawes Cl *DERBYW* DE22 ............ **25** G4
St Mellion *NORM/LIT* DE23 .......... **40** C5 3
St Michael's Cl *BPR/DUF* DE56 .. **12** D4 2
*DERBYSE* DE24 ........................... **54** B2 5
St Michael's La *DERBY* DE1 .............. **2** C2
St Michaels Vw *DERBYSE* DE24 .. **54** B2 6
St Nicholas Cl *DERBYW* DE22 ...... **33** G1 2
St Pancras Wy *DERBY* DE1 ........ **34** C4 6
St Peter's Churchyard *DERBY* DE1.. **2** C4
St Peter's Cl *BPR/DUF* DE56 ........ **6** B3 5
St Peters Cft *BPR/DUF* DE56 ........ **6** B3 6
St Peter's Rd *MELB/CHEL* DE73...... **63** H3
St Peter's St *DERBY* DE1..................... **2** D4
St Quentin Cl *NORM/LIT* DE23 .... **41** F3 1
St Ronan's Av *BPR/DUF* DE56 ........ **17** H2
St Stephens Cl
*BWSH/BRSTN* DE72 ...................... **45** G5
*NORM/LIT* DE23 ....................... **51** G3 4
St Swithin's Cl *DERBYW* DE22 ........ **41** G3
St Thomas Rd *NORM/LIT* DE23 ...... **52** B1
St Werburgh's Vw
*DERBYE* DE21 ............................ **44** C1 1
St Wystan's Rd *DERBYW* DE22 ...... **41** F3
Sale St *NORM/LIT* DE23..................... **42** C4
Salisbury Dr *BPR/DUF* DE56 ........ **7** E2 7
Salisbury La *MELB/CHEL* DE73 .. **76** A3 4
Salisbury St *NORM/LIT* DE23 ...... **42** B3 8
Sallywood Cl *DERBYSE* DE24 ...... **61** G2 6
Saltburn Cl *DERBYE* DE21................ **34** D2
Salter Cl *CDON/KEG* DE74 ............... **72** C3
Samantha Ct *DERBYE* DE21 ...... **36** A2 12
Sancroft Av *DERBYE* DE21 .............. **36** D5
Sancroft Rd *DERBYE* DE21.............. **37** E5
Sandalwood Cl *DERBYSE* DE24 .. **54** B2 7
Sandbach Cl *DERBYE* DE21 ........ **35** H2 6
Sandbed La *BPR/DUF* DE56 .............. **6** D5
Sanderson Rd *DERBYE* DE21 ...... **36** A5 3
Sandfield Cl *DERBYE* DE21 .......... **36** A3 2
Sandgate Cl *DERBYSE* DE24 ...... **54** A4 2
Sandown Av *MCKLVR* DE3 .............. **39** H3
Sandown Rd *DERBYSE* DE24 .......... **53** E1
Sandringham Dr *DERBYE* DE21...... **45** E2
Sandringham Rd *DERBYE* DE21 .... **35** F2
Sandyhill Cl *MELB/CHEL* DE73 ........ **63** H2
Sandy La *DERBYE* DE21 ................. **19** G1
Sandypits La *RDERBYSW* DE65 ...... **48** B5
Santolina Dr *DERBYE* DE21 ...... **35** G1 10
Sapperton Cl *NORM/LIT* DE23 .... **51** G4 3
Saundersfoot Wy *DERBYE* DE21.... **36** A1
Save Penny La *BPR/DUF* DE56 ...... **12** B5
Sawley Rd *BWSH/BRSTN* DE72 ...... **57** H2
*BWSH/BRSTN* DE72 ...................... **57** E2
Saxondale Av *MCKLVR* DE3 ........ **39** H2 1
Scarborough Ri *DERBYE* DE21 ...... **35** E2
Scarcliffe Cl *DERBYSE* DE24........... **63** F1
Scarsdale Av *DERBYW* DE22........... **25** F5
*NORM/LIT* DE23 .............................. **41** F4
Scarsdale Rd *BPR/DUF* DE56 .... **17** H2 4
School La *CDON/KEG* DE74.............. **72** D3
*MELB/CHEL* DE73 .......................... **63** H3
The Scotches *BPR/DUF* DE56 .......... **6** A2
Scott Dr *BPR/DUF* DE56 .................... **7** F2
Scott St *NORM/LIT* DE23................... **42** A5
Seagrave Cl *DERBYE* DE21 .............. **36** A3
Seale St *DERBY* DE1 ................... **34** C4 7
Searl St *DERBY* DE1 ........................... **2** A2
Seascale Cl *DERBYE* DE21................ **35** E2
Seaton Cl *MCKLVR* DE3 ............... **39** H3 4
Second Av *BWSH/BRSTN* DE72 ...... **47** H2
*MELB/CHEL* DE73 .......................... **63** H4
Sedgebrook Cl *DERBYE* DE21 .. **35** G1 11
Sefton Rd *DERBYE* DE21.................. **35** G5
Selborne St *DERBYSE* DE24 ........ **43** E4 2
Selina Cl *CDON/KEG* DE74 .......... **72** D3 3
Selina St *MELB/CHEL* DE73............. **75** H3
Selkirk St *DERBYE* DE21 .................. **35** F4
Selworthy Cl *DERBYE* DE21 ........ **35** H1 6
Selwyn St *DERBYW* DE22 ........... **33** F5 4
Serina Av *NORM/LIT* DE23 .......... **51** G1 1
The Settlement
*BWSH/BRSTN* DE72 ...................... **45** H1
Sevenlands Dr *DERBYSE* DE24........ **54** B5
Sevenoaks Av *DERBYW* DE22 ........ **40** C1
Severnale Cl *DERBYW* DE22 ............ **26** C3
Severn St *DERBYSE* DE24 ................ **53** G1
Seymour Cl *DERBYW* DE22 ........ **41** F1 5
Shacklecross Cl
*BWSH/BRSTN* DE72 ................. **45** H5 4
Shaftesbury Crs *NORM/LIT* DE23 .. **42** C5
Shaftesbury St
*NORM/LIT* DE23 ......................... **42** D5 1
Shaftesbury St South
*NORM/LIT* DE23 ............................. **52** C1
Shakespeare St
*DERBYSE* DE24 ........................... **52** B4 1
Shaldon Dr *NORM/LIT* DE23............ **41** G5
Shalfleet Dr *DERBYSE* DE24............ **54** B4
Shamrock St *NORM/LIT* DE23 ........ **41** H5
Shannon Cl *NORM/LIT* DE23............ **51** G3
Shardlow Rd *BWSH/BRSTN* DE72 .. **65** G5
*DERBYSE* DE24 ................................ **54** A3
Shaw La *BPR/DUF* DE56 .................. **12** C3
Shaw St *DERBYW* DE22..................... **33** H5
Shaw's Yd *BPR/DUF* DE56 .......... **13** G2 3
Sheffield Pl *DERBY* DE1 ............... **3** G6 1
Sheldon Rd *HEANOR* DE75 ................ **9** H2
Shelford Cl *MCKLVR* DE3.................. **39** H3
Shelley Dr *DERBYSE* DE24 .............. **52** B4
Shelmory Cl *DERBYSE* DE24............ **53** E4
Shelton Dr *DERBYSE* DE24 .............. **63** G1
Shenington Wy
*DERBYE* DE21 ........................... **36** A1 12
Shepherd's La *MELB/CHEL* DE73.... **75** E4
Shepherd St *NORM/LIT* DE23 .... **41** F5 4
Sherbourne Dr *BPR/DUF* DE56 .... **7** E2 8
Sheridan St *DERBYSE* DE24 ............ **52** A4
Sherston Cl *DERBYE* DE21 ........ **36** A1 13
Sherwin St *DERBYW* DE22 ............... **33** H3
Sherwood Av *BWSH/BRSTN* DE72.. **45** H4
*DERBYE* DE21 .................................. **35** G4
*NORM/LIT* DE23 ........................ **51** H4 6
Sherwood St *DERBYW* DE22 ...... **41** H3 2
Shetland Cl *DERBYE* DE21 .......... **34** D4 1
Shields Crs *CDON/KEG* DE74............ **72** C4
Shireoaks *BPR/DUF* DE56.................. **5** G2
Shireoaks Cl *NORM/LIT* DE23 ...... **51** F2 3
Shirley Cl *CDON/KEG* DE74 .............. **72** D3
Shirley Crs *BWSH/BRSTN* DE72 ...... **57** G1
Shirley Pk *BWSH/BRSTN* DE72 .. **65** G5 2
Shirley Rd *DERBYE* DE21 ................ **35** F2
Shop Stones *BWSH/BRSTN* DE72 .. **45** H1
Short Av *DERBYW* DE22 .................. **26** A3
Short Hl *MELB/CHEL* DE73 .............. **76** D4
Short Lands *BPR/DUF* DE56 ........ **6** B3 7
Short La *CDON/KEG* DE74................. **72** B3
Short St *BPR/DUF* DE56 ..................... **6** C3
Shorwell Gdns *DERBYSE* DE24........ **54** B4
Shrewsbury Cl *DERBYE* DE21 .... **36** B1 5
Shropshire Av *DERBYE* DE21 .......... **35** F4
Siddals La *DERBYW* DE22 ........... **26** A4 1
Siddals Rd *DERBY* DE1 ...................... **3** F4
Siddons St *DERBYSE* DE24 .......... **53** H2 2
The Sidings *DERBYE* DE21 .............. **43** H2
Sidmouth Cl *DERBYSE* DE24............ **54** B2
Sidney St *DERBY* DE1 ...................... **42** C3
Silverburn Dr *DERBYE* DE21............ **35** H1
Silverhill Rd *DERBYE* DE21 .............. **44** D3
Silver Hill Rd *NORM/LIT* DE23 ........ **42** B4
Silver La *BWSH/BRSTN* DE72 .......... **55** E4
Silverton Dr *DERBYSE* DE24 ........ **61** F2 2
Silvey Gv *DERBYE* DE21 .............. **44** C2 5
Simcoe Leys *MELB/CHEL* DE73 ...... **63** G2
Simon Fields Cl *ILK* DE7 ................. **21** F3
Sims Av *DERBY* DE1........................... **41** H1
Sinclair Cl *DERBYSE* DE24................ **51** H5
Sinfin Av *DERBYSE* DE24.................. **53** E5
Sinfin Fields Crs
*DERBYSE* DE24 ........................... **53** E4 3
Sinfin La *DERBYSE* DE24 .................. **52** A4
*MELB/CHEL* DE73 .......................... **68** B1
*NORM/LIT* DE23 ............................. **52** B2
Sinfin Moor La *DERBYSE* DE24 ...... **62** B2
*MELB/CHEL* DE73 .......................... **63** E2
Sir Frank Whittle Rd
*DERBYE* DE21 ................................. **34** D4
Siskin Dr *DERBYSE* DE24.................. **51** G5
Sister's La *BWSH/BRSTN* DE72 .. **45** H1 3
Sitwell Cl *DERBYE* DE21 .................. **44** C2
Sitwell Dr *BPR/DUF* DE56 .......... **13** H3 3
Sitwell St *DERBY* DE1 ........................ **2** D5
*DERBYE* DE21 .................................. **44** D2
Skiddaw Dr *MCKLVR* DE3 ................ **40** B5
Skylark Wy *DERBYSE* DE24 ............ **51** G5
Slack La *DERBYW* DE22..................... **34** A1
*DERBYW* DE22.................................. **41** G1
Slade Cl *RDERBYSW* DE65................ **48** B5
Slade Lands Dr
*MELB/CHEL* DE73 ...................... **63** H2 6
Slade La *MELB/CHEL* DE73 .............. **77** E4
Slaidburn Cl *MCKLVR* DE3 .......... **40** B5 9
Slaney Cl *DERBYSE* DE24 ............ **53** F2 2
Slater Av *DERBYW* DE22 .................. **41** H1
Sledmere Cl *DERBYSE* DE24 ........ **54** B2 8
Sleepy La *MELB/CHEL* DE73............ **76** A1
Slindon Cft *DERBYSE* DE24.............. **54** C3
Sloane Rd *DERBYW* DE22 ................ **32** D5
Smalley Dr *DERBYE* DE21 ................ **28** A5
Smalley Mill Rd *ILK* DE7 .................. **20** A1
Small Meer Cl
*MELB/CHEL* DE73 ...................... **63** G3 4
Smith Av *MELB/CHEL* DE73 ............ **76** A2
Snake La *BPR/DUF* DE56 ................ **17** G2
Snelsmoor La *MELB/CHEL* DE73 .... **64** A2
Snelston Crs *NORM/LIT* DE23.......... **41** F4
Snowberry Av *BPR/DUF* DE56.......... **6** C5
Society Pl *NORM/LIT* DE23 .............. **42** A4
Solway Cl *DERBYE* DE21 ............ **35** H1 7
Somerby Wy *DERBYE* DE21 ...... **35** G1 12
Somersal Cl *DERBYSE* DE24 ............ **63** F1
Somerset St *DERBYE* DE21.............. **35** E4
Somme Rd *DERBYW* DE22 .............. **25** E5
South Av *DERBYE* DE21 .................. **44** D2
*DERBYW* DE22.................................. **26** B5
*MELB/CHEL* DE73 .......................... **63** G1
*NORM/LIT* DE23 ............................. **41** G5
South Brae Cl *NORM/LIT* DE23 ...... **51**
Southcroft *NORM/LIT* DE23 ............ **51**
Southdown Cl *DERBYSE* DE24 .... **61** F2
South Dr *DERBY* DE1......................... **34**
*DERBYE* DE21 .................................. **43**
*MCKLVR* DE3 ................................... **40**
*MELB/CHEL* DE73 .......................... **63**
Southgate Cl *MCKLVR* DE3 ........ **39** H3
Southmead Wy *DERBYW* DE22 .. **41** E3
South St *BWSH/BRSTN* DE72 .......... **56**
*DERBY* DE1 ...................................... **41**
*MELB/CHEL* DE73 .......................... **75**
Southwark Cl *DERBYW* DE22 ...... **41** E1
Southwood St *DERBYSE* DE24........ **53**
Sovereign Wy *DERBYE* DE21 .......... **28**
*HEANOR* DE75 ................................. **15**
Sowter Rd *DERBY* DE1 ...................... **2**
Spa La *DERBY* DE1 ............................. **2**
Sparrow Cl *DERBYSE* DE24.............. **51**
Speedwell Cl *DERBYE* DE21 ...... **28** B5
Spenbeck Dr *DERBYW* DE22 .......... **26**
Spencer Av *BPR/DUF* DE56 ............. **6**
*DERBYSE* DE24 ................................ **53**
Spencer Rd *BPR/DUF* DE56 .............. **6**
Spencer St *DERBYSE* DE24 ........ **53** H1
*ILK* DE7 ............................................ **21**
Spindletree Dr *DERBYE* DE21 ........ **35**
Spinners Wy *BPR/DUF* DE56 ............ **6**
Spinney Cl *DERBYW* DE22 .......... **34** B1
Spinney Hl *MELB/CHEL* DE73.......... **75**
Spinney Rd *DERBYE* DE21 .............. **35**
*DERBYW* DE22 ........................... **41** H3
The Spinney *BPR/DUF* DE56 ............ **6**
*BWSH/BRSTN* DE72 ...................... **45**
*CDON/KEG* DE74 ........................ **72** D3
Spittal *CDON/KEG* DE74 ................. **72**
Spoonley Wood Ct
*NORM/LIT* DE23 .......................... **50** C2
Spring Cl *BPR/DUF* DE56 .................. **5**
*BWSH/BRSTN* DE72 ...................... **57**
Springdale Ct *MCKLVR* DE3 ...... **40** B5
Springfield *NORM/LIT* DE23............ **41**
Springfield Av *HEANOR* DE75............ **9**
Springfield Dr *BPR/DUF* DE56 .... **17** G2
Springfield Rd *DERBYE* DE21.......... **44**
*MELB/CHEL* DE73 .......................... **63**
*RDERBYSW* DE65 ........................... **58**
Spring Gdns *DERBYE* DE21.............. **35**
Spring Hollow *BPR/DUF* DE56........ **11**
Spring St *DERBYW* DE22..................... **2**
Springwood Dr *DERBYE* DE21........ **35**
The Square *DERBYW* DE22.............. **34**
*MCKLVR* DE3 ................................... **40**
Squires Wy *NORM/LIT* DE23............ **50**
Stables St *DERBYW* DE22 ................ **41**
Stadium Vw *DERBYSE* DE24............ **43**
Stafford Cl *ILK* DE7 .......................... **15**
Stafford St *DERBY* DE1....................... **2**
Staines Cl *MCKLVR* DE3 ............ **39** H4
Stainsby Av *ILK* DE7.......................... **14**
Staker La *MCKLVR* DE3 .................... **50**
Stamford St *DERBYSE* DE24 ...... **53** E3
Stanage Gn *MCKLVR* DE3 ........... **40** C5
Stanhope Rd *MCKLVR* DE3.............. **40**
Stanhope St *NORM/LIT* DE23.......... **42**
Stanier Wy *DERBYE* DE21................ **43**
Stanley Cl *DERBYW* DE22 ................ **34**
Stanley Rd *DERBYE* DE21 ................ **43**
*DERBYSE* DE24 ................................ **53**
Stanley St *DERBYW* DE22................. **41**
Stanstead Rd *MCKLVR* DE3 ............ **39**
Stanton Av *BPR/DUF* DE56 ............... **6**
Stanton Hl *MELB/CHEL* DE73.......... **74**
Stanton St *NORM/LIT* DE23 ............ **42**
Starcross Ct *MCKLVR* DE3................ **39**
Starkie Av *CDON/KEG* DE74 ............ **72**
Statham St *DERBYW* DE22............... **33**
Station Ap *BPR/DUF* DE56 .......... **18** A1
*DERBY* DE1 ........................................ **3**
Station Cl *MELB/CHEL* DE73............ **63**
Station La *RIPLEY* DE5 ....................... **9**
Station Rd *BPR/DUF* DE56 .......... **18** A1
*BWSH/BRSTN* DE72 ...................... **45**
*BWSH/BRSTN* DE72 ...................... **57**
*CDON/KEG* DE74 ............................. **73**
*DERBYE* DE21 .................................. **26**
*DERBYE* DE21 .................................. **44**
*ILK* DE7 ............................................ **21**
*ILK* DE7 ............................................ **27**
*ILK* DE7 ............................................ **29**
*MCKLVR* DE3 ................................... **40**
*MELB/CHEL* DE73 .......................... **63**
*MELB/CHEL* DE73 .......................... **76**
*RIPLEY* DE5 ....................................... **8**
Staunton Av *NORM/LIT* DE23........... **51**
Staunton Cl *CDON/KEG* DE74........... **72**
Staveley Cl *DERBYSE* DE24............... **63**
Staverton Dr *MCKLVR* DE3 .......... **40** A2

:eeple Cl *DERBYE* DE21 35 F1
:enson Av *NORM/LIT* DE23 51 H3
:enson Rd *DERBYSE* DE24 51 G5
*NORM/LIT* DE23 51 H1 1
:ephensons Wy *DERBYE* DE21 43 H3
'epping Cl *DERBYW* DE22 41 G1
epping La *DERBYW* DE22 41 G1
:evenage Cl *DERBYSE* DE24 53 G4
:evens La *BWSH/BRSTN* DE72 57 G1
:evenson Av
*BWSH/BRSTN* DE72 57 E1
evenson Pl *NORM/LIT* DE23 51 E1
ewart Cl *DERBYE* DE21 36 D5
iles Rd *DERBYSE* DE24 54 A2
irling Cl *DERBYE* DE21 34 D3 1
ockbrook Rd *DERBYW* DE22 41 G3
ockbrook St *DERBYW* DE22 41 H3
ocker Av *DERBYSE* DE24 54 B2
oke Cl *BPR/DUF* DE56 7 E3
onechat Cl *MCKLVR* DE3 40 D3
one Cl *DERBYE* DE21 36 D5
onehill *CDON/KEG* DE74 73 E5
one Hill Rd *NORM/LIT* DE23 42 A4
onesby Cl *DERBYE* DE21 35 G1
oney Cross *DERBYE* DE21 44 D3
oney Flatts Crs
*DERBYE* DE21 35 H3 1
oney La *DERBYE* DE21 44 D1
onyhurst Ct *DERBYSE* DE24 63 F1 2
ony La *BPR/DUF* DE56 12 D4
oodley Pike Gdns
*DERBYW* DE22 33 F1 5
:ores Rd *DERBYE* DE21 34 C4
:ornoway Cl *DERBYSE* DE24 61 G1 18
:ourport Dr *MELB/CHEL* DE73 63 H1
:owmarket Dr *DERBYE* DE21 35 E2
:rand *DERBY* DE1 2 C3
:ratford Rd *DERBYE* DE21 35 E1
:rathaven Ct *DERBYE* DE21 44 D1
:rathmore Av *DERBYSE* DE24 53 G3
:reatham Rd *DERBYW* DE22 32 D5
:reet La *RIPLEY* DE5 7 H1
:retton Cl *MCKLVR* DE3 40 A5 5
:roma Cl *DERBYSE* DE24 52 A5 4
:rutt St *BPR/DUF* DE56 6 A4
*NORM/LIT* DE23 42 B4
:uart St *DERBY* DE1 2 D2
:udbrook Cl *CDON/KEG* DE74 72 C4
'urges La *BWSH/BRSTN* DE72 55 E5
ıdbury Cl *DERBY* DE1 41 H1 2
ıdbury St *DERBY* DE1 41 H1
ıffolk Av *DERBYE* DE21 35 F4
ılleys Fld *DERBYW* DE22 25 G1 1
ımmerbrook Ct
*DERBYW* DE22 2 A6 2
ımmer Wood Ct
*NORM/LIT* DE23 51 G2
ınart Cl *DERBYSE* DE24 62 A2
ındew Cl *DERBYE* DE21 45 E2
ındown Av *NORM/LIT* DE23 51 G3
ınningdale Av *DERBYE* DE21 44 C1
ınny Bank Gdns
*BPR/DUF* DE56 6 A5 4
ınny Gv *DERBYE* DE21 43 H1
ınny Hl *BPR/DUF* DE56 12 A3
ınnyhill Av *NORM/LIT* DE23 51 H3
ın St *DERBYW* DE22 2 A6
ırbiton Cl *DERBYW* DE22 32 D5 4
ırrey St *DERBYW* DE22 33 G5
ıssex Circ *DERBYE* DE21 35 F3
ıtherland Rd *NORM/LIT* DE23 52 A1
ıtton Av *MELB/CHEL* DE73 63 G1
ıtton Cl *DERBYW* DE22 33 F5
ıtton Dr *DERBYSE* DE24 53 F5
ıtton La *RDERBYSW* DE65 48 A4
wallow Cl *MCKLVR* DE3 40 D3 3
wallowdale Rd *DERBYSE* DE24 51 G5
wanmore Rd *NORM/LIT* DE23 50 D1 5
wanwick *DERBYE* DE21 35 H2 7
warkestone Br
*MELB/CHEL* DE73 69 E2
warkestone Dr *NORM/LIT* DE23 51 F4
warkestone Rd
*MELB/CHEL* DE73 63 G3
*MELB/CHEL* DE73 68 B1
vayfield Cl *MCKLVR* DE3 39 G3
veetbriar Cl *DERBYSE* DE24 53 H4 3
vift Cl *MCKLVR* DE3 40 D3 4
vinburne St *DERBY* DE1 2 C7
vinderby Dr *DERBYE* DE21 36 A2 13
vinney Bank *BPR/DUF* DE56 6 B2
vinney La *BPR/DUF* DE56 6 B2
'camore Av *DERBYW* DE22 25 G5
*RDERBYSW* DE65 60 A2
'camore Cl *RDERBYSW* DE65 48 B5 4
'camore Ct *DERBYE* DE21 44 D1 3
'camore Rd *CDON/KEG* DE74 73 E2
'denham Rd *DERBYW* DE22 32 D4

Sydney Cl *MCKLVR* DE3 40 C3
Sydney Rd *BWSH/BRSTN* DE72 56 D2

## T

Taddington Rd *DERBYE* DE21 35 F3
Talbot St *DERBYW* DE22 2 A4
Talgarth Cl *DERBYE* DE21 36 B1
Tamar Av *DERBYW* DE22 25 G4
Tamworth Rd
*BWSH/BRSTN* DE72 67 G4
Tamworth St *BPR/DUF* DE56 17 H2
Tansley Av *ILK* DE7 21 F4
Tansley Ri *DERBYE* DE21 35 G2 2
Tants Meadow *BPR/DUF* DE56 13 F4
Tantum Av *HEANOR* DE75 9 H3
Tanyard Cl *CDON/KEG* DE74 73 E3
Taplow Cl *MCKLVR* DE3 39 H4 3
Tarina Cl *MELB/CHEL* DE73 63 H3
Tasman Cl *MCKLVR* DE3 40 C3
Taunton Cl *DERBYSE* DE24 54 B1 1
Taverners Crs *NORM/LIT* DE23 51 G1
Tavistock Cl *DERBYSE* DE24 61 G1
Tawny Wy *NORM/LIT* DE23 50 D2
Tay Cl *DERBYSE* DE24 61 G2
Taylor St *DERBYSE* DE24 43 E4
Tayside Cl *DERBYSE* DE24 61 G1
Tay Wk *DERBYW* DE22 25 H5
Tedworth Av *DERBYSE* DE24 61 G2
Telford Cl *MCKLVR* DE3 40 B5
Templar Cl *DERBYSE* DE24 61 F2
Temple St *NORM/LIT* DE23 42 A3 3
Tenby Dr *DERBYE* DE21 36 B1
Tennessee Rd *DERBYE* DE21 35 H4
Tennyson St *DERBYSE* DE24 53 E2 1
Terry Pl *DERBYSE* DE24 53 G2
Teviot Pl *DERBYE* DE21 35 H1 3
Tewkesbury Crs *DERBYE* DE21 35 E3
Thackeray St *DERBYSE* DE24 52 B4
Thames Cl *DERBYW* DE22 40 C1
Thanet Dr *DERBYSE* DE24 53 H3
Thirlmere Av *DERBYW* DE22 25 H5
Thirsk Pl *DERBYSE* DE24 53 E2
Thistledown Cl *DERBYW* DE22 34 B1 5
Thomas Cook Cl *MELB/CHEL*
DE73 75 H3 3
Thore Cl *DERBYE* DE21 36 A2 14
Thoresby Crs *BWSH/BRSTN* DE72 56 C2
Thorn Cl *DERBYW* DE22 25 G4
Thorndike Av *DERBYSE* DE24 53 H2
Thorndon Cl *MCKLVR* DE3 50 A1 2
Thorness *DERBYSE* DE24 54 B4 3
Thornhill Rd *DERBYW* DE22 41 F2
*NORM/LIT* DE23 41 F5
Thorn St *NORM/LIT* DE23 42 A4
Thorntree La *DERBY* DE1 2 D4
Thorpe Dr *MCKLVR* DE3 40 B3
Thorpelands Dr *DERBYW* DE22 33 H2 2
Thorpe Wy *BPR/DUF* DE56 6 C2
Thrushton Cl *RDERBYSW* DE65 59 H2 1
Thruxton Cl *DERBYSE* DE24 54 B3 3
Thurcroft Cl *DERBYW* DE22 33 F5
Thurlow Ct *DERBYE* DE21 35 H2 3
Thurstone Furlong
*MELB/CHEL* DE73 63 F3
Tiber Cl *DERBYSE* DE24 54 C4
Tickham Av *DERBYSE* DE24 61 F2
Ticknall La *RIPLEY* DE5 14 A1
Tideswell Rd *DERBYE* DE21 35 G2 3
Tilbury Pl *DERBYSE* DE24 53 H4
Tiller Cl *NORM/LIT* DE23 51 E3 2
Timbersbrook Cl *DERBYE* DE21 35 H2
Timsbury Ct *DERBYE* DE21 35 F1 10
Tintagel Cl *NORM/LIT* DE23 42 C4 3
Tipnall Rd *CDON/KEG* DE74 72 D4
Tiree Cl *DERBYSE* DE24 52 A5
Tissington Dr *DERBYE* DE21 28 A5 18
Tiverton Cl *MCKLVR* DE3 40 A2 4
Tivoli Gdns *DERBYW* DE22 33 H4
Tobermory Wy *DERBYSE* DE24 61 G1
Tonbridge Dr *DERBYSE* DE24 53 H4
Top Farm Ct *BPR/DUF* DE56 13 G2 4
Top Manor Cl *BWSH/BRSTN* DE72 45 H1
Torridon Cl *DERBYSE* DE24 51 H5
Tower St *DERBYSE* DE24 53 E2
Towle Cl *BWSH/BRSTN* DE72 45 G5
Towles Pastures
*CDON/KEG* DE74 72 D4
Town End Rd *BWSH/BRSTN* DE72 57 E2
Townsend Gv
*MELB/CHEL* DE73 63 H2 7
Town St *BPR/DUF* DE56 12 D4
*BPR/DUF* DE56 17 H2
The Town *DERBYE* DE21 26 D1 2
Traffic St *DERBY* DE1 2 E4
Trafford Wy *NORM/LIT* DE23 51 F1

Tredegar Dr *DERBYE* DE21 36 A1
Trefoil Ct *NORM/LIT* DE23 50 D2 10
Tregaron Cl *DERBYE* DE21 36 B1
Tregony Wy *DERBYSE* DE24 61 G2
Trent Bridge Ct
*NORM/LIT* DE23 51 F1 6
Trent Cl *DERBYSE* DE24 61 G2
Trent Dr *NORM/LIT* DE23 51 G4
Trent La *BWSH/BRSTN* DE72 70 D3
*CDON/KEG* DE74 72 D2
*MELB/CHEL* DE73 70 B5
Trenton Green Dr
*DERBYE* DE21 36 A5 4
Trent Ri *DERBYE* DE21 45 E2
Trent St *DERBYSE* DE24 53 H2
Tresillian Cl *DERBYW* DE22 33 H1
Treveris Cl *DERBYE* DE21 45 E2 2
Trinity St *DERBY* DE1 3 F6
Troon Cl *NORM/LIT* DE23 50 D1
Troutbeck Gv
*NORM/LIT* DE23 50 D2 11
Trowbridge Cl *DERBYE* DE21 35 F1 11
Trowels La *DERBYW* DE22 41 F2
Truro Crs *DERBYE* DE21 35 F3
Trusley Gdns *NORM/LIT* DE23 51 G4
Tudor Field Cl
*MELB/CHEL* DE73 63 H3 5
Tudor Rd *DERBYE* DE21 35 H5
Tufnell Gdns *DERBYW* DE22 33 E4 2
Tulla Cl *DERBYSE* DE24 61 H2
Turner St *DERBYSE* DE24 53 E3
Tuxford Cl *DERBYE* DE21 36 A2 15
Tweeds Muir Cl *DERBYE* DE21 35 G1 13
Twickenham Dr
*DERBYW* DE22 32 D5 5
Twin Oaks Cl *NORM/LIT* DE23 50 C2
Twyford Cl *HEANOR* DE75 15 H2
Twyford Rd *MELB/CHEL* DE73 68 B1
Twyford St *NORM/LIT* DE23 42 B3
Tyndale Cha *DERBYSE* DE24 61 F2 4

## U

Uffa Magna *MCKLVR* DE3 39 H5 3
Ullswater Cl *DERBYE* DE21 35 E1 5
Ullswater Dr *DERBYE* DE21 36 D5
Underhill Av *NORM/LIT* DE23 52 A2
Underhill Cl *NORM/LIT* DE23 51 H3
Union St *MELB/CHEL* DE73 75 H3
Uplands Av *NORM/LIT* DE23 51 F3
Uplands Gdns *NORM/LIT* DE23 41 H4 2
Upper Bainbrigge St
*NORM/LIT* DE23 42 A4
Upper Boundary Rd
*DERBYW* DE22 41 H2
Upper Dale Rd *NORM/LIT* DE23 42 A5
Upper Hall Cl *BPR/DUF* DE56 12 D4
Upper Hollow *NORM/LIT* DE23 41 F5
Upper Marehay Rd *RIPLEY* DE5 8 B1
Upper Moor Rd *DERBYSE* DE24 53 F3
Uttoxeter New Rd
*DERBYW* DE22 41 F3
Uttoxeter Old Rd *DERBY* DE1 41 G2
Uttoxeter Rd *MCKLVR* DE3 40 B5 11
*MCKLVR* DE3 40 B4 1

## V

Valerie Rd *BWSH/BRSTN* DE72 65 E5
Valley Rd *DERBYE* DE21 36 A5
*NORM/LIT* DE23 41 G5
Valley Vw *BPR/DUF* DE56 6 B5
Valley View Dr *ILK* DE7 21 F4
Vancouver Av *DERBYE* DE21 44 C3
Varley St *DERBYSE* DE24 53 E2
Vauxhall Av *DERBYW* DE22 32 D4
Verbena Dr *NORM/LIT* DE23 51 G5
Vermont Dr *DERBYE* DE21 36 B5 2
Vernon Dr *DERBYE* DE21 45 E2 3
Vernongate *DERBY* DE1 41 H1
Vernon St *DERBY* DE1 41 H1
Vestry Rd *DERBYE* DE21 35 F1
Vetchfield Cl *DERBYSE* DE24 62 A2 2
Vicarage Av *NORM/LIT* DE23 41 H4
Vicarage Cl *BPR/DUF* DE56 6 B3 3
*ILK* DE7 15 E4
Vicarage Ct *MCKLVR* DE3 40 A5 6
Vicarage Dr *DERBYE* DE21 35 H4
Vicarage La *BPR/DUF* DE56 17 H1
*DERBYE* DE21 18 C5
Vicarage Rd *BPR/DUF* DE56 12 A2
*MCKLVR* DE3 39 H4
*MELB/CHEL* DE73 63 G2
Vicarwood Av *BPR/DUF* DE56 12 D3 4

*DERBYW* DE22 34 A2
Victor Av *DERBYW* DE22 34 A3
Victoria Av *BWSH/BRSTN* DE72 45 G4
*BWSH/BRSTN* DE72 56 D2 3
Victoria Cl *MCKLVR* DE3 40 B2
Victoria Rd *BWSH/BRSTN* DE72 56 D2
Victoria St *CDON/KEG* DE74 73 E2
*DERBY* DE1 2 C4
*MELB/CHEL* DE73 75 H3
Victory Rd *DERBYSE* DE24 52 C2
Village St *NORM/LIT* DE23 52 A1
Villa St *BWSH/BRSTN* DE72 57 E2
Vincent Av *DERBYE* DE21 44 D3
Vincent Cl *BPR/DUF* DE56 13 H2 3
Vincent St *NORM/LIT* DE23 42 A5
Vine Cl *NORM/LIT* DE23 51 E2
Viola Cl *DERBYE* DE21 28 B5
Violet St *NORM/LIT* DE23 42 A5
Vivian St *DERBYE* DE21 34 C3
Vulcan St *NORM/LIT* DE23 42 C5 1

## W

Wade Av *NORM/LIT* DE23 41 F4
Wadebridge Gv
*DERBYSE* DE24 54 B4 7
Wade Dr *MCKLVR* DE3 40 B4
Wade St *NORM/LIT* DE23 41 F5
Wagtail Cl *DERBYSE* DE24 51 G5
Waingroves Rd *RIPLEY* DE5 9 G1
Wakami Crs *MELB/CHEL* DE73 63 H2
Wakelyn Cl *BWSH/BRSTN* DE72 66 C3
Walbrook Rd *NORM/LIT* DE23 42 A5
Walcote Cl *BPR/DUF* DE56 6 D2
Waldene Dr *DERBYSE* DE24 53 H3
Waldorf Av *DERBYSE* DE24 53 H2
Walk Cl *BWSH/BRSTN* DE72 56 D2
Walker La *DERBY* DE1 2 B2
The Walk *BPR/DUF* DE56 14 A2
Wallace St *DERBYW* DE22 41 F1
Wallfields Cl *RDERBYSW* DE65 60 A1
Wallis Cl *BWSH/BRSTN* DE72 56 D2
Walnut Av *DERBYSE* DE24 54 A2
Walnut Cl *BWSH/BRSTN* DE72 65 G4
*MELB/CHEL* DE73 63 H4
*MELB/CHEL* DE73 68 B1 1
*RDERBYSW* DE65 49 E4 1
Walnut Rd *BPR/DUF* DE56 6 C4
Walnut St *DERBYSE* DE24 52 D2
Walpole St *DERBYE* DE21 3 K1
Walsham Ct *DERBYE* DE21 34 D3
Walter St *BWSH/BRSTN* DE72 56 C2
*DERBY* DE1 33 H4
Waltham Av *DERBYSE* DE24 52 A5
Walthamstow Dr *DERBYW* DE22 33 E5
Walton Av *DERBYSE* DE24 53 F5
Walton Dr *NORM/LIT* DE23 51 H2
Walton Hl *CDON/KEG* DE74 72 C3
Walton Rd *DERBYE* DE21 43 G1
Wansfell Cl *MCKLVR* DE3 40 B5 12
Wardlow Av *DERBYE* DE21 35 H3
Ward's La *BWSH/BRSTN* DE72 57 G1
*MELB/CHEL* DE73 69 G5
Ward St *DERBYW* DE22 41 H2
Wardswood Cl
*BWSH/BRSTN* DE72 46 A5
Wardwick *DERBY* DE1 2 C3
Warner St *DERBYW* DE22 42 A3
*MCKLVR* DE3 40 A5 7
Warren St *DERBYSE* DE24 53 G1 3
Warsick La *MELB/CHEL* DE73 74 A2
Warwick Av *NORM/LIT* DE23 41 G5
Warwick Gdns *BPR/DUF* DE56 7 E2
Warwick St *DERBYSE* DE24 43 E4
Washington Av *DERBYE* DE21 36 A5 3
Washington Cl *MELB/CHEL* DE73 75 H3
Waterford Dr *DERBYE* DE21 43 H2
Watergo La *MCKLVR* DE3 49 H2
Watering La *BPR/DUF* DE56 13 E4
Waterloo Ct *DERBY* DE1 34 C4 3
Watermeadow Rd
*DERBYSE* DE24 53 H4
The Water Mdw
*MELB/CHEL* DE73 69 E1
Waterside Cl *DERBYW* DE22 34 B1 3
Watson St *DERBY* DE1 33 H5 3
*DERBYW* DE22 33 H4
Watten Cl *DERBYSE* DE24 62 A2
Waveney Cl *DERBYW* DE22 26 C3
Waverley St *DERBYSE* DE24 52 D2 4
Wayfaring Rd *DERBYE* DE21 35 H2
Wayzgoose Dr *DERBYE* DE21 3 H3
Weavers Cl *BPR/DUF* DE56 6 D1
*BWSH/BRSTN* DE72 46 A5
Webster St *DERBY* DE1 2 B6
Weirfield Rd *DERBYW* DE22 34 B1

Welbeck Gv *DERBYW* DE22 ..... 25 G5
Welland Cl *MCKLVR* DE3 ..... 40 A3
Welldon St *RIPLEY* DE5 ..... 9 F3
Wellesley Av *NORM/LIT* DE23 ..... 51 G2
Wellington Ct *BPR/DUF* DE56 ..... 6 A3 🖾
Wellington St *DERBY* DE1 ..... 3 G6 🖾
Well La *BPR/DUF* DE56 ..... 12 A3
Wells Rd *MCKLVR* DE3 ..... 40 B4
Well St *DERBY* DE1 ..... 34 B4 🖾
Welney Cl *MCKLVR* DE3 ..... 50 A1 🖾
Welshpool Rd *DERBYE* DE21 ..... 35 E2
Welwyn Av *DERBYSE* DE24 ..... 53 F5
  *DERBYW* DE22 ..... 25 C5
Wembley Gdns *DERBYW* DE22 ..... 32 D5
Wendover Cl *MCKLVR* DE3 ..... 39 H5
Wenlock Cl *MCKLVR* DE3 ..... 40 B5 🖾
Wensley Dr *DERBYE* DE21 ..... 45 E5 🖾
Wentworth Cl *MCKLVR* DE3 ..... 40 C5 🖾
Werburgh St *DERBYE* DE21 ..... 44 C2 🖾
Werburgh St *DERBYW* DE22 ..... 2 A5
Wesley La *BWSH/BRSTN* DE72 ..... 45 H1 🖾
Wesley Rd *DERBYSE* DE24 ..... 54 A4
Wessington Ms *DERBYW* DE22 ..... 33 H2 🖾
West Av *BWSH/BRSTN* DE72 ..... 56 C1
  *DERBY* DE1 ..... 2 A1
  *DERBY* DE1 ..... 34 A4 🖾
  *MELB/CHEL* DE73 ..... 63 F1
West Bank Av *DERBYW* DE22 ..... 34 A3
West Bank Rd *DERBYW* DE22 ..... 33 H3 🖾
West Bank Rd *DERBYW* DE22 ..... 25 H3
Westbourne Pk *DERBYW* DE22 ..... 32 C5
Westbury Ct *DERBYE* DE21 ..... 41 C3 🖾
Westbury Gdns *BPR/DUF* DE56 ..... 6 D2
Westbury St *DERBYW* DE22 ..... 41 G3
West Cl *DERBYW* DE22 ..... 33 H1
West Croft Av *NORM/LIT* DE23 ..... 51 C4
Westdene Av *DERBYSE* DE24 ..... 53 E4
West Dr *MCKLVR* DE3 ..... 40 A4
West End Dr *BWSH/BRSTN* DE72 ..... 66 B3
Western Rd *MCKLVR* DE3 ..... 40 B4
  *NORM/LIT* DE23 ..... 42 A3
Westgreen Av *DERBYSE* DE24 ..... 53 E4
West Gv *DERBYSE* DE24 ..... 53 E4
Westhall Rd *MCKLVR* DE3 ..... 40 A3
West Lawn *RDERBYSW* DE65 ..... 59 H2
Westleigh Av *DERBYW* DE22 ..... 33 F5
Westley Crs *DERBYE* DE21 ..... 19 E3
Westminster St
  *DERBYSE* DE24 ..... 53 G1 🖾
Weston Park Av *DERBYSE* DE24 ..... 63 E1
Weston Ri *MELB/CHEL* DE73 ..... 63 H4 🖾
Weston Rd *BWSH/BRSTN* DE72 ..... 71 E1
West Park Rd *DERBYW* DE22 ..... 33 H3
West Rd *DERBYE* DE21 ..... 44 C1
West Rw *DERBYW* DE22 ..... 34 B2 🖾
West Service Rd *DERBYE* DE21 ..... 43 H4
Westwood Dr *DERBYSE* DE24 ..... 53 E4
Wetherby Rd *DERBYSE* DE24 ..... 53 E2
Weyacres *BWSH/BRSTN* DE72 ..... 45 G5
Wharfedale Cl *DERBYW* DE22 ..... 26 C4
The Wharf *BWSH/BRSTN* DE72 ..... 66 D3
Wheatcroft Wy *DERBYE* DE21 ..... 34 D1
Wheathill Gv *NORM/LIT* DE23 ..... 50 D3 🖾
Wheatland Cl *DERBYE* DE21 ..... 61 F2 🖾
Wheatsheaf Cl *DERBYE* DE21 ..... 36 B1 🖾
Wheeldon Av *BPR/DUF* DE56 ..... 6 C3
  *DERBYW* DE22 ..... 33 H4
Whenby Cl *MCKLVR* DE3 ..... 39 H4 🖾
Whernside Cl *DERBYSE* DE24 ..... 54 B3

Whilton Ct *BPR/DUF* DE56 ..... 7 E3 🖾
Whinbush Av *DERBYSE* DE24 ..... 53 F4
Whiston St *NORM/LIT* DE23 ..... 42 B4
Whitaker Gdns
  *NORM/LIT* DE23 ..... 41 H4 🖾
Whitaker Rd *NORM/LIT* DE23 ..... 41 H4
Whitaker St *NORM/LIT* DE23 ..... 42 B4
Whitby Av *DERBYE* DE21 ..... 34 D2
Whitecross St *DERBY* DE1 ..... 33 H5 🖾
Whitehouse Cl *DERBYSE* DE24 ..... 53 E5
Whitehouse Ri *BPR/DUF* DE56 ..... 5 H1
Whitehurst St *DERBYSE* DE24 ..... 53 E2
White La *BPR/DUF* DE56 ..... 4 A4
Whitemoor Hall *BPR/DUF* DE56 ..... 7 E2 🖾
Whitemoor La *BPR/DUF* DE56 ..... 7 E2
White St *DERBYW* DE22 ..... 33 H4
Whiteway *DERBYW* DE22 ..... 33 H1 🖾
Whitewell Gdns
  *DERBYSE* DE24 ..... 54 B4 🖾
Whitmore Rd *DERBYE* DE21 ..... 35 G5 🖾
Whitstable Cl *NORM/LIT* DE23 ..... 51 G2 🖾
Whittaker La *DERBYE* DE21 ..... 19 E3
Whittington St *DERBYSE* DE24 ..... 53 E4
Whittlebury Dr *NORM/LIT* DE23 ..... 50 C2
Whyteleafe Gv *DERBYE* DE21 .. 36 A2 🖾
Wickersley Cl *DERBYW* DE22 ..... 33 H1 🖾
Wicksteed Cl *BPR/DUF* DE56 ..... 7 E2
Widdybank Cl *DERBYW* DE22 ..... 33 F1 🖾
Wigmore Cl *MCKLVR* DE3 ..... 39 H3 🖾
Wilders Lea Ct *BPR/DUF* DE56 ..... 6 B5
Wildpark La *ASHB* DE6 ..... 22 B2
Wildsmith St *DERBYSE* DE24 ..... 53 H1
Wild St *DERBYW* DE22 ..... 41 G1
Wilfred St *NORM/LIT* DE23 ..... 42 C4
Wilkins Dr *DERBYSE* DE24 ..... 53 F2
Willesden Av *DERBYW* DE22 ..... 32 D4
Willetts Rd *DERBYE* DE21 ..... 35 H4
William St *BPR/DUF* DE56 ..... 6 A3
  *DERBY* DE1 ..... 2 B5
Willington Rd *RDERBYSW* DE65 ..... 48 B5
  *RDERBYSW* DE65 ..... 59 H4
Wilin St *NORM/LIT* DE23 ..... 42 A5
Willowbrook Gra
  *MELB/CHEL* DE73 ..... 63 H3
Willow Cl *BWSH/BRSTN* DE72 ..... 65 G5
  *DERBYW* DE22 ..... 34 A1 🖾
Willow Cft *DERBYSE* DE24 ..... 54 B5
Willowcroft Rd *DERBYE* DE21 ..... 44 C3
Willow Gv *BPR/DUF* DE56 ..... 6 B5
Willowherb Cl *DERBYSE* DE24 ..... 62 A2 🖾
Willow Park Wy
  *BWSH/BRSTN* DE72 ..... 65 F5
Willow Rd *CDON/KEG* DE74 ..... 73 E2
Willow Rw *DERBY* DE1 ..... 2 B2
Willowsend Cl
  *RDERBYSW* DE65 ..... 60 A3 🖾
Willson Av *NORM/LIT* DE23 ..... 51 F1
Willson Rd *NORM/LIT* DE23 ..... 51 F1
Wilmington Av *DERBYSE* DE24 ..... 54 A4
Wilmore Rd *DERBYSE* DE24 ..... 52 B4
Wilmot Av *BWSH/BRSTN* DE72 ..... 70 D2
  *DERBYE* DE21 ..... 43 G1
Wilmot Dr *ILK* DE7 ..... 15 E5
Wilmot Rd *BPR/DUF* DE56 ..... 6 B3
Wilmot St *DERBY* DE1 ..... 2 D6
Wilmslow Dr *DERBYE* DE21 .. 36 A2 🖾
Wilne La *BWSH/BRSTN* DE72 ..... 57 F5
  *BWSH/BRSTN* DE72 ..... 67 E3
Wilne Rd *BWSH/BRSTN* DE72 ..... 56 D3
Wilson Av *HEANOR* DE75 ..... 9 G3

Wilson Cl *MCKLVR* DE3 ..... 49 H1
Wilson Ri *MELB/CHEL* DE73 ..... 76 D4 🖾
Wilson Rd *DERBYE* DE21 ..... 35 G3
Wilson St *DERBY* DE1 ..... 2 B5
Wilsthorpe Rd
  *BWSH/BRSTN* DE72 ..... 57 H1
  *DERBYE* DE21 ..... 57 H1
Wilton Cl *DERBYSE* DE24 ..... 61 F2 🖾
Wiltshire Rd *DERBYE* DE21 ..... 35 E4
Wimbledon Rd *DERBYW* DE22 ..... 32 D5
Wimbourne Cl *MELB/CHEL* DE73 ..... 63 H3
Wimpole Gdns *DERBYW* DE22 ..... 33 E5 🖾
Wincanton Cl *DERBYSE* DE24 ..... 43 E5
Winchcombe Wy *DERBYE* DE21 ..... 35 H1
Winchester Crs *DERBYE* DE21 ..... 35 E3
Windermere Crs *DERBYSE* DE24 ..... 25 H5
Windermere Dr *DERBYE* DE21 .. 44 D1 🖾
Windley Crs *DERBYW* DE22 ..... 34 A2
Windley La *BPR/DUF* DE56 ..... 10 B4
Windmill Av *BPR/DUF* DE56 ..... 14 A2
Windmill Cl
  *BWSH/BRSTN* DE72 ..... 45 H1 🖾
  *CDON/KEG* DE74 ..... 73 E5 🖾
  *DERBYSE* DE24 ..... 54 C5
Windmill Hill La *DERBYW* DE22 ..... 33 F5
Windmill La *BPR/DUF* DE56 ..... 6 B3
Windmill Ri *BPR/DUF* DE56 ..... 6 B2
Windmill Rd *RDERBYSW* DE65 ..... 58 A1
Windrush Cl *DERBYW* DE22 ..... 26 C3
Windsor Av *MELB/CHEL* DE73 ..... 75 H2
  *NORM/LIT* DE23 ..... 51 E1
Windsor Cl *BWSH/BRSTN* DE72 ..... 45 H5
Windsor Ct *MCKLVR* DE3 ..... 40 A3 🖾
Windsor Dr *DERBYE* DE21 ..... 37 E5
Windy La *DERBYE* DE21 ..... 18 D4
Wingerworth Park Rd
  *DERBYE* DE21 ..... 44 D1 🖾
Wingfield Dr *DERBYE* DE21 ..... 35 G2
Winslow Gn *DERBYE* DE21 ..... 36 A5
Winster Cl *BPR/DUF* DE56 ..... 6 C2 🖾
Winster Rd *DERBYE* DE21 ..... 35 F2
Wintergreen Dr *NORM/LIT* DE23 ..... 50 C3
Wirksworth Rd *BPR/DUF* DE56 ..... 10 B1
  *BPR/DUF* DE56 ..... 17 G2
Wisgreaves Rd *DERBYSE* DE24 ..... 53 G1
Witham Dr *NORM/LIT* DE23 ..... 51 G3 🖾
Witney Cl *DERBYSE* DE24 ..... 52 D1 🖾
Witton Ct *DERBYSE* DE24 ..... 51 G5
Woburn Pl *DERBYW* DE22 ..... 41 E1 🖾
Wolfa St *DERBYW* DE22 ..... 2 A5
Wollaton Rd *DERBYE* DE21 ..... 35 G3
Wolverley Gra *DERBYSE* DE24 ..... 54 B5
Woodale Cl *NORM/LIT* DE23 ..... 50 C3 🖾
Woodbridge Cl *MELB/CHEL* DE73 .. 63 G3
Woodchester Dr *DERBYSE* DE24 ..... 54 C3
Wood Close Camp
  *DERBYE* DE21 ..... 26 D1 🖾
Woodcote Wy *NORM/LIT* DE23 ..... 50 D2
Wood Cft *NORM/LIT* DE23 ..... 51 G1 🖾
Woodfall La *DERBYW* DE22 ..... 16 C3
Woodford Rd *DERBYW* DE22 ..... 32 D4
Woodgate Dr
  *MELB/CHEL* DE73 ..... 63 H3 🖾
Woodhall Dr *NORM/LIT* DE23 ..... 50 B1
Woodhouse Rd *BPR/DUF* DE56 ..... 13 H3
Woodhurst Cl *DERBYE* DE21 ..... 35 E2
Woodland Av *BWSH/BRSTN* DE72 .. 45 H4
Woodland Rd *DERBYW* DE22 ..... 33 H3
Woodlands Av *DERBYSE* DE24 ..... 53 F5

Woodlands Cl *DERBYE* DE21 ..... 18 C
  *MELB/CHEL* DE73 ..... 75
Woodlands La *DERBYW* DE22 ..... 25
  *MELB/CHEL* DE73 ..... 63
Woodlands Rd *DERBYW* DE22 ..... 25
The Woodlands
  *MELB/CHEL* DE73 ..... 76
Woodlands Wy *MELB/CHEL* DE73.. 75
Wood La *BPR/DUF* DE56 ..... 14
  *ILK* DE7 ..... 12
Woodlea Gv *DERBYE* DE21 ..... 18
Woodminton Dr
  *MELB/CHEL* DE73 ..... 63 G
Woodrising Cl *DERBYE* DE21 ..... 28 A5
Wood Rd *DERBYE* DE21 ..... 35
  *DERBYE* DE21 ..... 35
Woodshop La *MELB/CHEL* DE73 ..... 69
Woodside *ILK* DE7 ..... 20
Woodside Dr *DERBYW* DE22 ..... 26
Woods La *DERBYW* DE22 ..... 2
Woods Meadow
  *DERBYSE* DE24 ..... 54 C
Woodsorrel Dr *DERBYE* DE21 ..... 28
Woodstock Cl *DERBYW* DE22 ..... 25
Wood St *DERBY* DE1 ..... 2
Woodthorne Av *DERBYSE* DE24 ..... 53
Woodthorpe Av *DERBYE* DE21 ..... 35
Woolrych St *NORM/LIT* DE23 ..... 42
Worcester Crs *DERBYE* DE21 ..... 35
Wordsworth Av *DERBYSE* DE24 ..... 51
Wordsworth Dr
  *DERBYSE* DE24 ..... 52 B
Wragley Wy *DERBYSE* DE24 ..... 61
Wren Park Cl *BPR/DUF* DE56 ..... 5
  *RDERBYSW* DE65 ..... 60
Wretham Cl *MCKLVR* DE3 ..... 50 A
Wroxham Cl *DERBYSE* DE24 ..... 53
Wyaston Cl *DERBYW* DE22 ..... 33 H
Wye St *DERBYE* DE24 ..... 53
Wyndham St *DERBYSE* DE24 ..... 53
Wynton Av *DERBYSE* DE24 ..... 53
Wyvern Wy *DERBYE* DE21 ..... 43

# Y

Yardley Wy *BPR/DUF* DE56 ..... 7
Yarrow Cl *DERBYSE* DE24 ..... 61 H
Yarwell Cl *DERBYE* DE21 ..... 35
Yates St *NORM/LIT* DE23 ..... 42
Yeovil Cl *DERBYSE* DE24 ..... 54 B
Yewdale Gv *DERBYE* DE21 ..... 28 B5
Yews Cl *MELB/CHEL* DE73 ..... 63
Yew Tree Av *BWSH/BRSTN* DE72.. 46
Yew Tree Cl *DERBYSE* DE24 ..... 54 B2
Yew Tree La
  *BWSH/BRSTN* DE72 ..... 55 E
York Rd *DERBYE* DE21 ..... 35
York St *DERBY* DE1 ..... 41
Youlgreave Dr *DERBYE* DE21 ..... 35 G
Young St *NORM/LIT* DE23 ..... 42
Ypres Rd *DERBYW* DE22 ..... 33

# Z

Zetland Crs *DERBYSE* DE24 ..... 61

## Index - featured places

Allenpark Infant School
  *DERBYSE* DE24 ..... 53 F3
Alvaston & Boulton Sports Club
  *DERBYSE* DE24 ..... 43 H5
Alvaston Junior & Infant School
  *DERBYSE* DE24 ..... 54 B2
Alvaston Medical Practice
  *DERBYSE* DE24 ..... 54 A2
Appletree Medical Practice
  *BPR/DUF* DE56 ..... 18 A2
Arboretum Primary School
  *NORM/LIT* DE23 ..... 42 B4
Ashbrook Junior & Infant School
  *BWSH/BRSTN* DE72 ..... 45 G4
Ashcroft Primary School
  *DERBYSE* DE24 ..... 61 H2
Ashgate Junior & Infant School
  *DERBYW* DE22 ..... 33 H5

Assembly Rooms
  *DERBY* DE1 ..... 2 C3
Asterdale Leisure Centre
  *DERBYE* DE21 ..... 45 E3
Asterdale School
  *DERBYE* DE21 ..... 45 E3
Aston Hall Hospital
  *BWSH/BRSTN* DE72 ..... 71 F1
Aston on Trent Primary School
  *BWSH/BRSTN* DE72 ..... 65 F4
Audley Centre
  *DERBY* DE1 ..... 2 D4
Babington Hospital
  *BPR/DUF* DE56 ..... 5 H4
Beaufort Junior &
  Infant School
  *DERBYE* DE21 ..... 34 D3
Beaufort Street
  Business Centre
  *DERBYE* DE21 ..... 3 J1

Becket Primary School
  *DERBYW* DE22 ..... 2 A6
Belper Long Row
  Primary School
  *BPR/DUF* DE56 ..... 6 A2
Belper Meadows Sports Club
  *BPR/DUF* DE56 ..... 5 H3
Belper Natural Health Centre
  *BPR/DUF* DE56 ..... 5 H4
Belper Pottery Primary School
  *BPR/DUF* DE56 ..... 6 D3
Belper School
  *BPR/DUF* DE56 ..... 6 D3
Belper Sports Centre
  *BPR/DUF* DE56 ..... 7 E3
Belper Town Council
  *BPR/DUF* DE56 ..... 6 B3
Bemrose Community School
  *DERBYW* DE22 ..... 41 G2

Bishop Lonsdale C of E School
  *DERBYW* DE22 ..... 41
Bluebell Gallery
  *DERBYW* DE22 ..... 34
Boars Head Industrial Estate
  *DERBYE* DE21 ..... 3
Borrow Wood Junior &
  Infant School
  *DERBYE* DE21 ..... 45
Boulton Clinic
  *DERBYSE* DE24 ..... 53
Boulton Junior & Infant School
  *DERBYSE* DE24 ..... 53
Brackensdale Junior &
  Infant School
  *DERBYW* DE22 ..... 33
Bradshaw Retail Park
  *DERBY* DE1 ..... 2
Bramble Business Centre
  *DERBY* DE1 ..... 2

adsall C of E Primary School
ILK DE7 27 F4
adsall Hilltop Junior & Infant School
DERBYE DE21 35 F2
edon Priory Golf Club
MELB/CHEL DE73 76 D5
okfield Primary School
MCKLVR DE3 50 A1
okside School
ILK DE7 27 F4
omfield College
ILK DE7 28 A3
B
DERBY DE1 2 D5
lyle Infant School
NORM/LIT DE23 51 E1
stle Donington Community College
CDON/KEG DE74 73 E4
hedral Road Clinic
DERBY DE1 2 B2
vendish Close Infant School
DERBYE DE21 35 H3
vendish Close Junior School
DERBYE DE21 35 H3
addesden Medical Centre
DERBYE DE21 35 F5
arnwood Surgery
DERBY DE1 2 C6
ellaston Infant School
MELB/CHEL DE73 63 G2
ellaston School
MELB/CHEL DE73 63 G3
erry Tree Infant School
DERBYE DE21 44 A1
erry Tree Junior School
DERBYE DE21 44 A1
evin Golf Club
BPR/DUF DE56 11 H5
urch Wilne Water Sports Club
BWSH/BRSTN DE72 57 G4
ema
DERBY DE1 2 C5
y Road Industrial Park
DERBY DE1 34 B4
ckshut Lane Business Centre
MELB/CHEL DE73 75 H2
e College
DERBY DE1 41 H1
wn Court
DERBY DE1 2 C2
e Curzon C of E Primary School
DERBYW DE22 25 G2
e Medical Centre
NORM/LIT DE23 42 A4
e Primary School
NORM/LIT DE23 41 H4
me Catherine Harpurs School
MELB/CHEL DE73 74 B5
nby Free C of E Junior & Infant School
RIPLEY DE5 14 C1
e Derby Chest Clinic
DERBY DE1 2 C5
rby City Council
DERBY DE1 2 E5
rby City Council
DERBY DE1 2 E2
rby City Council
DERBY DE1 2 E3
rby City Council
DERBY DE1 2 B3
rby City Council
DERBY DE1 2 C3
rby City Council
DERBY DE1 2 B2
rby City Council
DERBYE DE21 35 E4
rby City Council
DERBYSE DE24 43 F5
rby City Council
DERBYSE DE24 52 D1
rby City Council
DERBYW DE22 32 D5
rby City Council
DERBYW DE22 34 A4
rby City General Hospital
DERBYW DE22 41 E4
rby College
DERBYE DE21 3 J2
rby College of Further Education
DERBY DE1 2 B6
rby College Wilmorton
DERBYSE DE24 43 G4

Derby County Football Club
DERBYSE DE24 43 F3
Derby County Football Club
NORM/LIT DE23 42 C5
Derby Crown Court
DERBY DE1 2 E3
Derby Independent Grammar School for Boys
NORM/LIT DE23 50 C2
Derby Moor Community School
NORM/LIT DE23 51 E2
Derby Playhouse Theatre
DERBY DE1 2 E5
Derby Regional Swimming Pool
DERBYSE DE24 52 D3
Derby Rowing Club
DERBY DE1 34 B4
Derbyshire County Council
DERBYE DE21 34 C4
Derbyshire County Council
DERBYE DE21 36 A5
Derbyshire County Council
DERBYW DE22 41 G3
Derbyshire County Cricket Club
DERBYE DE21 3 H1
Derbyshire Royal Infirmary NHS Trust
DERBY DE1 2 E6
Derbyshire Royal Infirmary NHS Trust
DERBYSE DE24 53 E1
Derby Small Business Centre
DERBY DE1 3 F6
Derby Small Business Centre
NORM/LIT DE23 42 C5
Derby & South Derbyshire Magistrates Court
DERBY DE1 2 D3
Derby Superbowl
NORM/LIT DE23 52 B2
Derby Trading Estate
DERBYE DE21 34 C4
Derwent Bus Centre
DERBY DE1 2 E1
Derwent Community School
DERBYE DE21 34 D4
Derwent Medical Centre
DERBY DE1 2 C1
Derwentside Industrial Estate
BPR/DUF DE56 12 A1
Draycott Parish Council
BWSH/BRSTN DE72 57 E2
Draycott Primary School
BWSH/BRSTN DE72 56 D2
Duffield Art Gallery
BPR/DUF DE56 18 A2
Duffield Road Industrial Estate
DERBYE DE21 26 D2
East Midlands Nuffield Hospital
NORM/LIT DE23 50 C3
The Ecclesbourne School
BPR/DUF DE56 17 H2
Ecclesbourne Surgery
BPR/DUF DE56 17 H2
Elvaston Castle Working Estate Museum
BWSH/BRSTN DE72 55 F3
Elvaston Cricket Club
BWSH/BRSTN DE72 55 E2
Endland Industrial Estate
DERBYW DE22 41 G2
Etwall Leisure Centre
RDERBYSW DE65 48 A5
Etwall Primary School
RDERBYSW DE65 48 A5
The Eye Gallery
DERBY DE1 2 C3
Family Medical Centre
DERBYSE DE24 53 H1
Findern CP School
RDERBYSW DE65 60 B4
Firfield Primary School
BWSH/BRSTN DE72 57 H2
Firs Estate Primary School
DERBYW DE22 41 H3
Flower Gallery
DERBYW DE22 33 H5
Friargate Gallery
DERBY DE1 2 B3
Friar Gate Surgery
DERBY DE1 2 A3
Friargate Surgery
DERBY DE1 2 A2
The Gallery
DERBY DE1 2 D4
Gayton Junior School
NORM/LIT DE23 51 G3

Green Lane Gallery
DERBY DE1 2 C6
Green Lane Surgery
BPR/DUF DE56 6 A3
Group Surgery & Clinic
DERBYW DE22 33 G1
The Grove Hospital
BWSH/BRSTN DE72 66 A3
Hardwick Infant School
NORM/LIT DE23 42 A5
Heanor Gate School
HEANOR DE75 15 H1
Hemington Primary School
CDON/KEG DE74 73 G2
Herbert Strutt Primary School
BPR/DUF DE56 5 H5
Holbrook C of E Infant School
BPR/DUF DE56 12 D3
Hollybrook Medical Centre
NORM/LIT DE23 50 C3
Horsley C of E Primary School
DERBYE DE21 13 G4
Horsley Lodge Golf Club
ILK DE7 20 A1
Horsley Woodhouse Primary School
ILK DE7 14 C4
Industrial Museum
DERBY DE1 2 D2
Ivy House School
NORM/LIT DE23 42 D3
John Flamsteed Community School
RIPLEY DE5 7 H5
John Port School
RDERBYSW DE65 48 A5
Junior & Infant School
BPR/DUF DE56 13 H2
Kedleston Hall (NT)
DERBYW DE22 24 B3
Kedleston Park Golf Club
DERBYW DE22 24 D2
Kings Mead Clinic
DERBY DE1 2 A1
Kingsmead Industrial Estate
DERBYW DE22 33 G5
Kings Mead Infant School
DERBY DE1 2 A1
Kingsway Hospital
DERBYW DE22 41 F2
Kingsway Industrial Park
DERBYW DE22 41 E1
Kingsway Retail Park
DERBYW DE22 41 F1
Kirk Langley C of E Primary School
ASHB DE6 31 E1
Ladylea Industrial Estate
ILK DE7 14 A3
Lancaster Sports Centre
DERBY DE1 2 B2
Landau Forte College
DERBY DE1 2 D1
Lees Brook Community School
DERBYE DE21 36 A3
Little Eaton Primary School
DERBYE DE21 18 D5
Littleover Community School
NORM/LIT DE23 50 C1
Littleover Medical Centre
NORM/LIT DE23 41 E5
Loscoe C of E Primary School
HEANOR DE75 9 G3
Lum Farm Leisure Centre
RIPLEY DE5 8 D2
Mackworth College Derby
DERBYW DE22 40 C1
Magistrates Court
DERBY DE1 2 E5
Main Shopping Centre
DERBY DE1 2 E4
Markeaton Primary School
DERBYW DE22 33 H4
Market
DERBY DE1 2 D4
Meadow Farm Community Primary School
DERBYE DE21 43 H2
The Meadows Primary School
BPR/DUF DE56 17 G2
Melbourne Junior & Infant School
MELB/CHEL DE73 76 A2
The Merrill Community School & Sixth Form College
DERBYSE DE24 53 F3
Mickleover Primary School
MCKLVR DE3 40 A4

Mickleover Surgery
MCKLVR DE3 40 B4
Milford County School
BPR/DUF DE56 12 B3
Millennium Business Centre
DERBYE DE21 43 F2
Montage Gallery
DERBY DE1 2 C2
The Moore Clinic
BPR/DUF DE56 6 A3
Moorhead Primary School
DERBYSE DE24 53 G3
Morley Primary School
ILK DE7 28 C1
Mosque
NORM/LIT DE23 42 A3
Murray Park Community School
MCKLVR DE3 40 C2
Museum & Art Gallery
DERBY DE1 2 C3
Newchase Business Park
DERBYSE DE24 42 D5
Nightingale Business Park
DERBYSE DE24 53 E1
Nightingale Infant School
DERBYSE DE24 52 D2
Nightingale Junior School
DERBYSE DE24 52 D1
Noel Baker Community School
DERBYSE DE24 53 G5
Normanton Junior School
NORM/LIT DE23 51 H2
Nursery
DERBY DE1 2 C1
Oakwood Infant School
DERBYSE DE24 53 H3
Oakwood Junior School
DERBYSE DE24 53 H3
Oakwood Leisure Centre
DERBYE DE21 35 H1
Oakwood Medical Centre
DERBYE DE21 35 G2
Oakwood Surgery
DERBYE DE21 35 H2
Ockbrook School
BWSH/BRSTN DE72 45 H1
Old Hall Mill Business Park
DERBYE DE21 26 D1
Old Vicarage School
DERBYW DE22 26 A5
Orchard CP School
CDON/KEG DE74 72 D3
Osmaston Road Surgery
DERBY DE1 2 D6
Parker Industrial Estate
DERBYE DE21 34 C3
Park Farm Medical Centre
DERBYW DE22 33 G1
Parkfields Surgery
DERBYSE DE24 53 H1
Park Lane Surgery
DERBYW DE22 26 A4
The Park Medical Practice
BWSH/BRSTN DE72 45 F4
The Park Medical Practice
DERBYE DE21 35 H5
Peartree Clinic
NORM/LIT DE23 42 B5
Pear Tree Junior & Infant School
NORM/LIT DE23 42 B5
Pear Tree Medical Centre
NORM/LIT DE23 42 B5
Perkins Industrial Estate
DERBYE DE21 34 D3
Peter Baines Industrial Estate
DERBYW DE22 2 B6
Pickfords House Museum
DERBY DE1 2 A3
Police Museum
DERBY DE1 2 C2
Portway Infant School
DERBYW DE22 25 H4
Portway Junior School
DERBYW DE22 25 H4
PO Sorting Office
DERBY DE1 3 F7
Prime Business Centre
DERBYE DE21 44 A2
Prime Industrial Estate
NORM/LIT DE23 42 D4
Queen St Baths
DERBY DE1 2 C2
Queens Leisure Centre
DERBY DE1 2 C2
Racecourse Industrial Park
DERBYE DE21 34 D3

Ramcharia Sikh Temple
 NORM/LIT DE23 .......................... 42 B4
Ravensdale Junior &
 Infant School
 MCKLVR DE3 ............................... 40 B3
Redhill Primary School
 BWSH/BRSTN DE72 ................... 46 A1
Redwood Junior &
 Infant School
 DERBYSE DE24 ........................... 61 H1
Reigate Junior & Infant School
 DERBYW DE22.............................. 32 C4
Richardson Endowed
 Primary School
 ILK DE7....................................... 15 E4
Ridgeway Infant School
 NORM/LIT DE23 .......................... 51 G3
Risley Lower Grammar
 C of E Primary School
 BWSH/BRSTN DE72 ................... 47 H2
Riversdale Surgery
 BPR/DUF DE56 ............................. 5 H3
Robinsons Industrial Estate
 NORM/LIT DE23 .......................... 42 D4
Rosehill Infant School
 NORM/LIT DE23 .......................... 42 C3
Royal Crown Derby
 NORM/LIT DE23 .......................... 42 C3
SAI Medical Centre
 NORM/LIT DE23 .......................... 42 B4
St Albans Primary School
 DERBYE DE21 ............................. 35 G5
St Andrews C of E
 Primary School
 ILK DE7....................................... 29 G3
St Andrews Special School
 DERBYE DE21 ............................. 35 F2
St Benedict School &
 Sixth Form Centre
 DERBYW DE22.............................. 34 A2
St Chads C of E Infant School
 NORM/LIT DE23 .......................... 42 A4
St Clares School
 MCKLVR DE3 ............................... 40 C4
St Edwards Junior School
 CDON/KEG DE74 ........................ 73 E4

St Elizabeths School
 BPR/DUF DE56 ............................. 6 A2
St Georges RC School
 NORM/LIT DE23 .......................... 51 F2
St Giles School
 DERBYE DE21 ............................. 34 D2
St Helens Business Centre
 DERBY DE1 ................................... 2 B1
St James C of E Infant School
 NORM/LIT DE23 ........................... 2 E7
St John Fisher RC
 Primary School
 DERBYSE DE24 ........................... 54 B1
St Johns C of E Primary School
 BPR/DUF DE56 ............................. 6 C2
St Josephs School
 NORM/LIT DE23 ........................... 2 B7
St Josephs School
 NORM/LIT DE23 .......................... 42 A3
St Martins School
 DERBYSE DE24 ........................... 53 G1
St Marys RC Primary School
 DERBY DE1 ................................... 2 B1
St Peters C of E Junior School
 NORM/LIT DE23 .......................... 41 F5
St Werburgh's Arcade
 DERBY DE1 ................................... 2 B3
St Werburghs C of E School
 DERBYE DE21 ............................. 44 C1
Sale & Davys C of E School
 MELB/CHEL DE73 ....................... 68 B2
Salvation Army
 DERBY DE1 ................................... 2 D5
Shardlow Business Park
 BWSH/BRSTN DE72 ................... 66 A3
Shardlow County
 Primary School
 BWSH/BRSTN DE72 ................... 66 B3
Sherwin Sports Centre
 NORM/LIT DE23 .......................... 52 C1
Showcase Cinemas
 NORM/LIT DE23 .......................... 52 B2
Silverhill Primary School
 MCKLVR DE3 ............................... 39 H3
Sinfin Community School
 DERBYSE DE24 ........................... 61 H1

Sinfin Primary School
 DERBYSE DE24 .......................... 52 A4
Sofa Gallery
 DERBYSE DE24 .......................... 43 E5
South Derbyshire
 Health Authority
 DERBY DE1 ................................... 3 F7
South Derbyshire
 Mental Health NHS Trust
 DERBYW DE22.............................. 41 E2
Southern Derbyshire
 Health Authority
 DERBY DE1 ................................... 2 D5
Southern Derbyshire
 Health Authority
 DERBY DE1 ................................... 2 D3
Southern Derbyshire
 Mental Health NHS Trust
 MCKLVR DE3 ............................... 41 E2
Southgate Infant School
 DERBYSE DE24 ........................... 53 G1
Springfield Primary School
 DERBYE DE21 ............................. 44 C1
Stanley Common
 C of E Primary School
 ILK DE7....................................... 21 F4
Stenson Fields
 Community Primary School
 DERBYSE DE24 ........................... 61 G2
Street Lane Primary School
 RIPLEY DE5 .................................. 8 A2
Sunnyhill Infant School
 NORM/LIT DE23 .......................... 51 H2
Swarkestone Boat Club
 MELB/CHEL DE73 ....................... 69 E3
Temple House Clinic
 NORM/LIT DE23 ........................... 2 C7
The Temple
 NORM/LIT DE23 .......................... 42 B4
Tomlinson Industrial Estate
 DERBY DE1 ................................. 34 C1
Trent Lane Industrial Estate
 CDON/KEG DE74 ........................ 73 E1
UCI Cinemas
 DERBYE DE21 ............................. 34 D2
University of Derby
 DERBY DE1 ................................... 2 A2

University of Derby
 DERBY DE1 ................................... 33
University of Derby
 DERBYW DE22.............................. 33
University of Derby
 DERBYW DE22.............................. 33
University of Derby
 DERBYW DE22.............................. 41
University of Derby
 MCKLVR DE3 ............................... 40
University of Derby
 NORM/LIT DE23 .......................... 41
Vernon Street Medical Centre
 DERBYW DE22.............................. 41
Vidya Medical Centre
 DERBY DE1 ................................... 2
The Village Community School
 NORM/LIT DE23 .......................... 52
Walter Evans C of E School
 DERBYW DE22.............................. 34
Waverley Street Clinic
 DERBYSE DE24 .......................... 52
Wellside Medical Centre
 DERBY DE1 ................................... 2
Weston on Trent Parochial
 Primary School
 BWSH/BRSTN DE72 ................... 70
West Park Community School
 DERBYE DE21 ............................. 44
William Gilbert End C of E
 Primary School
 BPR/DUF DE56 ........................... 17
Willow Sports Centre
 DERBY DE1 ................................... 2
Wilmorton Primary School
 DERBYSE DE24 .......................... 43
Wilson Street Surgery
 DERBY DE1 ................................... 2
Wilson Street Surgery
 DERBYE DE21 ............................. 35
Woodlands Community
 School
 DERBYW DE22.............................. 25
Wren Park Primary School
 MCKLVR DE3 ............................... 40
Wyvern Business Park
 DERBYE DE21 ............................. 43

## age 6

Birchview Cl
Elm Av
Honeycroft Cl
Lime Crs
Millbank Av
Redhill Ct

## age 28

Applegate Cl
Bardsey Ct
Bayleaf Crs
Benmore Ct
Brambleberry Ct
Brandelhow Ct
Cressbrook Wy
Field Head Wy
Glenorchy Ct
Holmoak Cl
Hucklow Ct
Kershope Dr
Kyle Gv
Meadow View Cl
Milburn Gdns
Oakdale Gdns
Oswestry Cl
Tissington Dr
Woodrising Cl

## age 34

Brook St
Edward St
Henry St
King's Mead Cl
Little Bridge St
Lodge La
Orchard St
Parker Cl
St Helen's St
St John's Ter
Walker La
Willow Rw

## age 35

Blackthorn Cl
Broadleaf Cl
Burdock Cl
Cedarwood Ct
Crofters Ct
Deacon Cl
Hornbeam Cl
Radstock Gdns
Ridgewood Ct
Timsbury Ct
Trowbridge Cl

Balleny Cl
Beardmore Cl
Celandine Cl
Cloisters Ct
Garthorpe Ct
Kingsland Cl
Markham Ct
Paddock Cft
Rutherford Ri
Santolina Dr
Sedgebrook Cl
Somerby Wy
Tweeds Muir Cl

Anstey Ct
Columbine Cl
Delamere Cl
Gleadmoss La
Hodthorpe Cl
Sandbach Cl
Swanwick
Thurlow Ct

## age 36

Armscote Cl
Barcheston Cl
Charingworth Rd
Churchdown Cl
Elkstone Cl
Lampeter Cl
Merthyr Ct
Mountford Cl
Oxwich Ct
Pontypool Cl
Radstone Cl
Shenington Wy
Sherston Cl

Appledore Dr
Ashcombe Gdns
Ashgrove Ct
Averham Cl
Bassingham Cl
Bickley Moss
Egmanton Cl
Gainsborough Cl
Grassthorpe Cl
Prestbury Cl
Roseberry Cl
Samantha Ct
Swinderby Dr
Thore Cl
Tuxford Cl
Whyteleafe Gv
Wilmslow Dr

## age 42

Becket St
Bramble St
Cavendish Ct
Cavendish St
Curzon St
Drewry Ct
Forman St
Friar Gate Ct
George St
Kensington St
Monk St
Newland St

### A5

1   Argyle St
2   Bailey St
3   Lime Av
4   Lorne St
5   Lower Eley St
6   Mill Hill Rd
7   Mount Carmel St
8   Temple St

### B1

1   Albert St
2   Amen Alley
3   Becket Well La
4   Cheapside
5   Corn Market
6   East St
7   Exchange St
8   Green La
9   Sadler Ga
10  St James's St
11  St Peter's
    Churchyard
12  Strand
13  Thorntree La
14  Wardwick

### B2

1   The Avenue
2   Babington La
3   Burton Rd
4   Crompton St
5   Degge St
6   Gower St
7   Green La
8   Harcourt St
9   Hill Brow
10  Leopold St
11  Osmaston Rd
12  Sacheverel St
13  Sitwell St

### C5

1   Arboretum St
2   Centre Ct
3   Litchurch St
4   Morleston St
5   Regent St

### D2

1   Leeds Pl
2   Midland Pl
3   Sheffield Pl
4   Wellington St

## Page 44

### C1

1   St Werburgh's Vw

## Page 51

### H4

1   Butterwick Cl
2   The Circle
3   Donington Cl
4   Invernia Cl
5   Roseheath Cl
6   Sherwood Av

## Page 61

### G1

1   Blackmount Ct
2   Bodmin Cl
3   Braemar Cl
4   Burnside Cl
5   Caerhays Ct
6   Campsie Ct
7   Chandwick Ct
8   Craiglee Ct
9   Dalness Ct
10  Edgelaw Ct
11  Hebrides Cl
12  Lindisfarne Cl
13  Lismore Ct
14  Mull Ct
15  Northfield
16  Padstow Cl
17  Rowan Cl
18  Stornoway Cl

**Notes**

**Notes**

**Notes**

**Notes**

**Notes**